STUDIES IN
INDUSTRIAL GEOGRAPHY

BELGIUM

Raymond Riley

DAWSON

ISBN 0 7129 0687 8

First published in 1976

© Raymond Riley 1976

Produced by Computer-controlled phototypesetting, using OCR input techniques, and printed offset by
UNWIN BROTHERS LIMITED
The Gresham Press, Old Woking, Surrey

Contents

List of Tables and Illustrations	page vii
Preface	xi
1 The Physical and Human Background	1
2 The Development of the Economy	26
3 The Declining and Slowly Growing Industries	55
4 The Growth Industries	90
5 The Brussels-Antwerp Axial Belt	114
6 The Brussels and Antwerp Industrial Regions	131
7 Flanders: Oost- and West-Vlaanderen and Limburg	145
8 The Coalfield Provinces: Hainaut, Namur and Liège	163
Conclusion	178
Notes and References	180
Bibliography	188
Acknowledgements	196
Index	197

List of Tables and Illustrations

TABLES

1	Lorenz Curve Coefficients of Population Clustering	14
2	Population Change in the Belgian Provinces, 1960–1970	15
3	Production Costs in Belgian, French and German Coalfields	31
4	Provincial Employment by Sector, 1955 and 1970	34
5	Unemployment by Linguistic Region, 1958–1972	36
6	Per Capita Incomes for 1966 and 1970	38
7	Growth Industries: Location Quotients and Provincial Employment	43
8	Industrial Diversification Coefficients, 1970	44
9	Output by Value in all Activities, 1962 and 1971	45
10	Employment Change in the Declining and Slowly Growing Industries	56
11	Physical Characteristics of Selected Coalfields, 1956	57
12	Output, Pits and Productivity in Coalmines, 1953–1972	60
13	The Consumption of Energy in Belgium, 1950–1971	61
14	Provincial Textile Employment in 1972	63
15	Employment in Smelting, Refining, Rolling and Forging, 1972	71
16	Location Quotients for the Brewing Industry, 1972	86
17	Employment in the Clothing Industry, 1955 and 1972	88
18	Employment in the Rapidly Growing Industries, 1955–1972	91
19	Employment in the Engineering Industry, 1960–1972	92
20	Employment and Turnover in Engineering in Foreign Plants	99
21	Employment in the Chemical Industry, 1960–1972	102
22	Location Quotients for the Paper Industry, 1972	111
23	Value Added in Antwerpen, Brabant and Brussels-Capital	115

24 Employment Change in Antwerpen and Brabant, 1960–1972   116
25 Manufacturing Employment in Antwerpen and Brabant, 1955–1972   120
26 Industrial Employment in Antwerp Docks, 1971   141
27 Traffic Handled by the Port of Antwerp, 1972   142
28 Value Added in Limburg, Oost- and West-Vlaanderen   146
29 Employment Change in Oost- and West-Vlaanderen and Limburg   146
30 Wages in Oost- and West-Vlaanderen and Limburg, 1955–1970   151
31 Industrial Employment in Oost- and West-Vlaanderen and Limburg   153
32 Value Added in Hainaut, Namur and Liège, 1966–1971   164
33 Employment Change in Hainaut, Namur and Liège, 1960–1972   164
34 Industrial Employment in Hainaut, Namur and Liège, 1955–1972   169

FIGURES

1 Relief and Drainage   3
2 January Isotherms   4
3 July Isotherms   6
4 Average Annual Rainfall   7
5 Density of Population   13
6 The Linguistic Divisions of Belgium   18
7 Freight Traffic on Belgian Railways, 1971   22
8 Freight Traffic on Belgian Inland Waterways, 1970   24
9 Average Monthly Unemployment in 1972   38
10 Per Capita Income in 1970   39
11 Changes in Manufacturing Employment, 1960–1971   40
12 Employment Change in the Growth Industries, 1960–1972   42
13 The Assisted Areas of Belgium in 1971   48
14 Population Potential Map of Belgium   52
15 Net Migration Balance, 1967–1971   53
16 Recent Closures and Output by Pit in Coalmining   59
17 The Belgian Textile Industry, 1972   64
18 The Belgian Iron and Steel Industry   73
19 The Belgian Non-Ferrous Metal Industry   80
20 The Belgian Brewing Industry   85

21	Employment Change in the Belgian Clothing Industry, 1960–1972	89
22	The Belgian Vehicle Industry	96
23	The Belgian Electronic Products Industry	100
24	The Belgian Oil Refining and Chemical Industries	104
25	The Belgian Pulp and Paper Industry	112
26	The Provinces of Antwerpen and Brabant: Location Map	117
27	Employment Change in the Leading Industries of Antwerpen and Brabant	123
28	The Brussels Industrial Region	132
29	The Antwerp Industrial Region	137
30	The Industries of the Port of Antwerp	138
31	The Provinces of Oost- and West-Vlaanderen and Limburg: Location Map	148
32	The Industries of the Port of Ghent	159
33	The Zeebrugge-Bruges Industrial Axis and Proposed Extensions	161
34	The Provinces of Hainaut, Namur and Liège: Location Map	166
35	The Liège Industrial Region	176

Preface

LIKE MANY COUNTRIES in Western Europe, Belgium has a high proportion of her workpeople engaged in manufacturing, but while some countries – the Netherlands is an outstanding example – have only recently industrialised, Belgium's manufacturing sector is of long standing. The Walloon coalfield was the scene of the first industrial revolution to take place on the continent of Europe, and the district shares with the British coalfields the problems of phasing out the old and introducing the 'neotechnic' industries which are expanding so rapidly. To exacerbate the regional problem, Flanders has received a large proportion of recent investment, especially that from abroad. This has added fuel to the flames generated by the linguistic controversy which has caused a very real schism between north and south: few advanced countries have to suffer such cultural restrictions on economic development. Yet at the same time intervention by the central government is minimal. More than any other country in the European Economic Community, Belgium is an example of industry operating very largely within the framework of the free play of market forces. At a time when unbridled opportunism in economic affairs is *démodé*, Belgium's prosperity may be irksome to many, but there are nevertheless lessons to be learned from her approach.

The linguistic division puts an author into something of a quandary regarding place-names, for most settlements have both a Dutch and a French name, in some cases quite dissimilar. An instance is the town known as Waremme to the Walloons but as Borgworm to the Flemings. Additionally, anglicisms exist for the better known cities; thus we have Ghent (English), Gent (Dutch) and Gand (French). The convention that has been observed is to use anglicisms where they exist, Dutch spellings for Flemish, and French spellings for

Walloon settlements, administrative areas and rivers. An exception is made in the case of Antwerp, where for ease of identification the form Antwerpen signifies the province, and Antwerp the city and *arrondissement*. Flanders is used to refer to the Dutch-speaking district of Belgium and not merely to the provinces of West- and Oost-Vlaanderen. A further potentially confusing issue is the existence of a Belgian province named Luxembourg. The treatment used here is to refer to the nation state as the Grand Duchy of Luxemburg and to the Belgian province as Luxembourg.

1

The Physical and Human Background

NOT ONLY IS Belgium a small country with an area of only 30,500 km², approximately one and a half times the size of Wales, but as a nation state it is of relatively recent origin. The independent state of Belgium was proclaimed in 1830 following the growing feeling of resentment at Dutch rule which followed the fall of Napoleon in 1815. The boundaries of the country as they exist today are very largely those of the 1831 treaty with the Netherlands, the only major subsequent changes having been the acquisition of the districts of Eupen, Malmédy and St. Vith from Germany at the Treaty of Versailles in 1919. For the most part the frontiers of the country are based not on natural phenomena, but rather on the results of political negotiations. Only the 65 km North Sea coastline, along the river Leie between Armentières (France) and Rekken, along the Maas between Lixhe and Kessenich, and along a short section of the Our south of St. Vith, do physical features shape the path of Belgian frontiers. Nor are the boundaries based on linguistic differentiation for, with the exception of the frontier between the province of West-Vlaanderen and France, they pass through territories where the same language is spoken on both sides of the political divide. This may not serve to provide a clear cultural identity, but the line traced by Belgium's frontiers endows the country with valuable proximity to a number of other nations, and with a common boundary with four of the five other original members of the European Economic Community. This centrality was the critical factor behind the choice of Brussels as the capital of the Community.

The physical attributes of any country make an important contribution to the operation of its economy, especially in the sense that distribution of population often reflects the period when man's activities were much more determined than they are today by the natural

1

2   BELGIUM

environment. In addition the distribution of natural resources, above all coal, has had a lasting effect on the geography of industry, and the Belgian transport network has been considerably influenced by the nature of the terrain.

Relief and Drainage

Lowland Belgium north of the Sambre-Meuse valleys essentially belongs to the North European Plain, while the southern third of the country, with the exception of the southernmost tip where the Liassic rocks of the Paris Basin intrude, is part of the Hercynian massif of the Ardennes which extend into France under the same name and into West Germany as the Eiffel mountains. As a consequence the Sambre-Meuse axis is very much a division between the densely populated, highly urbanised Belgian plain and the rural upland to the south. Inland from the dune coast, which has inhibited the development of any natural harbours, lie well established polders, the most recent of which are those at Nieuwpoort, Ostend and at the eastern end of the coastal strip, and which date from the seventeenth and eighteenth centuries. The polders are not now below mean sea level, but those in the vicinity of the Scheldt estuary in the absence of dykes would be flooded at very high tide. Behind the polders is the North European Plain, here very largely the drainage basin of the Scheldt and its tributaries the Leie, Durme, Zenne, Dyle and Nete, the latter originating in the low Kempische Hoogvlakte or Kempen plateau. (Fig 1) The sands and clays of the Flanders plain are not as suitable for agricultural production as the higher land to the south, but by dint of hard and persistent labour man has been able to develop a system of intensive cultivation capable of supporting a relatively dense population.

Above the 50m mark the plain gives way to the gently undulating landscapes of the low central *limon* plateaux, from west to east the Plateau Hennuyer, the Plateau Brabançon, the Plateau de la Hesbaye, and to the east of the Meuse, the Plateau de Herve attaining a height of 354m. North-flowing tributaries of the Scheldt such as the Dender, Zenne and Dyle have cut through the *limon* cover, which is part of the great north European loess (*limon*) belt located to the immediate north of the Hercynian uplands, and forming an important medieval routeway. The fertility of the *limon* soils, coupled with the absence of real restrictions on movement, allowing the development of trade, was conducive to the growth of population in the middle ages. Certainly by facilitating movement the terrain has contributed to the growth of the Brussels conurbation. In terms of relief the Kempische Hoogvlakte is similar to the low plateau, for it rises from the plain to a height of 104m near Lanaken, but in place of the fertile *limon* are found sour,

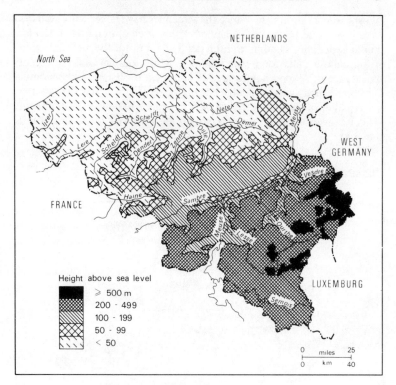

Fig 1. RELIEF AND DRAINAGE

ill-drained and infertile soils derived from alluvial gravels originating from the Maas. The circumscribed agricultural possibilities of the region have given rise to the phenomenon of part-time farming which is here especially well developed.

The Sambre and the Meuse form the southern margin of the low plateau for beyond them lie the Devonian and Cambrian rocks of the Ardennes. Although the northern part of this upland, known as the Condroz in the east and the Entre-Sambre-et-Meuse in the west, is very much a peneplain, varying in height from 260 to 290m, it is too high and climatically unfavourable to attract substantial settlement. This is also true of the High Ardennes which rise to 652m in the Plateau des Tailles and 694m at Botrange in the Hautes Fagnes. A rainfall regime which brings more than 190 rainy days each year (combined with up to 120 days of frost), and infertile, poorly drained, soils make this an inhospitable environment. Since the Ardennes have never witnessed the growth of large towns, it is inevitable that such a region of difficulty should experience continuing rural depopulation, for the mechanisation of agriculture calls for fewer workers, while tourism and the recent appearance of second homes are not sufficient to sustain the economy. The uplift that was experienced in Tertiary times has led to the rejuvenation of the rivers that flow across the Ardennes, causing them to incise deep valleys, many of which are followed by road and rail networks.

Climate

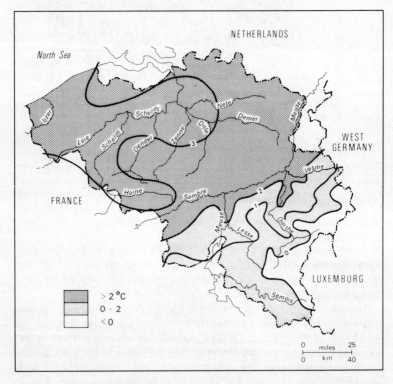

Fig 2. JANUARY ISOTHERMS

The Belgian climatic regime is that of the cool temperate oceanic type with abundant precipitation, mild winters and cool summers, although continental influences in the form of colder winters are apparent in the High Ardennes. Isotherms follow a generalised south-west north-east trend, influenced on the one hand by the line of the North Sea coast with its prevailing Gulf Stream Drift, and on the other by the main axis of the Ardenne massif in the southern third of the country. As Fig. 2 indicates, a narrow strip in the south-east has mean winter temperatures below freezing, and the 2°C January isotherm trends south-west north-east along the axis of the Sambre-Meuse valleys. Between the latter and the sea, mean winter temperatures rise to 4°C. The same broad pattern is repeated in the summer. The higher parts of the Ardennes have a mean July temperature of 15°C, contrasting with the valley of the lower Scheldt between Ghent and Antwerp which has a mean of 18°C. (Fig 3) The maritime influence of the North Sea ensures that there is a fall in temperature to the north of this belt, but the 17°C isotherm still trends south-west north-east. In spite of the upland nature of the Ardennes, there is thus a remarkably small range of average temperatures over the country at any given time during the year. Additionally, the difference between summer and winter temperatures in various parts of the country is strikingly similar. At Ostend, for instance, there is a seasonal variation of 13°C, yet at Bastogne in the Ardennes the figure is only 15°C.

The differentiation between upland and lowland is once more emphasised by the distribution of precipitation. Fig 4 shows that the highest regions of the Ardennes receive precipitation in excess of 1300 mm, although prevailing westerly winds ensure that the western sector of the massif above the Semois valley, only slightly above the 400m contour, receives more than 1400 mm per annum. The lower upland areas have a precipitation of between 900 and 1200 mm per annum, and lowland Belgium north of the Sambre-Meuse trough lies between the 750 and 900 mm isohyets. As a result of cyclonic activity, there is a seasonal peak of rainfall in autumn and winter.

Natural Resources

The natural resource base of any area dictates to a large extent the nature of its economic activities, which may reflect the absence or presence of such resources. The virtual absence of mineral resources in the Netherlands, for example, has shaped the path taken by Dutch manufacturing industry, which is largely of recent origin. Their presence and long-term working in Belgium by contrast, have contributed to the establishment of a number of industries typifying the industrial revolution and strongly associated with their source of materials. Examples are iron and steel production, metal industries and heavy engineering. Yet the former importance of the possession of

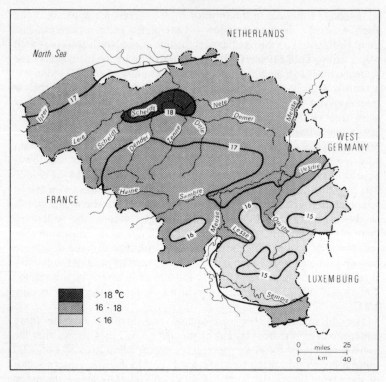

Fig 3. JULY ISOTHERMS

natural resources is being rapidly diminished for a number of reasons. Firstly, improvements in the means of transporting low-value commodities have reduced the friction of distance, allowing coal, oil, metallic ores and pulpwood to be moved many thousands of miles. Secondly, new cheap and transportable sources of energy such as oil and natural gas have ousted coal from its former monopolistic position, and together with electric power they have bequeathed to manufacturing industry a new mobility. Thirdly, industry has become increasingly complex and a diminishing number of factories are concerned with the processing of natural resources. However, although Belgium's natural resource endowment played a greater part in the country's production in the past than at present, it nevertheless retains a role in certain sectors of the economy.

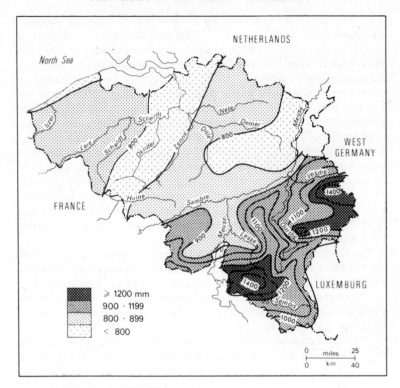

Fig 4. AVERAGE ANNUAL RAINFALL

Mineral Resources

Historically the most significant mineral resource in Belgium was coal, for this was the basis of the industrial revolution which took place earlier here than anywhere else except Great Britain. There are two coal mining areas, the Haine-Sambre-Meuse and the Kempen fields, the former worked since the thirteenth century and fully exploited in the nineteenth century, the latter developed between 1917 and 1938. The Haine-Sambre-Meuse field corresponds with the Carboniferous series which outcrop in a narrow band between Charleroi and Liège immediately to the north of the Devonian rocks of the Ardennes. The measures form the Namur coal syncline which is broken by the transverse anticline known as the *toit du Samson* causing Carboniferous Limestone to appear between Namur and Andenne. Because of this anticline, the coal measures dip away from the *toit du Samson*. Eastwards they reach a depth of 1500 m below Liège, only to rise sharply to the surface again; westwards they reach a depth of 2500m at the French frontier. To the west of Charleroi the measures are buried by an increasingly thick layer of chalk, sand and clay, but the thickness of the measures allows the whole range of coals, from anthracite at the lower level to gas coal at the surface, to be present. In the west there are some 160 separate coal seams, but only 85 at Liège. The gas and coking coal measures have been completely eroded east of Charleroi. The southern edge of the field is marked by a huge fault, the *faille du Midi*, representing the junction of the Carboniferous series with the Lower Devonian of the Ardenne massif.[1] Unfortunately the seams are thin, some being only 35 cm thick, and account for a mere 3 per cent of the total depth of coal measures. In addition the seams are badly folded and faulted and there are copious quantities of the dangerous gas methane. High production costs are the result.

The Kempen field differs in several respects from the older exploited region. Since it was opened up in the twentieth century it has failed to attract coal-using industry and the greater part of the fuel is exported from the area. The measures are overlain by Quaternary sands, gravels, alluvium, clays and Cretaceous rocks, giving an overburden of between 400 and 600 m. The seams dip gently from the Dutch border, where they occur at 500m, to 1000m near Turnhout, although no concessions have been granted this far west. They are relatively thick, reaching 3m at Beringen, and comparatively undisturbed, but the overburden of sands and gravels, unconsolidated and frequently waterlogged, require a special and costly shaft preparation technique, known as the shaft-freezing process, to be employed before coal may be reached. Productivity is much superior to that in the Haine-Sambre-Meuse field.

In the far south around Halanzy, the northern tip of the huge Lorraine iron ore field reaches into Belgium. The field is small and output of the silica-rich ore has never supplied more than 7 per cent of national requirements. Nevertheless the presence of the orefield was sufficient to prompt the construction of blast furnaces at Halanzy, Athus and Musson in the nineteenth century. Belgium formerly possessed another metallic mineral deposit which in the last half of the nineteenth century was of world significance. The zinc mines at Lontzen and Moresnet, north-east of Liège, were producing 70,000 tonnes a year in the 1860s and gave Belgium a world lead in the output of refined zinc. The deposits are now exhausted, but the presence of zinc refineries and rolling mills at Liège is testimony to the earlier influence of local materials.

If some mineral deposits are of only indirect importance today, the reverse is certainly true of chalk and limestone which are extensively worked to make Belgium an important producer of cement and the fourth largest exporter of cement in the world today. The deposits worked are the Carboniferous Limestone outcrop at Tournai and the Cretaceous series to the east of Mons and north of Liège where chalk can easily be quarried. The influence of the low-value materials upon the distribution of the cement industry is evident for with the exception of those at Zelzate and Charleroi, using blast furnace slag, the plants are close to the quarries and the location of markets is of secondary importance.[2] An outstanding deposit of glass sands in juxtaposition with coal measures has contributed to the growth of glass manufacture round Charleroi, although the present role of indigenous raw materials is much reduced. The largest single plant is in the Kempenland at Mol, adjacent to extensive deposits of white glass sands especially rich in silica. The presence of large deposits of clay at Bandour-Hautrage in the Borinage has given rise to the local manufacture of pottery and refractory products; there are other deposits in the Ardennes south of Charleroi and Andenne. China clay is mined at Libin in the western Ardennes and is sent to the Borinage and to La Louvière for processing, but clay suitable for brick-making is much more widely distributed, especially in the northern part of the country. Brickworks are strongly attracted to the source of their raw materials, yet three concentrations are notable: Turnhout in Kempenland, at Kortrijk and along the Rupel and Nete rivers between Duffel and Boom where long low kilns produce 2 million tonnes of bricks a year and with their tall slim chimneys create a most distinctive landscape.

Quarrying for stone has suffered greatly from the use of alternative materials for road-making and for the construction of buildings and bridges. Nevertheless building stones such as *petit granit* at Soignies, Ecaussinnes and Sprimont, road stones such as the porphyries of Lessines and Quenast and marble quarried at Gembloux, La Buissière and Philippeville, are useful additions to the national resource base.

Forest Resources

No less than one-fifth of the surface area of Belgium is forested, largely as a consequence of the physical nature of the Ardennes, and to a lesser extent, of Kempenland. In both the soil cover is conducive to tree growth, but a more important factor is that these areas have not encouraged human activities which would have increased the competition for land and curtailed forestry. The lower regions of the Entre-Sambre-et-Meuse and the Condroz are characterised by decid-uous plantations, particularly oak, but in the higher areas to the south, forestry is the dominant land-use in many districts, conifers such as spruce being the principal variety. Deciduous trees, especially beech, are located in the lower, southern margins of the Ardennes and in Jurassic hills of Belgian Lorraine. The forest cover of the other important regions of timber resources, the Kempenland, largely comprises silver birch and Corsican pine. Despite the density of the forest cover in some areas of the Ardennes, a pulp mill was not established there until 1964. However, Belgian forests provide 500,000 cubic metres of pulp wood annually, responsible for almost half the raw material base of the country's paper industry.

Water Resources

For long regarded as unimportant because of their apparently replaceable nature, water resources are now being viewed in a different perspective because of the rapidly increasing demands placed upon them. The introduction of household 'gadgets' has caused the domestic consumption of water to rise sharply in the last two decades, but the greatest demand has come from cooling installations, in particular those associated with the iron and steel, chemical and electric power industries. Approximately 90 per cent of industrial water in Belgium is used by these activities, and since the latter two are growth sectors the problem of water supply is becoming increasingly serious.

The central problem is the growing regional imbalance between supply and demand: Belgium has a maximum annual supply of 800 million cubic metres of ground water, but three-quarters of this originates from the southern half of the country. A longer term problem is that at present some 80 per cent of the total available supply is being consumed, and this figure is steadily rising. The aquifers of the dune coast, the sandy interior plain and eastern Kempenland are capable of meeting only a part of local demands, and this deficiency has to be made good from the more abundant supplies associated with the sands of eastern Brabant, the Cretaceous rocks of the Hesbaye and the Hainaut plateau, the Carboniferous Limestone of the Condroz and with the Jurassic strata in the province of Luxembourg. Thus the Brusselse Intercommunale Watermaatschappij takes its supplies from the plentiful aquifers of eastern Brabant. Other water transfers include the flows of water from the Borinage and the Carboniferous Limestone district round Tournai to Flanders and Brussels, and from Modave on the Hoyoux in the Condroz whence between 45,000 and 80,000 cubic metres, according to the season, are supplied daily to the capital. Inter-regional flows are further facilitated by the existence of a national water supply company which covers the whole of Belgium with the exception of the province of Antwerp – and the supply areas of the five regional water boards. The water grid is least developed in the province of

Luxembourg where there are still 525 municipal undertakings taking advantage of the local abundance of ground water supplies.[3]

Water pumped from underground sources accounts for three-quarters of total supplies, the remainder being surface water originating from rivers, canals, barrages and storage basins. The extent to which rivers and canals can supply water is limited by the need to maintain a minimum depth of water for navigation and by the cost of purification for drinking water. Fortunately the quality of the water is not an important consideration for industrial cooling plants, which almost exclusively employ very cheap surface water which is returned to the waterways after use. Indeed, rivers and canals supply 95 per cent of the water used by Belgian industry. Hydro-electric power stations utilise an annual volume of 14,000 million cubic metres, but this is not removed from the waterways and does not undergo any physical transformation.

The Meuse is by far the most important source of surface water. The river has important tributaries such as the Semois, Sambre and Ourthe, but unfortunately the Meuse leaves Belgium north of Liège and flows into the Netherlands. It is thus of great value to the southern but not the northern part of the country. The Meuse does, however, provide the water for the Albert Canal which uses 250 million cubic metres each year, and in this way canal-side industrial plants benefit although they may be distant from the Meuse itself. When the Albert Canal is widened in the mid-1970s, some 400 million cubic metres of Meuse water will be transmitted annually through the provinces of Limburg and Antwerpen.[4] Unfortunately the tidal and therefore saline nature of the Scheldt limits its use. In this context the availability of fresh and relatively unpolluted water from the Albert Canal is all the more valuable.

Since quality is not a primary consideration for industrial users, water may be used many times over by manufacturing plants. However, it is anticipated that industrial consumption of water will rise threefold between 1970 and 1980. Further, the situation will not be improved by the Scheldt-Rhine canal agreement of May 1963. Under this agreement Belgium agreed to supply the Dutch Delta region with a volume of fresh water equal to the volume of salt water passing into the otherwise fresh water Delta consequent upon the construction of the Scheldt-Rhine canal, which is due to be completed in the mid-1970s.[5] One solution to the problem of water shortage is the installation of purification plants by industry and by municipal sewage undertakings. Less than 20 per cent of all sewage passes through treatment plants, and cities such as Brussels, Antwerp and Ghent as yet have no plants, simply passing their sewage into rivers. Even though 80 per cent of the cost of treatment plants is met by the state, sewage is the concern of the *commune*, not the city, and in the past cooperation between *communes* has been difficult to achieve. Brussels-Capital (Greater Brussels) has nineteen *communes* and here agreement has proved impossible. It was to overcome such problems that river authorities were set up in 1972 to coordinate the policies of the many *communes* through which run rivers such as the Meuse and Scheldt. Further cause for optimism lies in the way in which Antwerp has taken the lead in the treatment of sewage, and is constructing six sewage farms with treatment plants which will be completed by 1977. Another strategy is likely to be the construction of reservoirs such as those that already exist on the Vesdre, Gileppe, Warche, Ourthe and Vierre in the Ardennes. Future supplies of drinking water will have to be largely met by mountain reservoirs for the consumption of ground water is almost equal to the content of the aquifers. Some aquifers are seriously depleted, for instance the water table beneath Brussels was virtually at surface level in 1885, but by 1956 had fallen to a depth of 61m. An experimental desalination plant is in operation on the coast at Bredene near Ostend, and it may be that in the next decade the shortage of ground and surface water will justify the introduction of large desalination plants.

Population

Since Belgian population statistics are gathered on the basis of administrative districts perhaps unfamiliar to English-speaking readers, a comment on these districts will not be out of place. The country is divided into nine provinces, mapped in Figure 6, each approximately equal to a British shire. The provinces are subdivided into *arrondissements*, of which there are forty-three. The four *arrondissements* of the province of Brabant, for example, are Brussels-Capital, Halle-Vilvoorde, Leuven and Nivelles. At a much smaller scale are the 2586 *communes*; nineteen such communes constitute Brussels-Capital.

With a population of 9.7 million in 1970, giving a density of 317 people per km,[2] Belgium is one of the most densely populated countries in Europe, lying fourth after the Channel Islands, Malta and the Netherlands if the city-principalities (for example, the Vatican and Monaco) are ignored. However, the average annual population increase of 0.6 per cent for the period 1963-1970 is one of the lowest recorded in Western Europe. Following upon earlier comments on the nature of the terrain, it is predictable that the population is far from uniformly distributed. Four areas of different population density may be identified in Fig 5. Firstly, the influence of relief is manifest in the Ardennes and the southern fringes of the central plateau which have less than 150 inhabitants per km.[2] Secondly, a region comprising the greater part of the Flanders plain, extending from the provinces of West-Vlaanderen

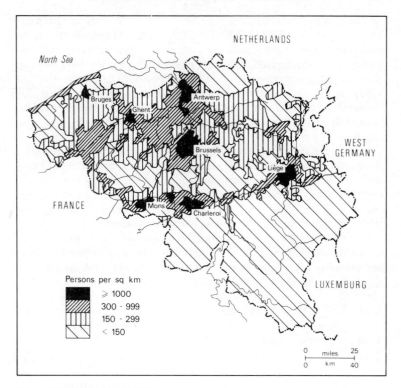

Fig 5. DENSITY OF POPULATION
SOURCE: *Atlas de Belgique*, plate 21

through Oost-Vlaanderen, through the southern half of Antwerpen province, through virtually the whole of Brabant to Limburg in the east, has a population density in excess of 150 per km.[2] This is a very high level for a largely rural district and helps to explain why urban areas in Belgium of 25,000 inhabitants and above account for only 57 per cent of the total population.[6] The industrialised Haine-Sambre-Meuse valleys form an arc of similar population concentration, its western and eastern margins meeting tentacles of the Flanders plain. Thirdly, there are a number of areas which might be called the larger city regions, where population density varies between 300 and 1000 per km.[2] To them must be added the coastal strip where tourist activities have given rise to settlements along its entire length. Finally the major agglomerations themselves – Bruges, Ghent, Antwerp, Brussels, Mons, La

Louvière, Charleroi and Liège – register above 1000 persons per km.^{2} The administrative area of Brussels-Capital supports some 6600 people per km^2, a level far in excess of any other area. A number of population axes suggest themselves, the most obvious of which is that between Antwerp and Brussels, with a southern extension to Charleroi, and that following the coalfield from east to west. Others are the axis tracing the medieval routeway from England to Westphalia via Ostend, Bruges, Ghent, Brussels, Leuven and Liège, and that following the Leie and Scheldt valleys from Kortrijk to Antwerp.

The extent of population concentration may also be considered by constructing Lorenz curves for each province. Where the population is well distributed high coefficients derived from the curves are registered, and conversely low coefficients are indicative of the dominant status of one city in the province. The values are set out in Table 1. The relatively high values for West-and Oost-Vlaanderen and for Limburg, indicating a tendency for dispersal, complement the findings of the population density map which shows high rural densities for these provinces. The high coefficient for Luxembourg illustrates the absence of a large town. On the other hand Brabant and Antwerpen have lower coefficients because of the presence of the major cities of Brussels and Antwerp. The province of Liège returns the lowest score because it has a single large city, Liège, and a large area of difficult upland terrain not conducive to settlement.

Table 1

LORENZ CURVE COEFFICIENTS OF POPULATION CLUSTER-
ING, BY PROVINCE

Liège	0.295	West-Vlaanderen	0.506
Brabant	0.325	Oost-Vlaanderen	0.530
Hainaut	0.382	Luxembourg	0.617
Antwerpen	0.400	Limburg	0.670
Namur	0.465	BELGIUM	0.357

Source: R. de Smet,'Degré de Concentration de la Population',
Revue Belge de Géographie, 86 (1962), 51

Population density patterns are very largely a reflection of the past masking more recent demographic changes, for the most densely peopled areas do not everywhere exhibit the most rapid growth. This is particularly true of the province of Limburg which, between 1960 and 1970, exhibited a population growth of 14.7 per cent, almost three times the national rate of 5.6 per cent. Limburg also has the highest provincial rate of natural increase, 9.43 per 1000 population in 1970. This somewhat unusual case of an essentially rural area exhibiting

THE PHYSICAL AND HUMAN BACKGROUND

marked population growth is in part a result of the continuing importance of coalmining and of the presence of many youthful immigrant mineworkers. As Table 2 indicates, the provinces of Brabant and Antwerpen also made substantial contributions to the growth of the national population between 1960 and 1970, yet neither Brussels nor Antwerp but peripheral areas of these two provinces contributed most of the increase. In Antwerpen it was the Turnhout region, adjacent to Limburg and sharing many of its characteristics, which grew most rapidly. The Antwerp *arrondissement* at least managed to increase its inhabitants during the decade (by 6.3 per cent), but the nineteen *communes* of Brussels-Capital suffered a decline, largely a result of central area redevelopment and of a concomitant preference for suburbia. It was Nivelles, to the south of the capital, that experienced the most marked population expansion in the province of Brabant. However, Nivelles had a very low rate of natural increase during the decade, and in 1970 registered a figure of —0.13 per 1000. Its substantial growth stems from in-migration, both from Brussels and from other areas of the country, and its migration balance (the number of immigrants less the number of emigrants) of 18.25 per 1000 was some twenty times greater than the mean for all Belgian *arrondissements*.

Table 2

POPULATION CHANGE IN THE BELGIAN PROVINCES, 1960-1970. '000.

	1960	1970	%		1960	1970	%
Limburg	572	656	+14.7	O-Vlaanderen	1,272	1,314	+3.3
Brabant	1,974	2,178	+10.3	Liège	1,010	1,015	+0.5
Antwerpen	1,430	1,536	+ 7.4	Luxembourg	219	219	—
Hainaut	1,264	1,331	+ 5.3	W-Vlaanderen	1,066	1,056	—0.9
Namur	371	385	+ 3.8	BELGIUM	9,178	9,691	+5.6

Source: *Annuaire Statistique de la Belgique,* 91, Brussels (1971)

During the decade 1960-1970 the population of the remaining six provinces expanded more slowly than the national mean, suggesting that the possession of major urban agglomerations is not always sufficient to ensure even average growth. Of the cities of Charleroi, Liège, Kortrijk, Bruges and Ghent, only Kortrijk and Bruges underwent substantial growth, but unlike Brussels and Antwerp they are insufficiently large to cause an important population increase in West-Vlaanderen. The loss recorded by the latter province was in part caused by the transfer of territory south of Ieper to Hainaut in 1965.

Despite the indifferent showing of Oost-and West-Vlaanderen, Table 2 hints at one of the major themes in the human geography of Belgium — the differences between the north, or Flanders, and the south, Wallonie. Not a single Walloon province reached the national level of population growth, and none of their rates of natural increase approached the national figure; indeed Liège had a natural decrease of 1.00 per 1000 in 1970. The two most populous Walloon provinces, Hainaut and Liège, have a higher percentage (15 per cent) of inhabitants of 65 years of age and above than any other province; the figure for Wallonie is also 15 per cent compared with only 12 per cent for the Dutch-speaking region.[7] Once again the data are indicative of the shift of dynamism from south to north.

Migration of population within Belgium may be considered under four headings. Firstly, there are flows from rural to urban areas, the continuation of a long-established process of rural depopulation. Rural areas such as Ieper, Tielt and Verviers are constantly losing inhabitants to the adjacent towns of Kortrijk, Bruges and Liège respectively. The numbers involved have been less than they would have been in many other advanced countries, chiefly because of the acceptance by the state in 1870 of the principle of cheap railway travel which allowed workpeople to take urban employment and retain a rural residence. Secondly, the two large cities of Brussels and Antwerp not only attract population from the encircling rural areas, but also from distant rural and urban areas, giving rise to an axis between the two cities characterised by an expanding population. The attraction of the capital is greater than that of Antwerp for it can offer a wider range of employment. The very rapid decline of coalmining and a number of other activities in Wallonie has caused some movement from Charleroi, Mons and Liège to Brussels. During the years 1967-1971, these *arrondissements* experienced an average net migration loss of 667, 430 and 402 respectively with Brussels-Capital. Walloon migrants effectively do not have the choice of settling in Antwerp or Brussels, for they are not welcome in Flemish-speaking Antwerp and must therefore head for the bi-lingual capital. Similarly, although Flemings can theoretically choose between the two cities, in practice they tend to select Antwerp. The third component of migration is suburbanisation. Improved means of transport, the need of industry for large areas of land for modern factories, and rising rents in built-up areas have all been conducive to accretion of population on the periphery of towns. The consequence has been that the old cores of the major cities have experienced a loss of inhabitants and suburbia has expanded simultaneously. Thus between 1947 and 1970 the population of the *commune* of Antwerp and the *commune* of Brussels, at the centre of these cities, suffered a decline of 16 and 14 per cent respectively, while peripheral *communes* such as Edegem in Antwerp and Ganshoren and Woluwe St. Pierre in Brussels returned increases in excess of 110 per cent. The same process is operating at Ghent, Bruges, Charleroi and Liège. Finally, the proximity of a number of Belgian border areas to important foreign industrial regions has given rise to cross-frontier commuting. The largest number of *frontaliers*, as they are known, live in West-Vlaanderen and work in the Lille-Roubaix-Tourcoing textile complex in France. There are also flows between the Borinage coalfield and the French steel-making district of Valenciennes, between Belgian Lorraine and the iron and steel district of French Lorraine, and between a number of Belgian towns in the provinces of Antwerpen, Limburg and Liège and the Netherlands.

The Language Problem

Although language is an attribute of population, special attention must be paid to it in Belgium for the differences between the two principal linguistic groups are by no means amicable, and have been instrumental in precipitating the fall of a number of governments since 1945. A crisis in 1973, for example, stemmed from the complete inability of the Social Democrat and Christian Social coalition to agree on a programme of improved economic autonomy for Flanders and Wallonie, and on a solution to the problem posed by Brussels, a nominally bi-lingual but effectively French-speaking exclave in Flanders. The Christian Socialists are split into Flemish and Walloon factions, the Liberal party is embarrassed by a splinter group of Brussels residents, the Bruxellois, while the existence of two extremist groups, the Flemish Volksunie and the Rassemblement Wallon, further aggravates the political situation. Examples of the difficulties are legion. There was a loud outcry from the Walloons over the provisions of the 1963 Scheldt-Rhine agreement since the fresh water to be pumped into the Dutch Delta originated in Wallonie, yet the canal, they argued, would benefit Antwerp. The expansion of the port of Zeebrugge was hotly resented by the Walloons who threatened to use the French port of Dunkirk, and were only placated when the government agreed to provide supplementary regional benefits for the south. Other, more vitriolic incidents include the rioting associated with the closure of the Zwartberg pit in the Kempen coalfield and with the campaign which eventually led to the departure to Ottignies of the French-speaking sector of Leuven university.

The origin of the Flemish-Walloon division goes back to the Roman period, for the linguistic border marks the junction of the sphere of influence of the Franks to the north and of the Romans to the south.

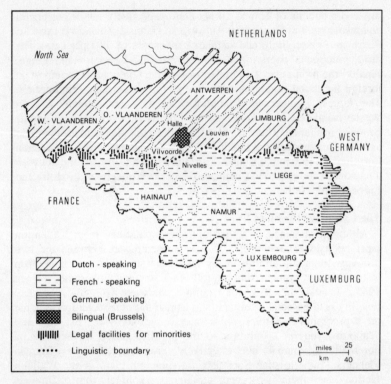

Fig 6. THE LINGUISTIC DIVISIONS OF BELGIUM
A. Mouscron
B. Ardennes
B. Ardennes Flamandes
C. Enghien
D. Herstappe
E. De Voerstreek

Fig.6 shows that there are four Flemish provinces (West-and Oost-Vlaanderen, Antwerpen and Limburg) and four Walloon provinces (Hainaut, Namur, Liège and Luxembourg). The ninth province, Brabant, has the officially bi-lingual Brussels-Capital at its centre, two Flemish-speaking *arrondissements* (Halle-Vilvoorde and Leuven) and one French-speaking *arrondissement* (Nivelles). The linguistic boundary thus crosses the centre of the country from west to east, although some Walloon and Flemish communities are marooned in the other's territory. In these cases there is special provision for the minority group.

Examples are Mouscron in northern Hainaut where the Flemish form the minority, and De Voerstreek or Les Fourons, a detached sector of Limburg, where the Walloons are in the minority. A further case was that of the Brussels *randarrondissement* which existed between 1963 and 1970, comprising three separate areas on the periphery of Brussels-Capital with Walloons as the minority group. The largest of the three was of particular significance in the language war for it separated Brussels-Capital from Walloon Nivelles, and the Flemings saw this as an important step in the containment of the spread of French-speakers into Flemish territory. Indeed the French-speakers of the *randarrondissement* lost the special provisions made for them when the administrative area was integrated with the Flemish district of Halle-Vilvoorde.

A second, fortunately peaceful, linguistic frontier lies in eastern Liège province and represents the transition zone between the use of French and German. However, complexities do exist for in the Welkenraedt region there are both Dutch-and German-speaking minorities, around Malmédy German is the minority language, and only in the larger areas of Eupen and St Vith is German the majority and French the minority language.[8]

Confrontation between Fleming and Walloon is constantly kept alive because of four underlying factors. Firstly, the Flemings are more fertile than the Walloons so that from a position of parity in 1880, the former now appreciably outnumber the latter. In 1970 the Flemings numbered 5.4 million (56 per cent of the national population) compared with 3.1 million (32 per cent) Walloons, bi-lingual Brussels-Capital accounting for 1.1 million (11 per cent) and the German-speaking group for 0.1 million (1 per cent). Between 1961 and 1970 the Flemish population increased 7.3 per cent, but the Walloon increased only 2.6 per cent. Their numerical strength allows the Flemings to claim a larger share of government funds and to achieve stronger parliamentary representation than the Walloons. Secondly, the core of the Walloon economy is the Haine-Sambre-Meuse coalfield whose industries are declining after a long period of great prosperity; on the other hand Flanders is experiencing rapid growth. Thirdly, the question of minority groups along the linguistic frontier causes educational and social problems. Fourthly, the Flemings dislike the presence of an affluent, almost entirely French-speaking Brussels in what they claim is their territory. They suggest that control of the officially bi-lingual capital should be equally vested in both factions, but the Walloons reject this since they muster 80 per cent of the city's population.

As a mollifying act, two Ministries of Regional Economy were created in 1971, and at the same time autonomy in respect of activities

such as education, television and radio services and the arts was
granted. A Ministry for Greater Brussels was mooted, but it has proved
impossible to define the region, let alone manage it. It is thought that
the Brussels region will have to be restricted to the nineteen central
communes of Brussels-Capital, but since this is only a small part of the
city, this solution is manifestly unsatisfactory. Despite the economic
disadvantages, there is strong support for an independent Flanders and
an independent Wallonie, and as time passes there is a lack of evidence
to suggest that the two sides are still looking for agreement.[9]

Transport

In a country such as Belgium which relies heavily on international
trade, ocean transport and, to a less extent, air transport are critical to
the operation of the economy. Indeed the port of Antwerp, which
handled 72 million tonnes in 1971, is second to Rotterdam in Western
Europe in terms of cargo handled and serves a much larger area than the
confines of Belgium. Although Brussels National airport at Zaventem
handled 1.5 million passengers in 1970 and SABENA (Société
Anonyme Belge d'Exploitation de la Navigation Aérienne) is an
important international airline, air transport is of less importance than
road or rail as a passenger-carrying medium. Inland transport has three
components: railways, navigable waterways and roads, and considering
the advantages of road transport, the movement of freight is remarkably
well distributed between the three media. In 1971 roads were
responsible for 44 per cent, railways for 29 per cent and inland
waterways for 27 per cent of the freight moved within Belgium.

Road Transport

The inexorable move towards universal car-ownership coupled with
the development of neotechnic industries (those with components and
products of high value in relation to their weight and bulk) have caused
a great increase in road traffic. It is estimated that there will be 4 million
cars on Belgian roads by 1980, and since the tonnage of road freight is
increasing by an annual rate of 6 per cent, the number of commercial
vehicles is steadily rising. The importance of major roads as part of the
essential infrastructure for new manufacturing industry has not been lost
on the government, and in 1962 the Ministry of Public Works produced
a 1000 km motorway plan to be implemented by 1980. The length of
motorway to be built was later amended to 2400 km, and on 1 January
1974, 1011 km of motorways were in use. When the net is complete the
density of motorways related to the area of the country will be second
only to that of the Netherlands. Since the Ardennes account for
one-quarter of the area of the country and lack any motorways, the

density of the network north of the Sambre-Meuse valley approaches the Dutch level.

Given that traffic flows are largely a function of the size of towns and the distance separating them, it is predictable that the motorway network should centre on Brussels, with Antwerp, the second largest city, as the major peripheral focus. The twin results are likely to be a continued increase in the importance of road traffic and the further improvement of the economic advantages to be obtained in Brussels and Antwerp. At present the net comprises two huge loops from Kortrijk to Liège via Ghent and Antwerp (E3, E39 and A13), and from Tournai to Liège via Mons, Charleroi and Namur (E41), intersected by the E5 between Ostend and Liège via Ghent and Brussels, and by the E10 between Antwerp and Mons also via Brussels. Since the network is an integral part of the larger motorway system linking Paris with Rotterdam and Amsterdam, and the French Nord manufacturing district with the Ruhr, it is likely that Belgium will be able to capitalise on its considerable nodality.

Railway Transport

The railways of Belgium are unusual in a country which still firmly believes in private ownership, for they have been controlled by the state since 1834. The system is an intensive one. Prior to the closure of many rural lines in the 1960s, there were 32 route kilometres for each 100 km^2 of the country, compared with figures of 15 and 7 route kilometres per 100 km^2 for the Netherlands and France respectively. In addition there is a 350 km remnant of the light railway system set up under an act of 1885 to serve areas where the density of traffic was low. Of the existing 4200 route kilometres of standard gauge track, only 2900 remain open for passenger traffic, but it is not only in terms of length that the freight and passenger systems differ.

The flows of goods traffic emphasise two factors, the degree of interaction between the two largest cities, Brussels and Antwerp, and the importance of the heavy industries associated with the Walloon coalfield. As Fig. 7 indicates, the densest flow of goods is between Brussels and Antwerp, approaching 32 million tonnes of freight in 1972; with the exception of the Ghent-Brussels traffic, the other flows of more than 14 million tonnes link Brussels and Antwerp with Mons, Charleroi and Liège, and Charleroi with Liège and Aachen in West Germany. The Walloon coalfield generates inwards shipments of iron ore and coal, and exports steel and steel products. Similarly it is the iron and steel industry that is responsible for the importance of the three flows through the Ardennes, for much iron ore is brought from Luxemburg and Lorraine by rail. The most significant route through the

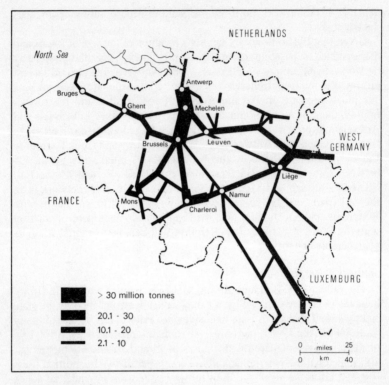

Fig 7. FREIGHT TRAFFIC ON BELGIAN RAILWAYS, 1971
Source: *Cartactual*, 38 no 6, 1972

Ardennes is that between Arlon and Marlois, a line which carried 14
million tonnes of freight in 1972, a total equal to that between Liège and
Mechelen (for Antwerp and Brussels).[10] This route handles both iron ore
imports and coke flows from the coalfield to the blast furnaces at Athus
in Belgian Lorraine. In contrast to the Ardennes, with its small number
of dense flows, the provinces of West-and Oost-Vlaanderen have a
large number of light flows, almost all of which comprise less than 1
million tonnes of freight annually. This is indicative of the unimportance of heavy industry in these two provinces.

   One single influence, the role of Brussels, dominates passenger traffic
in Belgium. Despite the Trans-Europe Exress services which link
Ostend and West Germany via Brussels and Liège, and the position of
Antwerp as a role of attraction in its own right, the national passenger

network is effectively a huge commuter system operating for the benefit of the capital. Some 185,000 people commute daily to Brussels, and two-thirds of these travel by rail. In general terms, lines with a daily traffic of more than 20,000 passengers are located within a 50 km radius of Brussels, and those of between 10,000 and 20,000 passengers within a 100 km radius.[11]. This remarkable situation has arisen, firstly, from government policy of cheap fares which cause *abonnements sociaux*, or fares reduced for social reasons, and *abonnements scolaires*, or schoolchildren's fares, to account for 55 per cent of passenger kilometres, though only 33 per cent of passenger revenue.[12] These fares encourage commuting over longer distances than would otherwise be the case, allowing Brussels to spread its sphere of influence. Secondly, Brussels has a high degree of nodality in respect of other cities, for Antwerp, Ghent, Mons, Charleroi and Leuven all lie within 70 km; flows between the capital and these points form the bulk of the total passenger traffic. Thirdly, Brussels offers a wide variety of employment, above all in the tertiary and quaternary sectors.

Inland Waterways

The Belgian waterway network has a total length of 1500 km, but although one-third of the system is capable of handling 1350-tonne barges, only half of the net can accommodate vessels larger than 400 tonnes. Viewed as a whole, it is apparent from Fig 8 that the system has considerable similarity to the railway freight net. This is not surprising since the largest settlements and industrial centres are located on rivers which have been canalised or modified to take barge traffic, and since some of the more important railway lines follow river valleys. In both systems the heaviest traffic flows are found in the lower Scheldt valley, the Sambre-Meuse valley and in the two links between these rivers from Charleroi, Brussels and beyond to the west and from Liège Antwerp in the east. Equally, in both systems traffic west of the Charleroi-Brussels-Antwerp axis is less important than traffic to the east of it. The principal differences between the two systems are the centrality of Brussels in the railway net and the centrality of Antwerp in the waterway network; the importance of railway routes in the Ardennes and the lack of navigable waterways there; and the presence of the 50,000-tonne capacity ship canal between Terneuzen in the Netherlands and Ghent.

The lower Scheldt below Rupelmonde carries the heaviest traffic, for at this point the Brussels-Rupel canal and the river Rupel, both of which have capacity for 2000-tonne barges, merge with the Scheldt. The tonnage handled in 1970 amounted to 47 million tonnes, which is some 15 million tonnes more than the freight hauled by the railways between

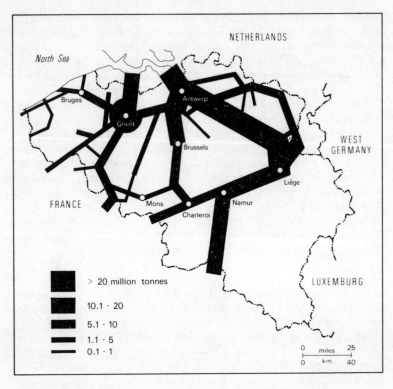

Fig 8. FREIGHT TRAFFIC ON BELGIAN INLAND WATERWAYS, 1970
SOURCE: *Annuaire Statistique de la Belgique*, 91, 1971

Mechelen and Antwerp. The 130 km-long Albert Canal, completed in 1940, is the second most important waterway, and moved some 38 million tonnes in 1970. In terms of tonne-kilometres, however, the canal returned a figure almost three times higher than that for the lower Scheldt, owing to the greater length of haul possible on the canal. The economies obtained from the use of push barges, a single unit of which is capable of shipping 5000 tonnes, are such that new locks, 200m long and 24m wide, capable of taking four push barges and their power vessel, are under construction on the Albert Canal. Further traffic may be generated by the construction of a section between Oelegem and the sea lock at Zandvliet which will by-pass the older Antwerp dock area. The Terneuzen-Ghent canal handled 21 million tonnes in 1970, largely a function of the integrated iron and steel plant at Zelzate. All other important waterways are part of the Antwerp-Charleroi-Liège-Antwerp loop.

2

The Development of the Economy

BELGIUM WAS THE first nation after Great Britain to experience the industrial revolution. The event that Rostow calls 'take-off', which occurs when investment reaches a level of more than 10 per cent of the national income,[1] was achieved during the 1840s, and it is therefore to be expected that not only has the industrialisation process played an important part in the shaping of the economy, but also that the location and nature of Belgian industry owes much to its nineteenth-century origins. Old established activities are frequently not among the most prosperous, with the result that if such activities represent a large part of a regional economy, as is the case in the Walloon coalfield and to a lesser extent in West-and Oost-Vlaanderen, local difficulties ensue. In order to understand the present it is necessary briefly to examine the past.

The Industrial Revolution

That Belgium was in the van of the introduction of large-scale manufacture was not so much a result of the possession of natural resources, for these, notably coal, were also available in neighbouring France and Germany, but rather the consequence of a number of other factors. Particularly important was the availability of capital and a willingness among entrepreneurs to invest in industry at a time when many other countries were at war. Entrepreneurs benefited from the enforced union with France (1793–1813) and from Bonaparte's war; Napoleon built the canal between Mons and Condé on the Escaut to facilitate the movement of coal to France, and he constructed Antwerp's first dock in 1811. The bank set up by William I of the Netherlands in

1824 for the promotion of industry (between 1815 and 1830 Belgium was part of the Netherlands) offered short-term credits to industrialists. After the revolution of 1830 a similar Belgian bank was opened, followed in 1835 by the Banque de Belgique. Hence some forty years prior to similar events in Germany, Belgian financiers were investing in industry to the considerable benefit of both. Although not so important as the supply of capital, the availability of labour in Belgium in the years down to the defeat of Napoleon gave the country no little advantage. France, Germany, Russia and Austria were involved in war and much of their labour force was locked up in their armies and enemy prisons. Additionally, the introduction of factories in the Flemish textile districts and the metallurgical area of the Sambre-Meuse valley caused the collapse of many domestic workshops, whose operatives then became available for factory employment. A striking example comes from the Liège region: some 40,000 domestic textile workers were thrown out of work, and drifted into factories, between 1800 and 1819.[2]

Entrepreneurial ability and a high degree of innovation seem to have characterised the Belgian metal workers, just as the former quality in particular typified the medieval merchants of Bruges, Ghent and Mechelen. By the eighteenth century the lower-Ardennes had become one of the most concentrated and important iron-making areas in Europe, thanks to easily worked ore deposits and to accumulated skills and ingenuity. That there should be between 12,000 and 15,000 nail-makers in the Namur district, and a similar number at Liège as early as 1737,[3] implies that these artisans were able, at a time of high transport costs, to compete successfully with other producers over a wide area penetrating deep into France and Germany. The craftsmanship exhibited by the Liège armourers from the fifteenth century onwards is an even more striking example of innovation. From the manufacture of armour they naturally diversified into production of guns, mortars and artillery pieces, and by 1850 they had made Liège the most important producer of ordnance in Europe. Ironically enough, they were helped by the traditional neutrality of the Bishopric of Liège (the city was part of an independent ecclesiastical territory until 1789) which allowed them to prosper and to acquire capital from their bellicose neighbours. Although the gun-makers included innovators such as Jean-Etienne Colleye de Sarolay, who invented the cartridge extractor for the breech loading rifle, theirs was largely a corporate genius stemming from their tight cluster of workshops at Herstal. Individual initiative of a high order was left to men like J.D. Dony who invented the zinc recovery process in 1798, and John Cockerill. Initially a textile machinery maker at Verviers, Cockerill came to Liège in 1807 and by 1812 was employing 2000 workers in his foundries and engineering

workshops at Seraing, where he confidently bought the palace of the
Prince-Bishops. In 1817 he built the first puddling furnace outside
Britain, and followed this in 1823 with the first successful coke-fired
blast furnace to be operated other than in Britain. Predictably it was
Cockerill who built the first Belgian railway locomotive in 1835.
Innovators such as Jaspar (electric arc lamp), Englebert (rubber
technology), Solvay (soda), Mélen (wool washing), Walschaerts (valve
gear) and Belpaire (boilers), came later and therefore did not account
for the early date of the Belgian industrial revolution, but they at least
ensured its momentum.

The events of the nineteenth century brought great changes to the
distribution of industry in Belgium, the most important of which was
undoubtedly the growth of factories along the Haine-Sambre-Meuse
axis, associated with the large-scale exploitation of coal measures. Coal
was used as a fuel in blast furnaces for example, and as a raw material in
the chemical industry, but more important, it was the principal source of
power; the nineteenth century has aptly been described as the era of
steam industrialism. In the Haine-Sambre-Meuse valleys coalmining
was ubiquitous and engineering was widespread, blast furnaces sprang
up at Charleroi, Liège and La Louvière, and also in the Borinage and in
towns such as Huy from which the activity has since migrated. The
fortuitous juxtaposition of raw materials and fuel gave rise to thriving
pottery and glass industries, above all in the Charleroi region. Towards
the end of the century the carbochemical industry was added to this
'Black Country', a landscape which became punctuated by spoil heaps,
and spread with grimy factories and cramped, insalubrious housing.
Peripheral to the coalfield, Verviers in the east witnessed the growth of
the largest cluster of wool textile mills in the country. Attractive though
the coalfield was to the factory masters, there was one industry which
expanded as fast as any, but did so in the valleys of the Scheldt and its
tributaries, the Leie and the Dender. The cotton and linen textile
industries were similar to many of the activities located on the coalfield
in that they were not new in the nineteenth century but merely embraced
the factory system. Power spindles and looms were introduced in Ghent
in 1798 and 1805 respectively, and cotton mills soon diffused to
Kortrijk, Oudenaarde, Ronse, Aalst and Ath. That steam driven mills
could exist other than on a coalfield was a result of the comprehensive
waterway system and the strength and adaptability of local skills dating
from the medieval period, of complex integration of the mills with the
existing domestic system and the use of efficient compound steam
engines.[4] The Flemish industrial districts differed from their counterpart
in the south in that they did not give rise to a Black Country, for

agriculture remained important and dispersed domestic textile workshops continued to function throughout the century.

Nineteenth-century Belgium was characterised by the appearance of a
number of manufacturing activities whose locational rationale poses
problems. Each of these activities was strongly associated with a single,
or exceptionally two, localities. In a number of instances it is reasonable
to expect an industry to exist in a particular region, even though the
explanation for the precise site is uncertain. Thus it is not surprising that
lace-making was carried on in Bruges, tapestry-weaving in Mouscron,
hat-making at Tournai and Leuze and the making of gloves at Ninove
and Oudenaarde, for such activities are associated with the textile
production and these towns are in, or adjacent to Flanders. Less easy to
explain is the Mechelen furniture industry, the clothing industry at
Binche, a small town south of the coalfield in Hainaut with fifty-four
workshops in 1896,[5] the Gembloux surgical instrument industry and the
Dender valley match industry. The reason for their location lies not in
the realms of material supply, markets and transport costs, but rather in
the sphere of chance and behavioural factors, the most important of
which is decision-making by manufacturers. The initial location was
fortuitous and stemmed in many cases from the simple fact that the
entrepreneur who made the decision to manufacture the item in question
lived at this location. The next pre-requisite was success sufficient to
induce others in the vicinity to enter the activity. Once this had been
achieved the 'swarm' could gather momentum to the disadvantage of
entrepreneurs located outside it. The external economies to be obtained
by such a swarm were very great, for many of the industries mentioned
were vertically disintegrated, with many processes, each one carried on
by small, specialist firms. There was much interdependence, the
product of one factory becoming the raw material of the next, and by
clustering at a single location, plants overcame the slowness of the flow
of information in an era before the telephone and motor vehicle. Some
of the clusters were very large indeed; no less than 150,000 lace-makers
were working at Bruges in 1875, and by 1906 Herstal was
manufacturing seven times more weapons than Birmingham, and thirty
times more than St Etienne. This was achieved by a labour force 73 per
cent of which worked in domestic workshops in 1896.[6]

The beginnings of most of these activities have not been recorded in
detail, but because of its more recent origin, it is possible to trace the
development of the Belgian match industry. Having learned the
methods of production in Germany, Mertens set up the first Belgian
match factory in 1832 at Lessines, where his brother ran a small
wax-making business. A family quarrel caused the brothers to leave
Lessines and to open a second factory 5 km to the north at Overboelare.

Both plants were successful, encouraging others in the locality to enter the activity, and by 1880 nine of the twelve plants in the country were located in the Dender valley. The strength of the Dender valley plants has persisted, and although there are only two still in operation, the larger is at Gerardsbergen-Overboelare, the site of the Mertens brothers' second factory. The other is downstream at Ninove.[7]

Competition and Adaptation in the Early Twentieth Century

Towards the end of the nineteenth century the productive capacity of nations such as Germany, the U.S.A. and France began to assert itself, not only in international markets, but also, since Belgium was dedicated to free trade, within Belgium itself. Prior to 1914 foreign investment by Belgian interests was greater than investment in Belgium by foreigners, but in the inter-war period the two became approximately equal. Innovatory dynamism passed to other industrial nations, and no longer could the Walloon coalfield expect an assured market for anything it produced. This had been the case with glass products for half a century, and indeed in 1880 the value of glass manufacture was twice that of steel. By 1900 there were 56 glassworks in Charleroi alone, employing 30,000 people. However, the introduction of mechanical glassblowing by Lubbers in the U.S.A. in 1903 severely undermined the Belgian hand blown industry, while other advances by Libbey-Owens, also in America, were likewise disadvantageous. In spite of its European importance, the Herstal ordnance industry was sufficiently cautious about the future to commence diversification in the last decade of the century. The major firm, Fabrique Nationale d'Armes de Guerre (FN), began the manufacture of bicycles in 1891 and other companies followed suit. Inevitably a number of firms went further and added engines to their cycles. Such a firm was Sarolea which diversified into cycles in 1892 and ceased making weapons in 1900 in order to concentrate on motorcycles.[8] But in spite of diversification almost all such companies closed down in the 1920s in the face of continuing foreign competition. FN itself followed a thoroughgoing policy of diversification which allowed it to survive; its range of production came to include cars, lorries, trolleybuses, aero engines, agricultural machinery and electric motors in addition to weapons.

The Flemish textile industry found more difficulty in diversifying the nature of its output: the principal reaction was the abandonment of the domestic system, which was still important even at the end of the century in linen and lace manufacture, and a growing reliance upon urban mills. Even so this was not sufficient to ensure a captive domestic market, and in the years prior to 1914 Russian linen accounted for two-thirds of all linen sales in Belgium. The wool sector of the industry at Verviers experimented with worsted cloth, and while this strategy had some success, it became apparent in the inter-war years that production costs were lower in Flanders owing to the lower wage levels prevailing there. The result was a northward migration of the industry. An augury of the impact that man-made fibres were to have on the manufacture of textiles was the opening of a rayon plant at Tubize in the late 1920s.

However desirable it may be as an answer to changing locational advantage, diversification is not always possible. It was unfortunate that the basic activity of the Walloon industrial district, coalmining, fell into this category. Largely because of their early start, Belgian pits were small and suffered from grossly uneconomic concessions. In one area of the Borinage there were fourteen concessions arranged one beneath the other. The Ruhr and Pas-de-Calais fields were exemplary by comparison, moreover they did not possess the unfavourable geological conditions which obtained in Belgium. By 1913 the output per manshift in the Ruhr was 1161 kg compared with 613 kg in the Borinage[9]. Table 3 illustrates the cost differentials between mines in the Borinage and those elsewhere at the beginning of the twentieth century. The situation was not helped by the practice of 'dumping' by the Germans, Poles and British. In 1928 Ruhr coal was being sold in Belgium at prices 26 to 36 per cent lower than at the pithead in the Ruhr as part of a campaign to ruin the Belgian collieries.[10] Tariff protection in the 1930s, World War II and the subsequent shortages of energy postponed real rationalisation in the Walloon coal industry; the result was that contraction was all the more drastic when it did take place in the 1960s.

Table 3

PRODUCTION COSTS IN BELGIAN, FRENCH AND GERMAN COALFIELDS, 1903-1906. BF PER TONNE

Borinage 1906	Béthune (Pas-de-Calais) 1903	Gelsenkirchen (Ruhr) 1906	Kölner Bergwerks Verein (Ruhr) 1906
12.92	11.0	9.50	8.50

Source: Georges de Leener, *Le Marché Charbonnier Belge*, Brussels, (1908), 39-41

The locational component of adaption to new competitive forces has been suggested above; two elements are apparent. Firstly, there was a concentration of production at the most favourable points, typified by the closure of small iron and steelworks, and by the clustering of large works at Charleroi and Liège. The same process was evident in the collapse of the domestic textile industry in rural areas, leaving a residual pattern of urban mills. Secondly, there has been a northward migration from Wallonie towards Flanders following the emergence of a wage differential between the two regions. An additional factor behind this northward industrial development was that imported coal was cheaper than Belgian coal in the north, and this was the reason for the construction of nine coking plants in Flanders during the first three decades of the century. One, at Zeebrugge, was within a port area, while all the others were located on canal bank sites at Zandvoorde, Zelzate, Ghent, Mol and along the Brussels-Rupel canal. The last plant to be completed, in 1932 was at Neder-over-Heembeek, and by the following year these Flemish plants were responsible for 32 per cent of Belgian coke production.[11] In spite of the external economies to be reaped in Wallonie, two large glassworks were established at Mol and Zeebrugge in the north, and there was a notable migration of smelting and refining of non ferrous metals to the Kempenland and Antwerp. The leading Liège zinc refiner, Vieille Montagne, built a plant at Balen in Antwerpen.

In addition to the specific industries mentioned, the inter-war period saw the development of a wide range of industries along the principal waterways of Flanders, above all along the lower Scheldt, the Brussels-Rupel and the Terneuzen-Ghent canals. Chemical works, paper mills, shipyards, engineering works and, at Antwerp, small oil refineries sprang up. Perhaps a more accurate indication of what was to come was the arrival of the two American vehicle companies, General Motors and Ford, which opened assembly plants at Antwerp, and the establishment of the Stampe and Vertongen aircraft factory at Deurne, Antwerp, in 1922. Similarly the Renard aero engine plant at Evere, Brussels, also suggested that engineering of some complexity could be undertaken outside Liège. This is not to say that Wallonie did not develop new technologies – FN and Ateliers de Construction Electrique de Charleroi (ACEC), for example were active there – but the dynamism once the prerogative of the south seemed to be diffusing northwards.

An important part of this process was the emergence of the Brussels conurbation as an important manufacturing region. By 1937 Brussels had 13 per cent and Brabant 20 per cent of the Belgian industrial labour force, and among the other provinces only Hainaut with 21 per cent made a larger contribution. Welded on to the craft-goods production associated with large cities was a growing range of neotechnic industries. These are industries not tied to raw materials nor restricted by onerous transport costs, for the goods produced are of high value. Such activities are attracted to major markets, which are also in a position to supply the relatively unskilled labour required. Typical of the new industries in Brussels were the Renault and Citroën assembly plants set up in the city in the 1920s.

The final, and in respect of numbers employed, the most important industrial trend in the early twentieth century was the opening up of the Kempen coalfield. Most pits were brought into production in the 1920s and 1930s, coal being first raised at Winterslag in 1917 and at the last pit to be sunk, Houthalen, in 1938. Each pit was built to mine approximately 1 million tonnes per annum, and at this size there were many economies of scale which the much smaller Walloon pits lacked. The concessions, granted by the state, were leased in a rational manner. They were large and did not overlap with the consequence that productivity was superior to that in Wallonie. Yet the Kempen field signally failed to attract substantial industrial development. Three reasons may be advanced for this phenomenon. Firstly, the geographical inertia of the Walloon industrial district was by now very powerful indeed, and, for many industries, to move to an entirely new region, almost entirely lacking an industrial infrastructure, would have been to incur great diseconomies. Secondly, water transport facilities for the shipment of coal from the Kempen were good, especially with the opening in 1940 of the Albert Canal, which can accommodate 2000-tonne barges. Thirdly, because of great improvements in the efficiency of the use of coal, a coalfield location was no longer as essential as it had been a century before.

Regional Economic Development Since World War II

Since World War II, Belgian regional economies have undergone a number of important changes which may conveniently be considered under the headings of employment, investment, unemployment and income.

Employment

At the national scale employment trends have been characterised by the growing importance, and ultimate domination, of the tertiary employment sector at the expense of manufacturing and the extractive industries. For the period before the late 1950s it is justifiable to emphasise the part played by the latter two sectors for they formed the basis of the country's economy, and were responsible for the development of industrial regions. In 1950, for example, the primary, secondary and tertiary sectors, the last including the construction industry, accounted respectively for 17, 38 and 45 per cent of total employment. But in the next two decades the tertiary sector became more important than the other two combined: 1971 saw the respective shares of national employment standing at 5, 33 and 62 per cent.[12] The decline of the primary sector has in large part been due to the drastic contraction in coalmining, whose labour force dropped from 143,000 in 1956 to 33,000 in 1972. Absolute employment in manufacturing has exhibited a small increase, but such have been the gains by the tertiary sector that manufacturing's share of total employment has fallen. Indeed, between 1950 and 1971 the number of jobs in the tertiary sector was nearly doubled.

Table 4

PROVINCIAL EMPLOYMENT BY SECTOR, 1955 AND 1970. %

	1955			1970		
	Primary	Secondary	Tertiary	Primary	Secondary	Tertiary
Antwerpen	1	59	40	0	46	54
Brabant	1	48	51	0	31	69
Hainaut	31	50	19	5	46	49
Liège	14	59	27	3	45	52
Limburg	56	21	23	15	37	48
Luxembourg	5	46	49	3	27	70
Namur	19	47	34	4	32	64
Oost-Vlaanderen	2	73	25	1	53	46
West-Vlaanderen	4	62	34	1	49	50

Source: Office National de Sécurité Sociale, *Rapport Annuel, 1955, 1970,* Brussels (1956, 1971)

The regional implications of these developments are considerable, for just as the demise of coalmining has not affected all areas equally, neither has the rapid growth of tertiary office employment. Table 4 summarises the situation in 1955 and 1970. The data for 1955 illustrate the importance of manufacturing compared with services at this time, and emphasize the four coalmining provinces of Hainaut, Liège, Limburg and Namur as large employers in this sector. These provinces, above all Hainaut, had weakly developed service sectors typical of many coalfield industrial districts. It is interesting to note that the highest figures for percentage employment in manufacturing were not found in the 'traditional' industrial areas, but rather in Oost-and West-Vlaanderen. Only in Brabant and Luxembourg was the service sector the leading employer, and the way in which this trend is reversed by 1970 is the outstanding feature of the table. There is evidence of a remarkable effort of diversification in the coalfield provinces and in Flanders, which has given rise to a much greater uniformity between the provinces than was the case in 1955. Some specialisation does remain, notably the extractive industry in Limburg, on manufacturing in Oost-Vlaanderen and the emphasis on services in Brabant and Luxembourg, but employment trends within the provincial economies do seem to be following a single path.

A comparison of the numbers employed in each sector by province is a fruitful exercise. In 1970 Brabant was still the leading manufacturing region with 22 per cent of the national total so employed, followed by Antwerpen with 19 per cent, Oost-Vlaanderen with 14 per cent and Hainaut with 13 per cent. Yet in 1955 Brabant claimed 25 per cent of the total; her relative decline has been due to increased industrial activity in Antwerpen, West-Vlaanderen and Limburg where there was a four-fold growth in manufacturing employment during the fifteen year period. Liège, the seat of the Belgian industrial revolution, actually experience a contraction in its manufacturing workforce and in 1970 could muster but 11 per cent of the national total. The overall tendency is thus for a more even distribution of manufacturing throughout the country. The same characteristic obtains for the tertiary sector, although not on quite the same scale for there are some activities such as banking, finance and insurance which congregate strongly in the largest cities. Thus Brabant, which includes Brussels, employs half the Belgian total in commerce and one-third of the total in the public services and the hotel trade, giving the province a 36 per cent share of the national tertiary sector as a whole. Despite the growth of the service sector elsewhere, the strength of Brabant and Antwerpen in the tertiary sector is formidable, for together they account for 53 per cent of the national total. Since they have 41 per cent of the country's manufacturing labour, it is clear that the Brussels-Antwerp axis is the national economic core. Fortunately there is evidence to suggest that the lag exhibited by the remaining provinces is showing signs of diminishing.

Investment

Investment is a good index of economic growth for it represents the expression of the businessman's views, albeit subjective, concerning locations most likely to produce the greatest profits. Government spending on projects such as roads, housing and financial support for industry influences the pattern somewhat, but since the greater part of investment in Belgium is private, the distribution of investment funds should highlight the regional problem. Until 1963 Brabant benefited most from investment in manufacturing, but without enjoying a clear lead over Antwerpen.[13] The two provinces accounted for 38 per cent of total industrial investment between 1955 and 1964, but Hainaut and Liège were not too far behind with a combined figure of 33 per cent. Of the other provinces only Oost-Vlaanderen received more than 10 per cent of manufacturing investment in any one year. In 1965 the huge sums sunk into the Sidmar steel plant at Zelzate, north of Ghent, were instrumental in Oost-Vlaanderen receiving more industrial funds than either Brabant or Antwerpen. The following year the same province had the highest total investment in Belgium, but 1966 was also the beginning of real expansion in petrochemicals in the port of Antwerp. In 1967 34 per cent of both manufacturing and total investment was placed in Antwerpen, and so long as the capital-intensive chemical industry continues to mushroom on the Scheldt, the province will attract large sums of money. The outburst of investment in Antwerp also ushered in an era of waning fortunes in Hainaut and especially Liège where combined investment could only equal that in Oost-Vlaanderen for the years 1966–8.

Table 5

UNEMPLOYMENT IN BELGIUM BY LINGUISTIC REGION, 1958-1972. %

	Wallonie	Flanders	Brussels	Belgium
1958	3.8	7.8	4.0	5.9
1960	4.7	7.0	4.4	5.9
1964	2.5	2.6	1.8	2.4
1968	6.5	4.5	2.7	4.8
1972	4.2	2.7	2.3	3.0

Source: Office National de l'Emploi, *Rapport Annuel, 1958-72,* Brussels
(1959-1973)

Unemployment

Economic prosperity is also reflected in unemployment trends which illustrate particularly well the fluctuations of regional development. There is certainly support from the unemployment figures for the contention that the old industrial regions of Hainaut and Liège began to exhibit stagnation in the mid-1960s, following a marked improvement in West-and Oost-Vlaanderen. As Table 5 indicates, in 1958 the Flemish provinces registered unemployment figures which were twice as high as those in Wallonie; two-thirds of those out of work were to be found in Flanders. In spite of the satisfactory investment performance of Wallonie in the early 1960s, the unemployment situation slowly worsened during the decade as coalmining contracted and as older industries underwent rationalisation. Unemployment in Flanders, on the other hand, followed the opposite path, falling sharply to a level below that in Wallonie in 1966. By the late 1960s, Wallonie had taken the place occupied by Flanders in the 1950s, and by 1969 half those out of work were in the French-speaking provinces. From a level of 2.9 per cent in 1966, unemployment in Liège rose to 7.6 per cent in 1972, substantially above the national level. Hainaut is rather better placed, with an unemployment rate of 4.2 per cent in 1972, but nevertheless compares unfavourably with Antwerpen, Brabant, and Oost-Vlaanderen. Only Liège and Limburg, now faced with the problem of absorbing redundant miners in addition to the difficulties posed by very high population fertility, have a higher level of unemployment than Hainaut. Fig 9 illustrates these recent trends, and also highlights the poor showing of the Walloon and Kempen coalfield *arrondissements* in comparison with other areas.

Income

Per capita income figures confirm the distributional tendencies noted in the case of investment and also the switch in the progress of West- and Oost-Vlaanderen on the one hand and Hainaut and Liège on the other. Table 6 indicates that although Brabant is the richest province, incomes in 1970 were not as far in advance of the rest of the country in 1970 as they were in 1966. Further, five provinces had an index greater than 90 in 1970 compared with only three in 1966. Both West- and Oost-Vlaanderen gained 7 points between 1966 and 1970, and would seem fast to be approaching the national average income level. Liège and Hainaut, however, lost ground, the former by 5 points. In spite of this Liège still had an income level above the national average, a situation arising from the strength of the basic metals sector which has by far the highest daily earnings of any industry in Belgium.[14] The table highlights the great disparity between Brabant and the two provinces of Luxembourg and Limburg, indicating that the centrifugal spread of prosperity from the economic core has not yet reached these peripheral areas. The low incomes prevalent in Luxembourg are not irreconcilable with relatively low unemployment (3.0 per cent in 1972) for much of the population is rural, a situation not conducive to high wages. That urban areas, however, are characterised by high incomes is seen in the index numbers for the major Belgian cities in 1970. The *arrondissements* of Brussels-Capital scored 145, Antwerp 120, Liège 108 and Ghent 103, well above the per capita incomes of their respective provinces. Fig 10 shows that apart from these areas, only the Brussels suburban districts of Halle-Vilvoorde and Nivelles had incomes above the national average. It is a hopeful sign that five of the eight *arrondissements* of West-Vlaanderen returned incomes in the band immediately below the national average.

Table 6

PER CAPITA INCOMES FOR 1966 AND 1970. BELGIUM = 100

	1966	1970		1966	1970
Brabant	130	125	Namur	89	89
Antwerpen	104	106	Hainaut	88	86
Liège	107	101	Luxembourg	75	76
Oost-Vlaanderen	89	93	Limburg	71	72
West-Vlaanderen	88	91			

Source: Institut National de Statistique, *Bulletin de Statistique*, no 3 (1969),
        no 4 (1973)

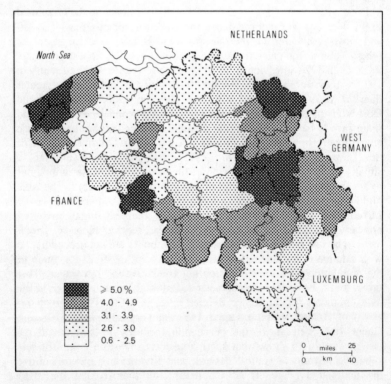

Fig 9. AVERAGE MONTHLY UNEMPLOYMENT IN 1972
SOURCE: Office National de l'Emploi, *Rapport Annuel 1972*, Brussels, 1973

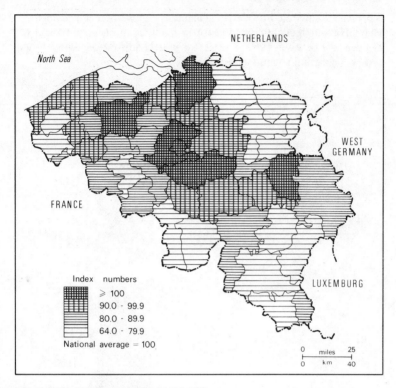

Fig 10. PER CAPITA INCOME IN 1970
SOURCE: Institut National de Statistique, *Bulletin de Statistique*, no 4, 1973

The Distribution of Manufacturing

There are two distinctive features to the distribution of Belgian industry. Firstly, many of the older industries are highly localised, and since it is precisely these industries which exhibit slow growth, the effect is to curb expansion possibilities in such localities. Secondly, the newer industries have for the most part been attracted to the Flemish provinces, thus avoiding the manufacturing districts established in the nineteenth century. These two facts combine to accelerate regional imbalance. The swathe of *arrondissements*, shown in Fig 11, exhibiting a loss or slow growth of manufacturing employment, extending from Thuin to Liège across the Walloon coalfield, is the result of specialisation in the older industries. On the other hand the striking expansion exhibited by West-Vlaanderen, Antwerpen and Limburg, where Hasselt recorded an increase in manufacturing employment of 273 per cent between 1960 and 1971, is largely attributable to the influx of new, neotechnic manufacturing.

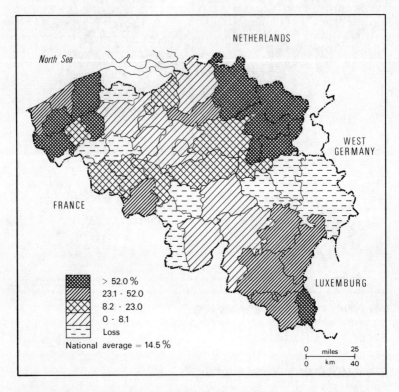

Fig 11. CHANGES IN MANUFACTURING EMPLOYMENT, 1960–1971
The Mouscron *arrondissement* did not exist in 1960 and no data can be computed. Data for Halle–Vilvoorde and Brussels–Capital are combined.
SOURCE: Office National de Sécurité Sociale, *Rapport Annual 1960, 1971*, Brussels, 1961, 1972

The Distribution of the Growth Industries

Using employment change between 1955 and 1972 as a measure, it is possible to isolate those industries which are growing rapidly from those exhibiting a modest performance. The increase in employment in all manufacturing industries was 15 per cent, and according to the classification drawn up by the Office National de Sécurité Sociale, only six industries underwent a faster rate of growth. These were: engineering (56 per cent), publishing (44 per cent), chemicals (32 per cent), paper (27 per cent), food processing (21 per cent) and metalworking (20 per cent). Changes in the employment in these industries between 1960 and 1972 appear in Fig 12, from which it is evident that the Flemish areas have indeed been most successful in attracting growth industry. Apart from Mons, Ath and Marche-en-Famenne, all the areas recording increases above 60 per cent lie in Flanders. Brussels, Halle-Vilvoorde and Antwerp, on the other hand, returned increases less than the national figure.

Although they describe the trend, changes in employment fail to indicate the absolute importance of the growth industries in particular areas. Table 7 sets out that proportion of employment in the growth industries on a provincial basis, and it is clear that for all Limburg's great strides, Antwerpen and Brabant still head the list. A further method of establishing the distribution of the growth industries is by the calculation of location quotients, using the formula:

$$Lq = \frac{100x_i}{x_t} \Big/ \frac{100y_i}{y_t}$$

where Lq is the location quotient, X_i is the number of workers in industry i in province X, X_t is the total industrial workforce in province X, Y_i is the number of workers in industry i in Belgium and Y_t is the total Belgian industrial workforce. Location quotients relate the share of an activity in the total employment of the province to the share of this activity in the total employment of the country as a whole. Quotients greater than 1 indicate specialisation in the activity concerned; quotients less than 1 indicate that the activity is underrepresented. Table 7 indicates that alone among the provinces, Antwerpen and Brabant specialise in all the growth industries, and between them they return the highest quotients in two of the six industries, publishing and chemicals. In contrast, West-and Oost-Vlaanderen and Hainaut do not have a single quotient greater than unity, and the latter province has only one score even approaching 1. Limburg has the highest score for the engineering industry, but Hainaut has four quotients of only 0.5 and one of 0.6. The performance of Liège reflects its strength in metalworking and engineering, but perhaps the most surprising finding is the excellent showing of the two remaining Walloon provinces, Namur and Luxembourg. The former has four scores greater than unity and the

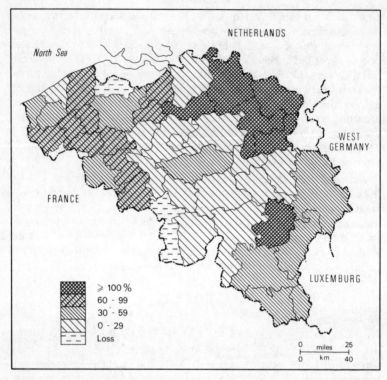

Fig 12. EMPLOYMENT CHANGE IN THE GROWTH INDUSTRIES
1960–1972
The Mouscron *arrondissement* did not exist in 1960 and no data can be computed
Data for Halle-Vilvoorde and Brussels-Capital are combined.
SOURCE: as for Fig 11

latter three, a situation redolent of Flanders rather than Wallonie which
is so burdened with the weight of old established industries.

By implication, provinces having a small proportion of their
workforce in growth industries will have a large part in the declining
and slowly growing industries. It may be hypothesised that the
provinces strong in the growth industries possess highly diversified
manufacturing sectors, giving them balance and minimising the risks
attendant upon undue specialisation. In order to test this proposition,
Lorenz curves, from which diversification coefficients may be
calculated, were constructed.[15] Absolute diversification results in the
highest coefficient of 1, and it may be observed from Table 8 that

Table 7

GROWTH INDUSTRIES: LOCATION QUOTIENTS AND SHARE OF PROVINCIAL
EMPLOYMENT. 1970

	Location Quotients						Share of Provincial Employment %
	Engin-eering	Publi-shing	Chemi-cals	Paper	Metal-working	Food	
Antwerpen	1.15	1.04	1.73	1.01	1.16	1.21	66
Brabant	1.05	2.02	1.50	1.92	1.38	1.17	63
Hainaut	0.93	0.69	0.51	0.58	0.52	0.57	37
Liège	1.17	0.62	0.36	0.69	1.35	0.94	50
Limburg	1.70	0.29	0.72	0.73	0.86	0.82	60
Luxembourg	0.43	0.58	0.14	2.59	1.28	1.76	40
Namur	0.74	0.70	1.40	1.45	2.03	1.19	53
O-Vlaanderen	0.53	0.59	0.91	0.76	0.48	0.95	33
W-Vlaanderen	0.98	0.58	0.21	0.15	0.62	0.90	38

Source: Office National de Sécurité Sociale, *Rapport Annuel, 1970,* Brussels (1971)

Antwerpen and Brabant do in fact have the greatest diversification. Oost-Vlaanderen is the third ranking province, but on the evidence of Table 7 there would seem to be a need to diversify into the growth industries to a greater extent than at present. At the other end of the spectrum, Liège is the least diversified province and yet half its working population is in the growth industries. In this case, however, the economy has a rather narrow base dominated by engineering and metalworking, and the high unemployment figures indicate that all is not well with the industrial structure of this province. Both Luxembourg and Hainaut have low coefficients, and since they also have modest percentages of workpeople in the growth industries, they must, with West-Vlaanderen, in spite of its slightly better diversification and higher per capita income, be regarded as the country's manufacturing problem areas. If social factors, reflected in incomes and unemployment, are considered critical, then Limburg must also be added to the list of problem regions.

Foreign Investment in Manufacturing

The speed of changes in the distribution of manufacturing is slowed down by the natural tendency of firms to expand *in situ* rather than to move to an entirely new site. Consequently the real potential of the Brussels-Antwerp axis has suffered from the inertia of investment decisions made by Walloon managers. A much more sensitive guide to regional potential is therefore new investment made by foreign firms, for as newcomers they are free to select what seems to them the most profitable area, unfettered by considerations of inertia or emotion. Belgium has sedulously encouraged foreign companies to establish themselves as a deliberate policy of employing foreign 'know how'.

Table 8

INDUSTRIAL DIVERSIFICATION COEFFICIENTS, 1970

Brabant	0.490	Limburg	0.339
Antwerpen	0.474	Hainaut	0.335
Oost-Vlaanderen	0.373	Luxembourg	0.328
Namur	0.358	Liège	0.326
West-Vlaanderen	0.351		

Source: Computed from Office National de Sécurité Sociale, *Rapport Annuel, 1970,* Brussels (1971)

Much of the capital is provided from Belgian sources, and although profits flow out of the country, at least the value added does not entirely do so, while the employment of Belgian labour by foreign companies has an important regional multiplier effect, jobs being created locally in support activities.

Between 1959 and 1972 foreign investment in new factories was twice that made by Belgian enterprises, and American organisations were responsible for 52 per cent of the foreign investment. Over the shorter period 1959–68 American investment accounted for 65 per cent of the total made by non-Belgian firms, the subsequent shortfall resulting from the recent American practice of setting up labour-intensive rather than capital-intensive factories. Wallonie failed to receive a single American factory between 1950 and 1960, indicative of the fact that although the region was still prosperous, Americans viewed the Flemish economic environment more favourably. Although Wallonie began to attract American firms after 1960, the most favoured area was the triangle comprising Brussels, Antwerp and Ghent, which received 65 of the 103 plants set up in Flanders and Brussels down to 1968.[16] In terms of total foreign investment, however, the province of Antwerpen was the greatest recipient between 1959 and 1968 with 40 per cent of the total followed by Oost-Vlaanderen (14 per cent) and Hainaut (13 per cent). 1969 saw a drastic change for in this year Hainaut took 40 per cent of all foreign investment, which in absolute terms was more than the province had received during the preceding eleven years. The reason was the establishment at Feluy by the American firm Chevron of an inland oil refinery and petrochemical complex, and this development has allowed Hainaut to continue to score over Antwerpen. The data for 1971 support the contention that Wallonie is on the threshold of new industrial expansion, for Hainaut took 26 per cent and Liège 24 per cent of foreign investment compared with Antwerpen's 25 per cent. Oost-Vlaanderen could only muster 3 per cent.[17]

Table 9

PER CAPITA OUTPUT BY VALUE IN ALL ACTIVITIES, 1962 AND 1971.
BELGIUM = 100

	1962	1971		1962	1971
Brabant	129	118	Liège	109	100
Antwerpen	108	114	Namur	91	86
West-Vlaanderen	91	101	Hainaut	89	82
Oost-Vlaanderen	80	88	Luxembourg	74	77
Limburg	68	82	WALLONIE	94	88
FLANDERS	89	97	Brussels-Capital	148	151

Source: Institut National de Statistique, *Bulletin de Statistique*, no 5 (1973)

The importance of foreign investment in Belgium may be attributed specifically to the system of direct taxation, the rate of which is the lowest among the EEC countries, the liberal legislation in respect of the repatriation of profits, the location of Belgium within the EEC, high labour productivity and the financial assistance made available to foreign firms by both the government and local authorities. This last factor seems to be less influential than is often thought, and an investigation carried out in Flanders in 1968 revealed that only 20 per cent of a sample of 203 foreign firms would not have invested in the absence of financial assistance.[18] The reasons for the attraction of Flanders rather than Wallonie during the 1960s are a function of the differences between the two regions. Until the 1950s the Flemish provinces had an important agricultural sector and they experienced considerable underemployment. The upshot was a level of wage rates very much lower than that of the Walloon industrial districts, and this was a powerful incentive for incoming enterprises. In 1955 average daily wages for male industrial workers in West-Vlaanderen, Oost-Vlaanderen and Limburg were 177, 179 and 189 Belgian francs (BF) respectively. (The 1975 exchange rates were: £1 = 84 BF, $1 = 40 BF). On the other hand the figures for Hainaut and Liège were respectively 215 and 231 BF, appreciably higher than even Antwerpen (209 BF) or Brabant (201 BF), where relatively high wages might be anticipated.[19] The high Walloon wage rates were a result of the favourable post-war economic situation, especially in the iron and steel and metallurgical industries which suffered from labour shortages and therefore from high labour costs. This Walloon prosperity led to an indifferent, perhaps antagonistic attitude to foreign investment by both entrepreneurs and local authorities, who had no wish to become dependent on outside help. There was admittedly some resentment in Flanders, but lacking the glittering industrial history of Wallonie, the Flemings were more easily persuaded. Indeed towns such as Mechelen, Bruges and St. Niklaas pursued an aggressive publicity policy from an early date. Inevitably success had led to a tighter employment situation in Flanders, and wages have begun to catch up with those in the south, helping to explain the recent movement of foreign firms to Wallonie. Labour in West-Vlaanderen, Oost-Vlaanderen and Limburg is still cheaper than in Wallonie, with daily rates of 594, 623 and 625 BF respectively in 1972, but rates in both Brabant (651 BF) and Antwerpen (677 BF) have overtaken those in Hainaut (649 BF) and are approaching those in Liège (696 BF).[20] The attitude of Walloons to the establishment of overseas firms is now beginning to change, but as Table 9 shows, productivity in relation to the national average is declining in the south, contrary to the situation in Flanders, where the index almost reached the national average in 1971.

Regional Policy in Belgium

The concept of regional planning developed later in Belgium than in many West European countries. In Great Britain, for instance, the Special Areas Act was passed in 1934, but similar legislation was not enacted in Belgium until 1959. There are several reasons for this. Firstly, there has always existed a dislike of governmental intervention in economic affairs. Secondly, the Flemish-Walloon problem made it especially difficult to assist particular areas of the country without giving the impression of partiality, and indeed each of the two factions would have eagerly looked for loopholes in any legislation with an eye for attacking each other. Thirdly, the traditional mobility of the Belgian labour force, both within the country and as *frontaliers*, allowed regions of poor economic health to derive an income from more prosperous areas. The government did introduce legislation in 1947, 1953, 1955, 1957 and 1959 making grants and credit facilities available to newly established factories, but this was blanket assistance to industry throughout the country. The same was true of the section set up at the Ministry of Economic Affairs in 1955 to help attract foreign investment, and it was not until an act of July 1959 that the principle of regional policy was established.

Prior to this date, regional renovation was more the result of collaboration between private individuals, manufacturers' organisations and local public bodies, with results which were usually unsatisfactory. Local initiative was behind the formation of the Conseil Economique

Wallon in 1945 and the Economische Raad voor Vlaanderen in 1952, but although they published pamphlets and periodicals they lacked funds materially to influence the location of economic activity. Real success was limited to a small number of outstandingly dynamic towns such as Bruges and Mechelen, where the first Belgian industrial estate was established, largely owing to the influence of the mayor, M. Spinoy, who on several occasions was also the Minister of Economic Affairs. The estates included the provision of roads, gas, electricity and water supplies, thereby helping to reduce construction costs to new firms, and municipal rates were waived for an initial period.

The 1959 act consolidated much of the earlier legislation concerning economic development in all areas of the country. Assistance was made available for factory premises, plant and equipment, for research and development and for the modernisation of existing production lines. The aid was in the form of low interest loans, the rate of interest depending upon the government's assessment of the potential of the investment. The general rebate allowed for the loan to be repayable at 2 per cent less than the market rate; the special rebate, for a particularly suitable investment, also amounted to 2 per cent, and could be used in conjunction with the general rebate, giving a 4 per cent rebate. Rebates were allowed to run for three years although the loan repayments could be made over ten years. The government undertook to guarantee the capital repayment and interest charges on the loans, thus removing much of the risk to the lender and avoiding a shortage of loan funds. Other provisions of the act included interest-free loans of up to 50 per cent of the cost of research and development projects, a five year tax exemption on buildings constructed under the act, the establishment of advance factories and the organisation of social and economic studies.[21]

The above provisions, which affected the whole country, received royal assent on 17th July 1959. The regional package became law on the following day. Some 322 *communes* in West-and Oost-Vlaanderen, south-eastern Antwerpen, western Limburg, the Borinage and Centre coalfields, the Andenne and Verviers industrial districts and parts of Luxembourg were designated as development areas. (Fig 13). These *communes* contained 1.7 million people or 18 per cent of the national population. Four criteria were employed in their selection. Development areas were required to exhibit consistently high unemployment, a high level of out-migration, well developed seasonal, weekly or daily out-commuting, and a major decline in the working population. Loans of up to 20 per cent of the cost of new buildings and 7.5 per cent of the cost of equipment could be granted, and the government undertook to finance the establishment of industrial estates. In addition a new type of *intercommunale* was proposed. The first *intercommunales* were created in 1922 in response to the inability of single *communes* to provide a range of services efficiently. The new *intercommunales* were effectively economic planning units, as their title *sociétés d'équipement économique régionale*, suggests. Their creation was the most important element of the legislation for they represented an acceptance of the notion that regional planning is not only possible, but is also an essential part of economic growth.

Fig 13. THE ASSISTED AREAS OF BELGIUM IN 1971

The effect of the 1959 regional policy was marginal, largely because the differential between the development area incentives and those obtaining elsewhere was insufficient. Between 1959 and 1964 investment under the act amounted to a mere 6 per cent of total investment in the country.[22] The consequence was a second act, passed in August 1966, which amplified the earlier regional incentives. Interest rebates went up to 5 per cent and remained in force for five years; in some cases loans were free of interest in the first two years. Guarantees covering 75 per cent of loans from private institutions were provided by the government, depreciation allowances were raised, property taxes were waived for the first ten years of operation, grants for buildings were increased to 30 per cent of the total cost, and those towards equipment were raised to 10 per cent of the initial cost. At the same time development areas were extended to include a number of hitherto unassisted districts, and some *communes* which benefited from the 1959 act, which remained in force, were also included. The legislation was applicable to 679 *communes* with a population of 3.4 million, or 35 per cent of the national total, located for the most part in six areas: Westhoek, that is the westernmost part of West-Vlaanderen, southern Oost-Vlaanderen, virtually the whole of Kempenland, the Borinage-Centre-Charleroi coalfield, the Liège coalfield and the southern tip of Luxembourg. These areas are mapped in Fig 13. No less than 33 criteria were employed in the selection of the new development areas, but unfortunately they were never published. The EEC Commission did not approve of the extent of the assisted areas, nor of the level of assistance available, but the Belgian government ultimately managed to prevail, arguing that to tamper with the law as it stood would be to interfere with the delicate balance between Flanders and Wallonie.

The laws of 1959 and 1966 were superceded by fresh legislation which came into operation on 1st January 1971. The interest rebates, grants and various forms of tax relief were substantially similar to those already in force; in addition, preferential treatment was allowed for firms signing agreements with the government to conform with the 1971 Economic Plan, irrespective of whether they were in development areas or not. Philips Electrologica and Siemens were among the first companies to enter into this kind of contract.[23] Regional employment premiums were introduced, the amount of the premium depending on the number of jobs created, on whether or not the firm was considered to belong to a technologically advanced industry and on whether the plant was located in a category I or category II development area. Category I areas were those designated in 1966 and received greater financial aid than the category II regions, areas assisted by the 1959 but not by the 1966 legislation. More innovatory, however, was the attempt to forge stronger links between regional developments and national economic planning. An Economic Programming Office had been set up in 1968 to coordinate regional planning. Prior to this the national economic plans had ignored regional development and the proposals tabled by the regional planning bodies such as Groupe l'Equerre for Liège and Mens en Ruimte for Leuven-Tienen, and submitted to the Service de la Politique Générale d'Aménagement du Territoire, had gone unheeded by the economic planners. It must be said, however, that owing to a combination of opposition, mistrust and disinterest, the economic plans for 1962–65 and 1966–70 were not outstandingly successful.[24] More important than this decentralisation of economic planning was the abandonment in 1971 of the earlier narrow view of the encouragement of manufacturing as the sole panacea. The new legislation made funds available for infrastructural developments, and accepted that some regions may benefit more than others through tourism or even agriculture or forestry. As an OECD report on Belgium observed, 'excessive and widespread industrialisation can have disastrous effects on the economic, human and ecological equilibrium of the whole country'.[25]

The 1971 legislation was not without its critics. The most influential of these was the EEC Commission which objected to the level of financial incentives in an area of the Community which could hardly be said to be backward. There was also some suspicion that the rules in respect of aid both within and without the development areas were not always strictly enforced, ensuring that Belgium obtained more than her fair share of foreign investment.[26] The Commission ruled that aid should not exceed 20 per cent of the total investment and in April 1972 it was agreed that the benefits under the act be limited to 28 of the 43 *arrondissements*. The strength of the EEC Commission's criticism certainly indicates that Belgian regional policy has exerted a powerful influence on the distribution of manufacturing.

Membership of the EEC ensured that regional assistance did not spring from Belgian sources alone. The contraction of coalmining in accordance with Community policy was accompanied by reconversion aid. This comprised loans of up to 30 per cent of investment repayable over 13 years at low rates of interest, provided the investment was made in coalfield regions.[27] The European Coal and Steel Community (ECSC) was responsible, with the central government, for the establishment of the first industrial estates in the Walloon coalfield. In addition, unemployed miners were paid 80 per cent of their former wages for six months and 75 per cent for a further two years while retaining for other work. Salary supplements were paid to those who found lower paid jobs. Between 1954 and 1968 some 69,000 miners benefited from these arrangements. The European Investment Bank has been another source of funds both for manufacturing industry and for infrastructural projects such as the E10 motorway linking Rotterdam, Antwerp and Brussels and extending south towards Paris. It is likely that some areas will benefit from the European Regional Development Fund set up by the EEC in 1972, but they will be restricted to regions whose economic health is poor by the standards of the Community. Proposals tabled by the

EEC Commission late in 1973 suggest that the provinces of Limburg, Liège, Namur and Luxembourg and the *arrondissements* of Diksmuide, Ieper, Tielt and Veurne in West-Vlaanderen, Aalst, Eeklo and Oudenaarde in Oost-Vlaanderen and Ath, Charleroi, Mons and Thuin in Hainaut would benefit. Aid from the Regional Fund is likely to be limited to 15 per cent of the total investment in industrial projects, and will be no more than half the sum granted under Belgian regional policy.

Conclusion

Two major themes emerge from the changing distribution of economic activity in Belgium since World War II. The first is the relative decline of the Walloon coalfield industrial districts, contrasted with the emergence of the Flemish provinces as important manufacturing areas. The second theme is that in spite of regional policy aimed at encouraging expansion in peripheral areas, the greatest economic progress has been made by the Brussels-Antwerp axis. Almost invariably, whatever index is employed to describe regional economic health, the provinces of Brabant and Antwerpen show up most favourably. It is a case of nothing succeeding like success. The strength of this economic core area may be demonstrated in a number of ways, but to conclude, maps of population potential and net migration balance are offered as causes and results of the development of the axial belt. Both indices synthesize the interaction of a number of factors.

A population potential map is a measure of consumer accessibility portraying proximity to the aggregate of population.[28] It provides an indication of the number of people, as consumers, within the reach of all the different localities in a country. Large towns have high values, but small towns adjacent to large towns have higher values than small towns without such proximity, for they suffer from the effect or 'friction' of distance. The values are computed using the formula.

$$V_i = \sum_{j=1}^{n} \frac{P_j}{d_{ij}}$$

In the case of Belgium, the potential (V) at the *commune* of Borgerhout (i) is equal to the population (P) of, say, Ixelles (j), divided by the distance (d) between Borgerhout and Ixelles, plus the result of the application of the formula to all the remaining (2,585) *communes*. The process is then repeated for all 2,585 *communes*. The computation, which clearly calls for the use of a computer, has been carried out by Nadasdi and Fig 14 is based on his work.[29] The highest values are in Brussels, but less predictably the 250 isoline completely encircles not only the capital but also Antwerp, Aalst, Leuven and Mechelen, as well

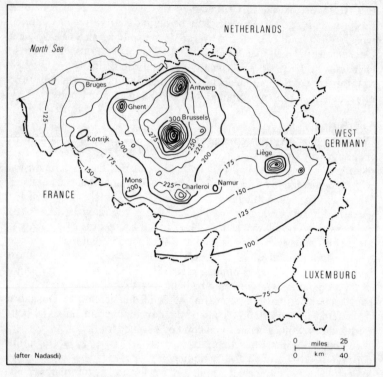

Fig 14. POPULATION POTENTIAL MAP OF BELGIUM
SOURCE: I. Nadasdi, 'Carte de Potentiel de Population de la Belgique', *Bulletin de la Société Belge d'Etudes Géographiques*, 40 (1971), 240

as the rural areas separating them. On the other hand, many urban areas such as Ostend, Bruges, Kortrijk, Mons and Namur score less than 250; only Liège and Ghent of the settlements outside the axial belt score 300. The implication is that the axial belt represents a market for consumer goods and services so powerful that it must be very much less profitable for new consumer goods factories and servicing facilities to open up in the regions outside it. Possible exceptions are Liège and Ghent, but access to consumers in the centre of Liège and Ghent is less than half that of central Brussels.

The second map, Fig 15, depicting net migration balances during the period 1967 and 1971, reflects decisions made in respect of employment opportunities and residential desirability, and as such

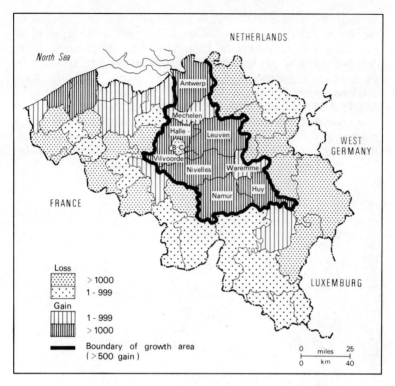

Fig 15. NET MIGRATION BALANCE, 1967–1971 B–C = Brussels–Capital
SOURCE: Institut National de Statistique, *Annuaire Statistique de la Belgique*,
88–92, Brussels, 1969–73

sharply distinguishes the economically expanding from the less
fortunate areas. The map indicates that migrants' view the Brussels-
Antwerp axis and its southern extension as the most potentially
rewarding region, as the economic indicators would suggest. Outside
this region a number of Flemish towns, in particular Bruges and Ostend,
have proved attractive to many living in adjacent rural areas. High net
out-migration from the coalfield areas of Mons, Charleroi, Liège and
Hasselt, many areas in western Flanders, from the Kempenland and the
eastern Ardennes reflect a lack of confidence in their potential. There
are several growth points in Flanders; in Wallonie the favourable
in-migration balances registered for Namur, Huy, Waremme and
Soignies have been influenced by the expansion of Brussels as much as

by their own economic growth. Brussels represents a special case, for the losses suffered by Brussels-Capital are equal to the gains of the encircling *arrondissement* of Halle-Vilvoorde, these trends reflect suburbanisation of the population, rather than dissatisfaction with the employment opportunities available in the centre. The map, then, confirms earlier findings and allows the national growth area to be delimited on the basis of perception by individuals of their economic environment. Using the criterion of contiguous *arrondissements* with a positive migration balance between 1967 and 1971 of more than 500, the growth area therefore comprises Antwerp, Mechelen, Halle-Vilvoorde, Leuven, Nivelles, Namur, Huy and Waremme.

3

The Declining and Slowly Growing Industries

THOSE INDUSTRIES WHOSE labour force is contracting, or expanding more slowly than the national average for all manufacturing, are old established activities which were in the van of Belgian economic development in the nineteenth century. Some such industries processed indigenous raw materials, for the most part more abundant in Wallonie, and were thus located close to these supplies. This was true of the iron and steel and metallurgical industries, the processing of non-metallic minerals such as ceramics and glass-making, and most fundamentally of all, coalmining itself. There was one very important activity – textile manufacture – which, with the exception of linen, did not transform local materials, and which was very largely located in Flanders. A number of other activities, of which brewing was one, were not exclusively located in Wallonie or in Flanders, but were related to the distribution of population, and their contraction has affected all parts of the country. It is not entirely true, therefore, to say that declining industries are to be found in Wallonie alone; rather that this region had, and still does have a large share of the declining and slowly growing industries.

In almost all of the industries considered in this chapter, the contraction, relative or absolute, of employment is not a corollary of decreasing production, but is part of rationalisation normally involving the installation of labour saving equipment. Textiles, which as Table 10 shows, have suffered heavy contraction of employment in recent years, are a good example of this trend. At the foot of the table, the manufacture of clothing is a sector which has undergone a new lease of life, and employment is increasing almost as rapidly as the national

Table 10

EMPLOYMENT CHANGE IN THE DECLINING AND SLOWLY GROWING INDUST-
RIES, 1955-1972

	1955	1972	%
Coalmining	142,978	32,800	−303
Textiles	164,778	118,602	− 39
Brewing & Soft Drinks	27,060	23,585	−15
Non-metallic Minerals	66,191	63,779	−4
Metallurgy	113,850	123,249	+8
Clothing	83,804	92,374	+10
All manufacturing*	998,690	1,151,093	+15

*Excludes coalmining

Source: Office National de Sécurité Sociale, *Rapport Annuel 1955, 1972,* Brussels
       (1956, 1973)

average, despite the use of expensive machinery. Two activities,
coalmining and ceramics, a sub-sector of non-metallic minerals, exhibit
both contracting production and employment, the former having
suffered a deterioration of massive proportions.

Coalmining

Coalmining in Belgium is a declining industry *par excellence.* Table
10 indicates that between 1955 and 1972 some 110,000 jobs were lost, a
total only slightly smaller than the present workforce in textiles, the
third largest industry. This three-fold decline in employment was
accompanied by a two-fold contraction in output from 29.5 to 10.5
million tonnes; in Wallonie employment fell from 92,000 to 12,000,
and output contracted from 19.1 to 3.2 million tonnes. Peak output in
Wallonie occurred in 1927 when 25.1 million tonnes were mined, but at
this time the Kempen field was still being developed and output there
was only 1.9 million tonnes. Subsequently trends in the two fields were
in opposite directions. The Kempen grew to achieve maximum
production in 1956, with an output of 10.5 million tonnes, while the
trend in Wallonie was one of contraction. 1956 was a turning point for
Belgian coalmining. Unrelenting contraction ensued in Wallonie, with
production falling to 7.5 million tonnes in 1967, and to 3.2 million
tonnes in 1972. Assuming a continuation of this rate of decline, the end
cannot be far from sight. The same cannot be said for the Kempen, for
although the field has experienced a steady fall in production since
1956, this has amounted to only a 44 per cent contraction. Indeed, since
1970 the Kempen mines have registered a slight increase in output, and
in the light of the meteoric rise in world oil prices at the end of 1973,
there is every possibility that further expansion will take place.

Table 11

PHYSICAL CHARACTERISTICS OF SELECTED COALFIELDS, 1956

	Borinage	Kempen	Ruhr
Density of seams, tonnes p.m^3	1.4	8.4	8.0
Average seam thickness, m	0.99	1.04	1.22
Average depth of pit, m	780	825	700
% output from seams whose slope is			
1°-19°	48.5	96.7	70
20°-34°	38.9	3.3	10
>34°	12.6	0	20
Methane per tonne coal mined, m^3	3.8	0.6	1.2
Output per shift, kg	965	1492	1591

Source: R. C. Riley, 'Recent Developments in the Belgian Borinage', *Geography*,
        228 (1965), 261

The two fields are very different both geologically and in terms of organisation so that it is not surprising that their fortunes should have followed different paths. Table 11 compares some of the physical attributes of the Borinage, a not untypical Walloon mining region, with those of the Kempen and the German Ruhr. It is clear that the Borinage is at a disadvantage on every count with the exception of the average depth of pit. The early date of the commencement of mining in Wallonie was not conducive to efficiency either in respect of the size of the pits or of the nature of the concessions. In 1850 there were 408 pits, some working concessions beneath those of other pits, and with this legacy it is predictable that the rational concessions, drawn up by the state, and the large size of the Kempen pits ensured higher productivity. In 1953 there were still 136 pits in Wallonie compared with only 7 in the Kempen and by 1959 Wallonie had but 15 profitable pits out of 54. By comparison, four of the seven Kempen pits were profitable and the field as a whole declared a profit of 12 BF per tonne.

The superior efficiency of the Kempen enabled it to compete favourably for markets on the Walloon coalfield itself. Virtually all the coal consumed by the coke ovens of the Liège and Charleroi steelworks was supplied by the Kempen. The Kempen field was not alone in providing problems for Wallonie, however, for there were other influences at work. Firstly, the ending in 1958 of the ECSC's five year transition period, introduced to prepare collieries to face competition on the open Community market, made it likely that Walloon coal would have to face severe competition from the lower cost collieries of the Ruhr and Zuid-Limburg. Production costs in the Ruhr in the late 1950s were two-thirds of those in Wallonie. Secondly, the introduction of the

international through rate by the ECSC in 1956, by abolishing
discriminatory freight rates charged by member countries, removed an
element of the distance-protection enjoyed by the Walloon mines.[1]
Thirdly, the use of large bulk carriers on the North Atlantic route,
coupled with the very high productivity of mines in the USA have
meant that American coal sells on the Walloon field at prices lower than
those charged by local pits. Fourthly, the increasing availability of oil at
low prices in the 1960s caused many coal consumers to switch to the
new energy source. In 1960 crude oil was being landed at Antwerp at
870 BF per tonne, compared with a price of 895 BF for a tonne of
general purpose Walloon coal.[2] Since oil has a calorific value one and a
half times that of coal, the calorifically adjusted price of coal would be
1342 BF per tonne. Small wonder that consumers reacted against coal.
The use of oil in electric power stations reduced coal's chance of
participating in the expansion of this industry. The decision to import
natural gas from the Netherlands and to construct a country-wide gas
grid was a further blow to the prospects for Walloon coal. Natural gas
transmission began in October 1966. Since Walloon production costs
were actually higher than prices charged, and since only some of the
difference was made up by subsidies from the government and the
ECSC, it was quite inevitable that the 1960s should witness an
accelerated rate of contraction in this field, especially in the light of the
ECSC's declared intent to pursue a cheap energy policy.

Such were the economic forces working against coal in the 1960s that
the Kempen as well as Wallonie became unprofitable. By 1970 the
Kempen made a loss of 190 BF on every tonne of coal mined, although
this pales into insignificance beside the deficit of 563 BF per tonne
recorded by Wallonie.[3] That mining has been able to continue in
Wallonie is the result of the demand for anthracite which accounted for
85 per cent of the output from Charleroi, and for all that from Liège in
1970. Anthracite prices are twice those of coking coal, and for this
reason some of the Charleroi and Liège pits were able to remain
profitable while the more efficient Kempen mines, which lack
anthracite, returned deficits. That the Walloon fields do not mine the
same range of coal is the principal cause of the more rapid cut back in
output in the Borinage and the Centre compared with the two fields to
the east, a trend evident in Table 12 and Fig 16.

Faced with such a hostile economic environment, there was little the
Walloon colliery companies could do to make themselves viable. Some
with more than one pit tried to effect economies by amalgamating their
operations, while others merged to form relative large firms. An
example of this strategy was the creation in 1960 of Charbonnages du
Borinage, a consortium of six colliery companies working nine pits.

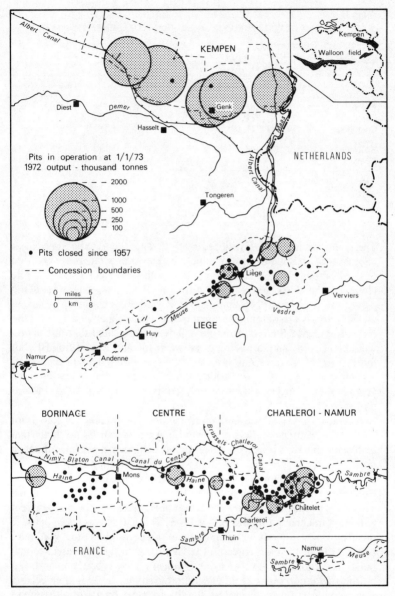

Fig. 16. RECENT CLOSURES AND CURRENT OUTPUT BY PIT IN THE
    COALMINING INDUSTRY
SOURCE: *Annales des Mines de Belgique*, 1958, 1974

Table 12

OUTPUT, PITS AND PRODUCTIVITY IN BELGIAN COALMINES, 1953-1972

	Production '000 t		No. of Pits		Output per Pit '000 tonnes		Productivity Kg per shift	
	1953	1972	1953	1972	1953	1972	1953	1972
Borinage	4,621	282	23	1	201	282	936	1,827
Centre	3,678	221	17	1	216	221	1,025	
Charleroi	7,275	1,717	58	7	125	245	1,043	1,827
Liège	5,003	956	36	6	139	159	900	1,642
Wallonie	20,578	3,176	136	15	151	212	977	1,767
Kempen	9,483	7,323	7	5	1,355	1,046	1,298	2,643

Source: *Annales des Mines de Belgique*, (1954, 1973)

The company immediately closed two pits and integrated operations at another four, but it was only a palliative. The same strategies were tried in the Kempen, but, as had been noted, without financial success. The Houthalen and Helchteren-Zolder pits merged in 1964, the former being closed the following year, and in 1966 Zwartberg was shut. At the end of 1967 the five remaining Kempen collieries amalgamated to form the N.V. Kempense Steenkolenmijnen. It was anticipated that this action would lead to an annual saving of between 150 and 200 million BF, but the receipt of government subsidies was conditional upon an annual reduction of capacity by 600,000 tonnes in each of the following three years. Production was therefore duly cut back from 8.8 million to 7.0 million tonnes in 1970.

Although physical and economic factors have played an important role in the fortunes of Belgian coalmining, there can be no doubt that action by the ECSC and the government had been a critical influence upon the levels of production. In 1958 the inefficiency of the Walloon pits within the Community forced the ECSC partially to isolate the Belgian coalmining industry from the ECSC market and to continue subsidies for five years on condition that there was a 40 per cent reduction in capacity by the end of 1963. This action was taken because of the poor alternative employment opportunities in Wallonie, particularly in the Borinage and the Centre, with the consequence that policy on production levels was determined not by production costs but by the social costs of a rapid closure programme. In 1964 the decision was taken to reduce capacity by 5 million tonnes by 1970, although in practice the speed of the closures in particular areas largely depended upon the local success of governmental and ECSC regional policy.

Grants for the retraining and rehousing of miners and for industrial development schemes are still being paid (aid given to coalmining in 1971 was equivalent to 310 BF per tonne mined), and it reflects great credit on the government, the ECSC and the regional development associations that the switch from mining has been effected so smoothly.

The Kempen field has also been influenced by governmental and ECSC policy decisions. Belgium has been concerned to retain a large proportion of the capacity of her most efficient mining region. For this reason the Kempen receives operational subsidies and is guaranteed markets at power stations. Assistance also comes from the ECSC which allows the imposition of import quotas on coal from non-Community countries, and which since 1967 has sanctioned subsidies for coking coal in order not to jeopardise the competitiveness of the iron and steel industry. Domestic coking coal also attracts a rail freight subsidy which in 1970 was 28 BF per tonne, although this was reduced to 16 BF per tonne in 1972. In the light of world shortage, and consequent increase in the price of coking coal that became apparent in 1970, and the drastic rise in the cost of oil at the end of 1973, it would seem that ECSC policy in respect of coking coal and Belgium's maintenance of markets for Kempen coal are more than justified.

Table 13

THE CONSUMPTION OF ENERGY IN BELGIUM, 1950-1971 %

	Coal	Oil	Natural Gas	Hydro-electric power
1950	91	9	0	0
1962	66	34	0	0
1971	34	51	15	0

Sources: ECSC, High Authority, *Eleventh General Report on the Activities of the Community*, Luxembourg, 1963. Economic Commission for Europe, *The Coal Situation in Europe in 1971 and its Prospects*, United Nations, New York, 1972

Some Changes Associated with the Decline of Coalmining

The manner in which other sources of energy have grown in importance at the expense of coal may be seen in Table 13. Domestic coal accounts for only two-thirds of the total consumption of coal, so that Belgian mines which once supplied virtually all the energy used in the country, are now responsible for a mere 23 per cent. Oil has made great inroads into markets previously the province of coal, and the advent of natural gas has eroded the market for coal gas. The natural gas grid supplied from the Netherlands now serves the principal industrial districts and the net is continually being extended. In 1971 alone some 436 km of pipeline were laid, including a 154 km section of 400 mm pipe from Huy to the steelworks town of Athus in Belgian Lorraine. As Belgian imports rise so the frontier price falls. In 1971 the price was 6 per cent lower than that obtaining the previous year[4], a trend which may persuade more electric power generating companies to burn this fuel. Seven of the twenty power stations with a capacity of 100 MW and above were equipped to deal with natural gas in 1970. For many years the generation of hydro-electric power was restricted to a number of small stations on Ardenne rivers such as the Amblève and Warche, and to a few larger projects such as Ivoz-Ramet on the Meuse at Liège. However, as part of the policy of developing indigenous resources a large pumped storage station is being constructed at Coo on the Amblève. The lower storage lake has been fashioned from a former meander channel of the river, and when it is complete in 1974 the plant will have a capacity of 400 MW, making it one of the largest power stations in the country. Nuclear power is at present of little importance for the 11 MW plant at Mol (Turnhout) is really part of an experimental establishment, while the joint Franco-Belgian plant on the Meuse at Chooz (282 MW) is actually in France. However the electric power generation programme for 1971–7 calls for the opening of nuclear plants at Tihange (870 MW) near Liège and at Doel (790 MW) near Antwerp. Off-peak power from these stations will be used at the Coo hydro-electric plant to pump water from the lower to two upper lakes. This complementarity between water power and atomic fuel will help to reduce the role of coal still further.

The Textile Industry

It was the manufacture of woollen cloth that formed the basis of the extraordinary prosperity of Flemish towns in the Middle Ages, but the first textile mills did not arrive until the nineteenth century. The domestic system lingered for many decades and there remained 150,000 domestic lace workers in the Bruges region in 1875.[5] The switch from the domestic to the factory system gave rise to a great concentration of labour, and this has been a continuing trend as firms have concentrated production into a few large and efficient mills. Taken in the round, textile output is increasing and the improved sales possibilities resulting from membership of the EEC have caused exports to rise. But because this is an old industry undergoing modernisation, its workforce is dwindling: as has been noted earlier employment fell 39 per cent between 1955 and 1972. During this period the textile industry's share of manufacturing employment dropped from 16.5 to 10.3 per cent, and after running a close second to engineering in 1955, the activity was relegated to third place after engineering and iron and steel in 1972. In this sense it is a declining industry.

Table 14

PROVINCIAL TEXTILE EMPLOYMENT IN 1972

	Workers	%		Workers	%
Oost-Vlaanderen	51,447	43.4	Limburg	1,657	1.4
West-Vlaanderen	32,634	27.5	Antwerpen	1,142	1.0
Hainaut	16,333	13.8	Luxembourg	263	0.2
Liège	7,451	6.3	Namur	236	0.2
Brabant	7,439	6.3	Belgium	118,602	100.0

Source: Office National de Sécurité Sociale, *Rapport Annuel 1972,* Brussels (1973)

A characteristic of many industries developed before and during the nineteenth century is the way in which they clustered about particular points. Textile manufacture exemplified this principle, and because few mills have been built in the twentieth century we are left with a pattern of distribution inherited from an earlier era. The two Flemish provinces of West-and Oost-Vlaanderen can still claim 70 per cent of all textile employment, if the Mouscron *arrondissement*, which was formerly Flemish, is included. The activity spills over into the neighbouring provinces of Brabant and Hainaut, bringing the share of all these areas of the total textile workforce up to 91 per cent. Some 6 per cent of the remainder is accounted for by the province of Liège.

The clustering exhibited at the provincial level is even more pronounced when the finer mesh of the *arrondissement* is used. Two of these, Kortrijk (19.5 per cent) and Ghent (11.8 per cent), have between them almost one-third of the entire workforce, and the addition of seven others, St. Niklaas, Mouscron, Oudenaarde, Dendermonde, Aalst, Verviers and Tournai accounts for four-fifths of the national total. In many of the towns in these areas textile production is the dominant industrial activity, giving rise to very real specialisation. The extent to which this is the case is conveniently expressed by location quotients, which relate the importance of an activity in a locality to its importance in the country as a whole. Fig 17 shows that there are thirteen *arrondissements* exhibiting specialisation, that is, scoring quotients greater than 1; with the exception of Verviers, they form a contiguous belt coinciding with the Scheldt and Leie valleys. Only one of these *arrondissements*, Roeselare, with a quotient of 1.38, has less than twice as many jobs in textiles as would be expected if the activity were spread uniformly throughout Belgium.

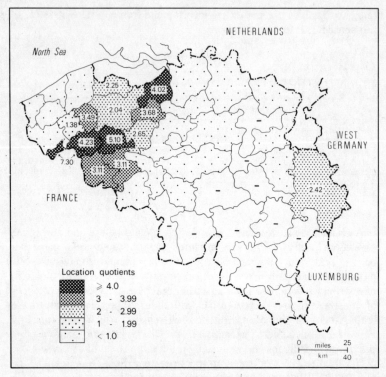

Fig. 17. THE BELGIAN TEXTILE INDUSTRY, 1972
A dash is used to signify *arrondissements* with negligible textile employment
SOURCE: Office National de Sécurité Sociale, *Rapport Annuel, 1972*, Brussels, 1973

Woollen and Worsted Manufacture

Woollen cloth manufacture is the oldest of the textile branches and yet the foundations of the modern industry were laid not in Flanders, where it was so important in the Middle Ages, but in Verviers in the pre-Ardennes. While the Flemish spinsters and weavers gradually forsook woollen cloth for linen during the eighteenth century, it was left to Verviers to meet the competition from cheap English cloth which had been a main cause of the Flemish diversification. By 1797 Verviers had become one of the leading textile districts of Napoleonic France, and 1846 saw the area claiming 78 per cent of employment in the Belgian woollen industry.[6] By the end of the century Verviers's share of woollens and worsteds had fallen to 62 per cent, and it now stands at 30 per cent. The reasons for the localisation of the industry in Verviers have been the subject of some controversy which has certainly emphasised the dangers of specious assumptions about the influence of the physical environment. The Ardennes are said to have been a source of raw materials, but while concentration on the rearing of sheep could certainly be justified on the poor soils of parts of Flanders, the Verviers region by contrast is well suited pedologically and climatically to the growth of grass, making cattle rearing more remunerative than sheep farming. As early as 1772 local wool supplies were sufficient only to meet one-tenth of local needs and wool was imported from Spain, Portugal and Saxony.[7] Likewise the soft water qualities of the Vesdre have been quoted as an important attractive influence for manufacture of woollens, yet the water is in fact relatively hard with a pH value of between 7.5 and 8, and further is no different from that of other rivers in the area such as the Warche, Ourthe and Amblève whose valleys did not attract textile manufacture. Soft water with a pH value of 5 was not available until the construction of the Gileppe reservoir in 1878, but as Sporck remarks, the advantage of soft water for scouring, dyeing and finishing was not appreciated until the nineteenth century, by which time these activities were well established.[8] The Vesdre and its tributaries did provide a useful source of power for the early mills, but to no greater extent than other, untapped, rivers in the region.

Some writers attribute the origin of Verviers cloth-making not to these physical factors but to the arrival of Ghent weavers in the early fourteenth century. Vanex, however, has shown that there is no evidence of such in-migration in the town records, that there is no trace of Flemish terminology in the technical language of the locality, and that perusal of the Ghent records fails to support the hypothesis of an out-migration from the city.[9] If in-migration did take place it was from nearby Aachen. The initial impetus is more likely to have stemmed from the interest of the Prince Bishops of Liège in promoting cloth production, from the location of the valley astride the route between Liège and Westphalia, and in the early stages of the industry, from the presence of important innovators like William and John Cockerill, brought in by the dynamic entrepreneurs Simonis and Biolley.

Having established a position of primacy in Belgium, the Verviers mill owners became one of the world leaders in one aspect of woollen cloth-making, scouring and carbonising, for which the copious supplies of water in the Ardennes streams were an undoubted asset. The Verviers scourers adapted their plant to handle dirty Latin American wool and became specialist exporters of clean wool to Germany, France, Italy and Great Britain. An important factor was the invention in 1863 of the

'Leviathan' scouring machine by J. Melen so that the amount of wool scoured rose from 13,000 tonnes in 1860 to 40,000 tonnes in 1868. A method of chemical carbonisation was introduced in 1869 and shortly after, this small town was scouring and carbonising one-tenth of the world total. Although the Verviers region continues to dominate the scouring and carbonising process, accounting for 90 per cent of the national and 30 per cent of the EEC (the Six) output, its share of woollen and worsted production has dwindled. As recently as 1948 Verviers produced 65 per cent of Belgian woollen yarn, 52 per cent of combed wool and 20 per cent of worsted yarn, but at present the respective shares are only 25 per cent, 29 per cent and 9 per cent.[10] There is thus a clear indication that the Verviers textile district is declining and the implication is that the Flemish manufacturing area is both increasing its importance within Belgium and becoming increasingly diversified in the process.

The migration of wool textiles to Flanders first began to assume important proportions during the last quarter of the nineteenth century, largely because of labour cost differentials within Belgium. The presence of highly paid metallurgical and engineering trades in Liège close to Verviers, forced textile wages up, in many cases, to prohibitive levels. In 1937 Verviers mills had to pay 46 per cent of their workforce more than 5 BF an hour, but in rural areas like Eeklo only 13 per cent received this top rate.[11] The Flemish mills made greater use of female labour which received lower remuneration than male labour, and restrictive practices by the Verviers unions further reduced productivity. Although the wool textile industry is the least clustered of all the textile branches in Flanders, there is nevertheless specialisation in a number of towns such as Eeklo, Ronse, Oudenaarde, St. Niklaas, Termonde, Zulte and Kortrijk; outside the two Flemish provinces, Mouscron, Tournai and Brussels-Capital, despite the high wage levels prevailing in the latter, have important wool sectors. The reason for the growth of the activity in these particular towns is difficult to establish, for they do not possess special advantages over many other locations. The answer probably lies in a whole complex of factors, such as the accident of residence, which influenced entrepreneurs to make the selection in the first place. Once the first arrival was seen to be successful it is easy to hypothesise that others would follow suit. This seems to have been the case with Ronse which received a large share of the woollen and worsted mills migrating from Verviers.[12]

Because wool textiles in Belgium are for the most part made in small family-owned mills, the industry has found difficulty in withstanding competition from cheap foreign imports, those from the Prato district of Italy in particular. The trend towards more casual clothing has favoured man-made fibres (cotton, suède and knitwear, for example) further restricting outlets. Contraction has been the result, but at the same time there has been some reorientation. The worsted spinners of Mouscron, Tournai and Brussels have chosen to become specialist exporters of yarn, which is then woven abroad; more than half their output is directed to foreign markets. The woollen spinners of St. Niklaas, Termonde and Verviers supply yarn to the carpet, upholstery, hosiery and knitwear industries rather than to woollen weaving mills. Carpet mills now take 65 per cent of the yarn spun by the woollen spinning mills, some of which are integrated with carpet firms.[13]

Linen Manufacture

The linen sector now employs only 2 per cent of Belgian textile workers, and as such is one of the least important branches. It is taken after wool because its growth followed that of the latter activity. Before its decline in the 1840s, some 278,000 were involved in the manufacture of linen. The industry was taken up in place of woollens in the fifteenth and sixteenth centuries by the rural population of Flanders. The declining fortunes of woollen cloth was a contributory factor, but more important was the local availability of the basic raw material, flax. The cultivation and preparation of this crop was labour-intensive as was the domestic linen industry itself; together they relieved the Flemish population pressure problem. Flax was particularly suited to the soils of the Leie valley and of Waasland which effectively restricted the distribution of its cultivation. Much has been written on the part played by the waters of the Leie, 'the Golden River', in the location of linen production, but the Leie was in fact no more suitable for the preparatory process of retting than other Flemish rivers. In practice the most important areas for flax preparation were Oudenaarde and Dendermonde on the Scheldt, Aalst on the Dender and Waasland adjacent to the lower Scheldt.[14] The first linen mill was not set up until 1838, and although ten were in operation by 1846, the industry was in no position to compete successfully with the products of the highly mechanised British mills.

The preparation of flax has remained a craft industry based on the family unit, only 16 of the 511 firms at work in 1970 employing more than 20 workers. The greatest concentration is now to be found in the Leie valley in the vicinity of Kortrijk, whereas the largest spinning and weaving mills are clustered round Ghent and Lokeren to the east. The small mills of West-Vlaanderen are highly clustered between Kortrijk and Roeselare.[15] The spinning mills are largely concerned with the production of coarse yarns used in the manufacture of furnishing fabrics and only a small number of weaving mills are still involved in the exclusive production of pure linen cloth. The industry is increasingly turning to the use of man-made fibres, a trend which tends to blur the distinction that formerly existed between cotton and linen manufacture. It has been assisted, however, by the advent of the EEC, for it can now penetrate French markets which were formerly heavily protected; but since 40 per cent of the total output is sold in the USA, the industry is still very much at the mercy of changes in international trading policies.

Cotton Manufacture ·

The production of cotton cloth in Belgium owes much to the efforts of Lieven Bauwens who surreptitiously removed cotton spinning machinery from England in 1798 and re-erected it in Ghent. Although some cotton spinning mills were established in rural areas like Eeklo and Wetteren, there was remarkably little diffusion from Ghent, and in 1900 the city still had 90 per cent of all Belgian employees in this sector. This domination was substantially eroded in the first three decades of the present century as spinning spread westward to the Kortrijk region. In 1970 Ghent's share of employment in this sector was down to 54 per cent; it was followed by Kortrijk and Oudenaarde with 21 and 16 per cent respectively.[16] Ghent still exercises a compelling attraction for the large cotton spinning mills by virtue of its nodality, the presence of a port complex, local labour supplies and other external economies such as machinery supplies and maintenance services. The area returns a location quotient of 4.53 for cotton spinning, and Oudenaarde immediately to the south has a score of 2.19 Kortrijk, on the other hand scores 1.19, suggesting that the area is not one of specialist cotton spinning.

Weaving firms tend to be smaller than those in spinning, and are thus encouraged to proliferate in small towns, but the Kortrijk region nevertheless has a marked concentration of weaving, dating from the early years of this century. Indeed, the Kortrijk district exhibits the reverse of the normal employment trend in textiles, for the numbers employed in weaving are rising. The Kortrijk *arrondissement* has a cotton weaving location quotient of 2.63, superior to that of Ghent with 1.54, and Kortrijk employs 44 per cent of Belgian weavers compared with only 16 per cent in the case of Ghent.[17] Other specialist weaving areas are Tielt, Oudenaarde and to a lesser extent Eeklo. Ronse, in the *arrondissement* of Oudenaarde, has a number of large integrated mills in which both spinning and weaving is carried out, in addition to its weaving activities.

Competition from imported fabrics, the paucity of export markets and the introduction of equipment requiring less supervision have caused the industry to contract, but it is nevertheless still the leading textile branch with a quarter of all textile employment. Rationalisation has been more effective in spinning than in weaving, and a number of public companies have concentrated production into a small number of large mills. The largest of these firms is UCO, based at Ghent, operating twelve spinning mills. A further strategy is product diversification and a number of mills, especially in the Kortrijk and St. Niklaas regions, now manufacture upholstery fabrics, normally containing a high proportion of man-made fibres. A small selection of mills at Aalst and Kortrijk produce cotton sewing thread, but there is a limited domestic market for this product.

Hosiery and Knitwear Manufacture

In terms of numbers employed, this is the third largest textile sector after cotton and wool. It is an old established activity dating from the late seventeenth century, following the introduction of William Lee's knitting frame at two quite separate locations: the adjacent towns of Leuze and Quevaucamps to the east of Tournai and Arendonk near Turnhout in Kempenland. Competition from the newly mechanised Nottingham mills towards the middle of the nineteenth century resulted in the collapse of the Arendonk firms, but increasing demand in the 1860s and 1870s caused fresh expansion. By this time Arendonk had turned to the manufacture of cigars, and although the two Hainaut centres continued to develop, a number of entirely new centres sprang up, for the most part in Oost-Vlaanderen. The three most important were St. Niklaas, Aalst and Zottegem, and once again the cause may be attributed to behavioural rather than strictly economic factors. These towns have enjoyed a measure of what is termed initial advantage and, with Leuze and Quevaucamps, continue to be the leading production centres. St. Niklaas alone has a quarter of the workers in the industry. Location quotients for the industry reflect this specialisation. The *arrondissement* of Ath, which includes Quevaucamps, scores 2.76, St. Niklaas 2.61, Aalst 2.06 and Tournai, which includes the town of Leuze, scores 1.69. The growing popularity of knitwear has recently led to the establishment of mills in a number of new locations such as Mechelen and Brussels. Most of the plants in Brussels are knitting mills which, rather than remain merely producers of wool, have integrated forwards into the making up of jerseys and pullovers.[18] To a much greater extent than either wool or cotton textiles, this industry is characterised by small size of firm. Only 44 of the 397 mills working in 1970 employed more than 100, representing just under half the total workforce.[19] No less than 163 firms employ less than 20 workers and there certainly seems scope for rationalisation in this profitable activity.

Other Textile Manufacture

The Flemish textile region is one of very considerable diversity, possessing virtually all the various textile sectors which, in many other countries, exhibit much greater dispersal. Yet, as has been suggested, there is considerable regional specialisation, a characteristic which applies equally to the less important branches. Thus carpet manufacture, which has 6 per cent of textile workers, is concentrated almost entirely in two areas: the Kortrijk region with almost two-thirds of the workforce, and St. Niklaas, where nearly all the remainder are employed. The Belgian jute industry is the fourth largest in the world, although it employs only 5 per cent of Belgian textile operatives. It grew out of linen manufacture in the second half of the nineteenth century, and the location pattern is strikingly similar to that of linen. Problems of raw material supply and foreign competition plague this industry and help to explain its decline. Finally, mention must be made of three textile branches, none of which accounts for more than 1 per cent of total textile employment, but which exhibit 'swarming' to a remarkable degree. The town of Hamme, south of St. Niklaas, has 80 per cent of all Belgian workers in hemp manufacture. Deinze, south-west of Ghent, has an even higher proportion of those engaged in elastic web production[20], and Aalst and Hamme have a majority of operatives in the ribbon and tape industry.

The Iron and Steel and Associated Industries

Ferrous metallurgy, no less than the textile industry, was established as an important activity at an early date in Belgium, and the techniques employed by the Belgian forge masters were in the van of medieval progress in iron-making. It was here at the end of the fourteenth century that one of the most fundamental innovations, the indirect method of production which introduced a defining stage, was pioneered, causing the term 'Walloon method' to be given to the process. The presence of iron ore in close proximity to streams (which provided power for bellows and hammers), abundant supplies of wood for charcoal, coupled with the innovative characteristics of the workers, caused the Ardennes to become one of the leading iron-making areas in the whole of Europe.[21] The ingenuity of the Liège armourers was as widely accepted as that of the Sheffield cutlers, and it is not surprising that the first successful experiments with puddling and coke-smelting outside Great Britain were undertaken in the city.

Employment in the iron and steel, metal-rolling, forging and drawing industries places this sector in second position behind engineering. In 1972 123,000 workers were employed, representing an 8 per cent increase over the total for 1955, but the present trend is in the reverse direction for since 1965 there has been a contraction in the labour force. Steel production has steadily risen from 4.5 million tonnes in 1953 to 14.5 million tonnes in 1972, itself eloquent testimony of the improvement in productivity during the last decade and a half. Despite the diffusion of the finishing stages in particular from the traditional centres of Liège and Charleroi, these two localities continue to dominate the activity. Between them the provinces of Liège and Hainaut account for 57 of total employment, as Table 15 indicates. However, both West-and Oost-Vlaanderen exhibited considerable expansion between 1955 and 1972, both trebling their metallurgical workforce. At the same time Liège registered an absolute decline from 43,000 to 36,000 workers. Hainaut's workforce remained stationary during this period, and it would seem that even in the two entrenched iron and steel centres external economies are not powerful enough to attract new growth.

Table 15

PROVINCIAL EMPLOYMENT IN SMELTING, REFINING, ROLLING, FORGING AND DRAWING, 1972

	Workers	%		Workers	%
Liège	35,753	29.0	West-Vlaanderen	8,512	6.9
Hainaut	34,997	28.4	Limburg	3,314	2.7
Brabant	14,269	11.6	Luxembourg	2,604	2.1
Antwerpen	13,682	11.1	Namur	1,254	1.0
Oost-Vlaanderen	8,864	7.2	Belgium	123,249	100.0

Source: Office National de Sécurité Sociale, *Rapport Annuel, 1972*, Brussels (1973)

The computation of location quotients at *arrondissement* level confirms Liège and Charleroi as specialist metallurgical areas, their respective scores being 3.34 and 3.22, but it also emphasises specialisation in the entire coal furrow. Mons in the west has a quotient of 1.54, Soignies further east scores 2.59, in part a function of the integrated works at La Louvière, while Thuin, south of Charleroi, returns a score of 1.36. Huy, to the west of Liège, has a quotient of 2.97, completing the string of specialist coalfield districts. There are also some other specialist metallurgical areas, and indeed the highest quotient is achieved by Arlon in Belgian Luxembourg. The score is 6.42, the result of *minette* smelting at Athus in otherwise rural surroundings. Somewhat similar in principle if not in scale is Nivelles (2.84). Here there is an integrated works at Clabecq and a large steelworks at Court St. Etienne. That Ghent returns a quotient of only

1.07 is a result of the relatively small number of workers required to operate the new SIDMAR integrated plant at Zelzate and the strength of other manufacturing in the area. The heavy sector of the industry is characterised by considerable 'swarming' round Liège and Charleroi, and by a small number of outlying plants such as those at Athus, Clabecq and Zelzate. Fig 18, which maps the principal works, indicates that of the 10 steelworks, only 4 – those at Court St. Etienne, Lembeek, Genk and Langerbrugge (Ghent) – are not on the Walloon coalfield. Of the 15 rolling mills, only those at Paliseul, Nivelles and the suburban Antwerp plants at Schoten and Boechout, are not on this coalfield. Certainly in terms of the major works, the metallurgical industry has maintained its close association with the Walloon industrial axis. To facilitate the understanding of the changing location of the industry, it is convenient to consider each of the four distinctive categories of site in turn. These are: iron ore sites, coalfield sites, intermediate sites and coastal sites.

Iron Ore Sites

The metallurgical industry based on the lean phosphoric ores of Belgian Luxembourg is not of major significance, and there is some doubt as to the long-term future of the activity in the region. Iron-and steel-making here owes its origin to the lean qualities of the ore in a small 300 ha orefield, for with an iron content of only 35 per cent, there have always been advantages in smelting the ore *in situ* in order to avoid onerous transport costs. Three blast furnace works, at Halanzy, Musson and Athus, arose in the nineteenth century, sending their pig iron to be refined on the Walloon coalfield. As local ore production contracted, their *raison d'être* was removed for they were obliged to rely upon Lorraine ore. Halanzy was the first to shut, followed by Musson in 1967. The third plant, Athus, however, was owned by the Liège firm John Cockerill which, far from cutting back output, was able to find the necessary funds to expand operations there. Bessemer converters were added to the blast furnaces in the 1930s, and their capacity is now 0.6 million tonnes of steel a year. A 354 mm mill for the production of reinforced bars was opened in 1971,[22] and the firm clearly has no intention of abandoning the location in spite of the paltry local ore output of 90,000 tonnes per annum, the rising cost of French ore and the need to import coking coal from the Ruhr. Although the plant may be isolated within Belgium, it does benefit from the external economies of the great Lorraine-Luxemburg metallurgical district. The future of the plant is therefore linked with that of Lorraine-Luxemburg, but the fact remains that ore can be delivered to coastal works at prices below those of Lorraine ore at Athus, placing the works at some disadvantage.

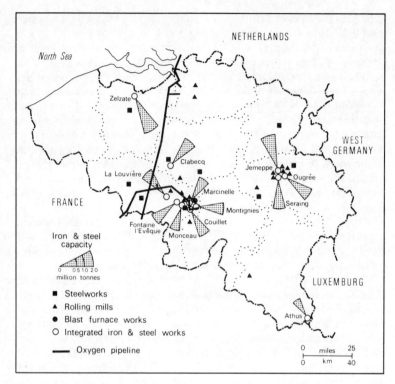

Fig 18. THE BELGIAN IRON AND STEEL INDISTRY
SOURCES. H. G. Cordero (Ed), *Iron and Steelworks of the World*, London, 1969.
  Various issues of *Metal Bulletin*, London

Coalfield Sites

The remarkably fortuitous juxtaposition of the Ardennes and the Walloon coalfield caused only a slight northward shift to be required to enable the Belgian iron industry to survive and then to expand during the nineteenth century. Coking coal of high quality was mined in the Borinage and the Centre, and when local ores were exhausted, recourse was made to the *minette* of Luxemburg and Lorraine. Of great assistance to transport was the presence of the rivers Sambre and Meuse following the trace of much of the coalfield. As the economies of large-scale production became clear, blast furnaces migrated to Liège and Charleroi, steelworks and rolling mills often remaining at the old sites. Such a case was Huy which could claim two blast furnaces, three puddling furnaces and four rolling mills at mid-century.[23] Now a steelworks and rolling mill alone survive, both operated by Tôleries Delloye-Matthieu, under whose control production has shifted from standard steels to galvanised sheeting. Such product diversification has often been a necessary strategy on the part of small firms unable to reap economies of scale. Meanwhile technical advances affecting the optimum size of plant have cause a number of works at both Charleroi and Liège to be closed; since 1952 the Cockerill steelworks at Grivegnée (Liège) and the Providence blast furnace works at Dampremy (Charleroi) have disappeared. Sometimes it has proved impossible to raise output by the rationalisation of existing works and new plants have been built. Thus Espérance-Longdoz, the Liège firm, built a large steelworks downstream of the city at Chertal in 1963, while the new Armco-Pittsburgh cold strip mill at Liège represents foreign investment in the industry. In numerical terms there were thirty major works on the Walloon coalfield in 1938[24] compared with twenty-seven at present, but the output achieved is three times larger.

As in Belgian Luxembourg, so in Wallonie the local raw material base of the industry is now non-existent for coking coal is no longer mined. Fortunately the Kempen field is a producer of coking coal and is linked to both Liège and Charleroi by a waterway with a capacity for 1350-tonne barges. Some 4.27 million tonnes out of a total of 7.76 million tonnes of coking coal delivered to Belgian steelworks in 1970 came from this source. Even so, since 1.78 million tonnes originated from West Germany and 1.45 million tonnes from the USA, the delivered cost of these imports would have been less at coastal sites than at Liège or Charleroi. However the Centre National de Recherches Métallurgiques has developed a method of oil and natural gas injection which will reduce the coke rate, that is, the quantity of coke required to produce 1 tonne of pig iron, from 638 to 372 kg,[25] thus greatly reducing the locational pull of coal upon blast furnaces.

As long as the coalfield blast furnaces smelted Lorraine-Luxemburg ores, they were at no disadvantage compared with coastal works. In 1952, 74 per cent of the ore smelted originated from the *minette* field,[26] but the rising price of these ores has resulted in a switch to Swedish ore which now accounts for 60 per cent of blast furnace consumption as against 25 per cent from the *minette* area. The consequence has been that inland plants must meet a transport charge from the importing port on an increasingly large proportion of their iron ore; coastal works have no such burden. Swedish ore prices have themselves risen sharply in recent years and some steelworks are considering moving from Thomas steel into LD steel refined by oxygen injection techniques, allowing the use of cheap, non-phosphoric ores from West Africa, Brazil and Venezuela, but this will still favour coastal plants. Only in the third fundamental raw material, scrap, does the Walloon coalfield enjoy an advantage, for a large proportion of the 3 million tonnes consumed in Belgium originates there.

The question arises as to the rationale behind the continued existence of the Sambre-Meuse metallurgical industry. Its greatest advantages are the external economies obtaining in an area devoted to the activity for nearly two centuries. The strength of metallurgy has resulted in a host of specialist services, the most recent of which is an oxygen pipeline serving works in Hainaut, and illustrated in Fig 18. At the same time the vast sums of money invested, more especially since 1945, substantially add to geographical inertia. In 1970 the steel industry embarked upon a five year, 30,000 million BF modernisation programme which includes new blast furnaces at the Boël plant at La Louvière, the installation of additional oxygen steelmaking equipment at the Hainaut-Sambre plants at Charleroi and at Cockerill's Marchiennes works, and the provision of a 120 tonne electric arc furnace at Thy-Marcinelle et Monceau, Charleroi.

As a reaction to the growth of large integrated coastal works in countries to which Belgian firms have long exported steel products, Walloon companies have participated in a number of mergers to bring their combined output closer to that achieved by Klöckner at Bremen, Hoogovens at Ijmuiden and Usinor at Dunkirk. Usines Métallurgiques du Hainaut merged with Société Métallurgique de Sambre et Moselle in 1955 to create a Charleroi group known as Hainaut-Sambre, whose output in 1971 was 1.76 million tonnes. Similarly SA des Hauts Forneaux, Forges et Aciéries de Thy-Le-Château et Marcinelle have combined with Aciéries et Minières de la Sambre to give a second Charleroi group, Forges de Thy-Marcinelle et Monceau, with a capacity of 1.1 million tonnes. The amalgamation of firms has been more active in the Liège region, and at the root of events has been SA John Cockerill. Even in 1955 this firm merged with the then second largest Belgian steel company, Ougrée-Marihaye, creating a group with 40 per cent of the national steelmaking capacity. Cockerill-Ougrée then took over the Charleroi firm of Forges de la Providence in 1966, and finally Cockerill-Ougrée-Providence combined in 1970 with SA Métallurgique d'Espérance-Longdoz. Cockerill made 6.13 million tonnes of steel products in 1970, the greater part coming from its Liège mills. The firm is now larger than most coastal EEC plants, and with the exception of the Armco-Pittsburgh strip mill, controls the entire output of the Liège district. Because these mergers have for the most part been on a regional basis, this has allowed the new groupings to effect plant specialisation giving important economies of scale. Within the Cockerill group, the Liège works are assigned to two divisions, one for hot rolled products (Tilleur, Jemeppe and Liège-Longdoz) and the other for cold rolled and coated flat products (Chertal, Seraing, Ougrée and Flémalle); the Marchienne and Athus divisions produce sections and bars.[27] The use of 150 tonne hot metal railway wagons allows the separation of steelworks from blast furnaces, formerly not desirable owing to the need to reheat the pig iron. Pig railed from the Cockerill works at Seraing to the Chertal steelworks 22 km distant loses only $8-12°C$ en route, and a similar hot metal service is operated between the Marcinelle and Monceau plants of Thy-Marcinelle et Monceau.[28]

A number of coalfield works, particularly the steelworks, are highly specialised, and in this way their inland location is in no way disadvantageous. Fabrique de Fer de Charleroi installed a 150 tonne electric arc furnace for the production of alloy steels in 1957, Jadot Frères at Beloeil have been making manganese steels since the World War I, and as we have seen, Delloye-Matthieu at Huy produce galvanized sheet. Some of the plants operated by the larger companies are also specialised: Cockerill has an electrolytic tinning line at its Ferblatil works at Tilleur, electric steel sheets are made at the Tolmatil works, also at Tilleur, galvanized metal sheet is produced at the wholly-owned Phenix Works at Liège, and the company has 90 per cent of the shares of the Allegheny-Longdoz stainless steel plant at Genk in Kempenland. Other evidence of forward integration by the Cockerill group is its interest in the rapidly growing Flemish wire-drawing firm, NV Bekaert, and in Usines à Tubes de la Meuse which makes small diameter welded tubes at Jemappes and Flémalle.

Regional policy provides a further reason for the continuation of metallurgy on the Walloon coalfield; since 1959 and 1966 all firms have been eligible for financial assistance. Although the steel industry is privately owned (largely by financial institutions such as Société Générale), the government is involved in the industry through its participation in the Comité de Concertation de la Politique Sidérurgique (CCPS), set up in 1967.[29] This body coordinates development plans submitted by various companies in an attempt to avoid duplication of investment, and this itself is conducive to inertia for domestic competition is greatly reduced. However the CCPS is not an entirely reactionary body for shortly after it was set up it recommended that rationalisation be effected at Hainaut-Sambre. The threat of unemployment was such that eventually 1600 million BF were advanced to allow the firm to reorganise without the contraction of its labour force. It would appear that social pressures are now a powerful contributary influence upon the maintenance of the metallurgical industry on the coalfield.

Intermediate Sites

Fig 18 indicates that there are a number of works whose location is not explicable in terms of orientation towards raw materials. The steelworks at Genk, for instance, opened in 1961 on the Kempen coalfield, uses electric arc furnaces and the presence of local coal is irrelevant. Nor can the location of those works not sited on coal and ironfields be held to be a function of proximity to markets, for these are to be found within the EEC rather than within the country itself. Four works, Allegheny-Longdoz at Genk, Sadacem at Langerbrugge, Fabrique Belge d'Aciers Rapides et Spéciaux at Lembeek and Forges de Clabecq are adjacent to large capacity canals, but it is doubtful whether transport costs alone provide the answer to the question of their location. Further, although the plants at Langerbrugge, Schoten and Boechout are in the cities of Ghent and Antwerp, they cannot be regarded as coastal sites since they do not obtain their supplies through these ports. Only one of the nine above-named plants, which may be considered as occupying intermediate sites, is an integrated works, namely Forges de Clabecq. The others are steelworks and rolling mills and this does allow them relative freedom in their choice of site, especially where the steels produced are high grade, for then transport costs are a small part of total costs. The Lembeek plant is an exclusive producer of special steels, Sadacem at Langerbrugge makes ferromanganese, Allegheny-Longdoz manufactures stainless steel and Usines Emile Henricot at Court St. Etienne is an established electric steel specialist. Although Forges de Clabecq is an integrated works and lacks the degree of specialisation of the plants so far mentioned, it is significant that the plant was one of the first in Belgium to install electric arc furnaces, in 1947, and by 1958 was responsible for 38 per cent of Belgian electric steel.[30]

Because of the locational flexibility and the ability of relatively small works to benefit from urban external economies, the rationale behind the precise location of the intermediate plants can only be satisfactorily explained by recourse to behavioural considerations. The Paliseul rolling mill, which dates back to 1786, is the residual feature of the entire Ardennes iron-making industry, and has remained not because of site characteristics but rather because its owners have managed more successfully than others to adapt their works to changing economic circumstances. The continuation of metallurgy at Court St. Etienne, rather than at the many other towns in Brabant once possessing foundries, was largely due to the injection of capital into a failing business in 1859 by a local aristocrat, le Comte Goblet d'Alviella, and by a director of Belgian railways.[31] Further impetus was obtained from the appointment in 1866 of an innovative works manager, Emile Henricot, under whose guidance, and eventual ownership, the plant flourished. The success of the Clabecq iron and steelworks followed the same pattern. The works was controlled by Goffin and Warocqué, both of whom came from families with extensive financial and business interests so that capital for modernisation was not in short supply. After the death of the partners, Goffin's son took over in 1851 and such was his success that the plant was acquired by a consortium of Brussels financiers in 1888. The arrival of Germeau in 1909 set the plant on its present path for he built blast furnaces and supplementary coke ovens at Vilvoorde which use cheap imported coal.[32] The Genk steelworks owes its existence to the desire of Espérance-Longdoz to expand and to diversify, to its inability to do so in the cramped Meuse valley at Liège and to the interest of Allegheny-Ludlum in producing stainless steel in the EEC. These were cases of entrepreneurs choosing sites rather than of sites 'suggesting themselves' to entrepreneurs.

Coastal Sites

The advantages enjoyed at the present time by an integrated iron and steelworks located on the coast have been considered above under the heading of coalfield sites, and need no elaboration here. The speed with which the single Belgian coastal works, SIDMAR, on the Ghent-Terneuzen Canal at Zelzate to the north of Ghent, has expanded its output is itself a commentary on the profitability of such locations. The first blast furnace was blown in on 2 May 1967, and the second followed in May 1968; yet at the end of the latter year no less than 1.2 million tonnes of steel sheets were produced. By 1970 output reached 1.9 million tonnes and 1972 saw a total of 2.5 million tonnes of steel leaving the works. This was achieved by a workforce of some 5000, giving a productivity ratio markedly superior to that obtaining in Wallonie. Steel is exclusively made by the LD process and no phosphoric ores from either Lorraine or Sweden are employed. The principal ore suppliers in 1971 were Brazil, Australia, Mauritania and Algeria.[33] To allow 60,000 dwt ore carriers access to the plant, the Ghent-Terneuzen Canal has been widened to 400 metres adjacent to the works, and although these vessels are smaller than many that serve other coastal works, landed ore prices are below those of Lorraine ore at Liège and Charleroi.

The plant is operated by a consortium of financial groups and by steel firms all wishing to benefit from the economies stemming from a coastal site. These firms include the otherwise land-locked Cockerill group, the French Schneider firm, the Italian group of Falck and ARBED from the Duchy of Luxemburg. Participation by the last was in part responsible for the precise siting of the plant, for ARBED had had the foresight to purchase a 300 ha plot on the right bank of the canal in 1929. That Ghent rather than Antwerp was selected was also a result of the high unemployment in the former region, causing government pressure to be brought to bear upon the location decision.[34]

The Non-Ferrous Metal Industry

The smelting and refining of non-ferrous metals is a particularly distinctive industry in Belgium both in terms of absolute production and location within the country itself. In 1972 Belgium was the world's fourth producer of cadmium, seventh producer of refined zinc, eighth producer of both copper and tin, and held tenth place in respect of lead. This is an almost anomalous position for a country lacking in sources of these minerals. Although output is expanding, this has been achieved from a decreasing number of plants and a contracting labour force. Most of the plants pre-date World War II, and indeed the only new site to be developed since then, at Ehein near Liège, was not begun until 1970. Thus using employment as the criterion, the activity cannot be regarded as a growth industry.

Fig 19, which maps the distribution of plants, reveals three clusters, at Antwerp, in Kempenland and in the Liège district. Plants in Kempenland have a combined annual capacity of 686,000 tonnes, compared with 188,000 tonnes in the case of Antwerp and 100,000 tonnes in the Liège region, suggesting that the attractions of Liège are not highly regarded by the industry. This was not always the case, for the process by which zinc could be separated from its ore was invented in 1805 by Daniel Dony in Liège, and the first zinc ingots were produced by his firm five years later. Using local coal and ores mined to the east of the city, the firm of Vieille-Montagne began smelting zinc in Liège in 1837 and by the end of the century had become the largest zinc-producing firm in the world, operating some forty plants in the Liège district. This number had been reduced to ten by 1927, but by this time there were also three plants at Balen (1889), Overpelt (1893) and Lommel (1904) in the Kempen at this time. Since the first Kempen coal was not mined until 1917 the reasons for the migration from Liège had nothing to do with the cost of fuel.

The advantages of the Kempenland were considerable and were accepted by Vieille-Montagne to whom the Balen works belonged. The Liège ores were reaching their economic margins, causing an increasing reliance to be placed upon imports, so that a location closer to Antwerp

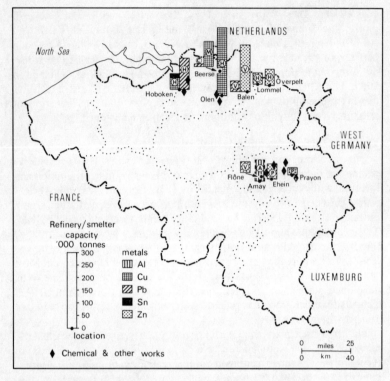

Fig 19. THE BELGIAN NON-FERROUS METAL INDUSTRY
The capital letters in the columns represent company names as follows:
A. Alusuisse
C. Métallurgie de la Campine
H. Hoboken-Overpelt
M. Métallo-Chimique
P Prayon
V. Vieille-Montagne
SOURCE: *Yearbook of the American Bureau of Metal Statistics, 1972*, New
   York, 1973

than Liège would save some transport charges. Since a large proportion
of output was exported, mostly through Antwerp, further savings
accrued from proximity to the port. Water transport links with Antwerp
were available through the Antwerp-Turnhout and Schelde-Maas
canals. Land could be bought at very low cost in the Kempen, and firms
could consequently make adequate provision for future expansion.

Rural poverty was such that labour costs were much lower than those in Liège, an area of high wages. After 1917 the availability of local coal made the Kempen even more attractive. So far the assumption has been that the migration was from Liège northwards, but one firm, SA Métallurgique de Hoboken, established its first plant at Hoboken south of Antwerp in 1887, and subsequently expanded at Olen in Kempenland. Thus not even a site at Antwerp, the probable least transport cost location, could overcome the low land values and labour costs of the area to the east.

Belgian supremacy in zinc refining owed much to the availability of zinc ore, now exhausted. Similarly an important influence in subsequent diversification into the recovery of other non-ferrous metals was the discovery of extensive deposits of copper, tin, cadmium, cobalt and radium in the Belgian Congo. The introduction in the 1920s of electrolytic refining in place of the cruder heat treatment allowed the recovery of a wider range of metals and broadened the base of the firms involved. Métallurgie Hoboken-Overpelt, formed in 1970 from a merger of the former with Overpelt-Lommel, now produces more than 20 different metals. Many metals such as gold, antimony, germanium, tantalum and uranium are produced in small quantities, but the output of one metal, copper, has doubled since 1945 and is now manufactured in large quantities. Hoboken-Overpelt has an annual capacity of 315,000 tonnes, and its plant at Olen is the largest electrolytic copper refinery in Europe.

Metals are not the only products of non-ferrous metal works, and for some time large quantities of chemicals have been produced. Vieille-Monatagne, for example, manufactures 470,000 tonnes of sulphuric acid each year. The firm also makes calcium arsenate, zinc oxide which is used in the manufacture of photocopying paper, thallium sulphate and magnesium oxide.[35] Prayon's plant at Engis manufactures chemicals such as sulphuric acid, phosphoric acid and a range of fertilizers. Hoboken-Overpelt appears to be integrating forwards into the metal using industries in addition to possessing chemical interests. The firm owns Usines à Cuivre at à Zinc at Liège, and in association with this subsidiary it opened a 100,000 tonne continuous casting and rolling plant for quality copper rod at Olen in 1973. Should Alusuisse decide to go ahead with their smelter at Amay near Huy, it will be instructive to see whether or not the availability of crude aluminium will further accelerate the growth of the secondary aluminium industry, concerned with the fabrication of semi-finished products by rolling and stamping. Firms such as Sidal at Duffel, Alcan at Raeren, Aleurope at Ghlin and Affinerie du Hainaut at Tournai have helped to make this the fastest growing sector within the entire metallurgical industry.

The Ceramic and Glass Industries

The localisation of ceramic and glass manufacture has been very largely determined by the distribution of raw materials which are normally bulky, of low value and therefore uneconomic to move long distances. The existence of cheaply worked coal measures in the Haine-Sambre-Meuse valleys both aided the rapid development of the two industries there and ensured their concentration in the coal furrow. The twentieth century has witnessed great changes in the fortunes of these once prosperous, exported-oriented activities, and indeed ceramics have exhibited a contraction in employment second only to that experienced by coalmining. At the same time coalfield areas have become relatively more important as contraction elsewhere has proceeded more rapidly. Between 1937 and 1970 employment in ceramics fell from 25,160 to 7421. At the earlier date Hainaut had only 33 per cent of the total workforce, compared with 53 per cent in 1970. Antwerpen, the second province in 1937 with 20 per cent of the total, employed only 11 per cent in 1970, illustrating the Walloon dilemma of 'strength' in the declining industries.

The collapse of the ceramics industry is the result of a number of factors. A large proportion of the foreign markets that formerly accounted for the bulk of sales has now been lost to other competitors. The introduction of plastic materials has also reduced the scope for ceramic goods. In the light of these compelling influences, the industry has necessarily diversified. A not untypical example of this trend is the strategy adopted by NV Koramic at Kortrijk. The firm now turns out eight varieties of roofing tiles, decorative facing bricks, window sills, prefabricated walls, flooring materials and a range of artistic pottery ware. A rather more specialist approach is taken by NV Ostyn-Marke, also at Kortrijk, which produces prefabricated chimneys and fireplaces.[36] The old established sector producing heavy clay goods remains localised in the vicinity of Charleroi, in particular at Bouffioulx, and all the principal pottery firms are either at Hautrage and Baudour in the Borinage or La Louvière in the Centre. Similarly the production of refractory goods for the metallurgical industry remains in the Borinage and in the neighbourhood of Philippeville in the Ardennes, while the manufacture of tiles is divided between the Hainaut coalfield and the specialist brick-making region on the Rupel to the east of Boom.

Like the ceramics industry, the manufacture of glass was a well established activity prior to the industrial revolution, although output was small. A map produced by Olyslager shows that in the second half of the eighteenth century there were glassworks in many of the larger towns such as Bruges, Brussels, Leuven, Liège and Namur, but also that there was a remarkable concentration round Charleroi. Some twenty-two works appear on the map, but no less than twelve of these are clustered round the town.[37] The region was admirably endowed with the necessary materials: glass sands, coal, chalk and refractory clay for the melting pots. Additionally it seems likely that local skills had been engendered by the arrival of Venetian glass blowers in the fifteenth century. The nineteenth century saw the diffusion of the industry throughout the Walloon coalfield, and although works of the highest repute such as Val St. Lambert, Liège, were set up outside Charleroi, by 1896 the Hainaut coalfield still accounted for 65 per cent of the total workforce.[38] However the Walloon monopoly was soon to be broken for a number of works were established to use the sand and coal of the Kempen: at Lommel in 1910, Mol-Donk in 1922 and Mol-Gompel the following year. Also in 1923 the sheetglass plant at Zeebrugge began operations. From a total of 21,699 workers in 1869, there was an increase in this industry to 23,156 in 1937, and in 1970 there were still some 22,571 employed. Clearly this is not a growth industry, but it has fared very much better than ceramics.

The maintenance of a labour force of nineteenth-century proportions has been achieved by the retention of export markets following the ability to produce glass at low cost. Some three-quarters of the glass currently made is exported. The Belgian market for safety glass is ensured by the government stipulation that such glass used by the vehicle industry must originate from indigenous plants. Glass manufacture lends itself to large scale production and this was achieved at a relatively early date by a series of amalgamations. The first merger took place in 1930 between 13 firms operating 17 plants, creating the Univerbel group. In 1931 Glaver was formed and Glaceries de St. Roche followed in 1932. The largest subsequent amalgamation has been that between Univerbel and Glaver, to form Glaverbel, in 1961. The consequence is that the Belgian glass industry is dominated by large groups, some of which are themselves associated with glassworks in other countries. The French groups St. Gobain and BSN have between them 42 per cent of Glaverbel's capital, so that the sheer size and international ramifications of these firms ensure that they are competitive. It is not surprising that it was Glaverbel which first took up the licence for the Pilkington float glass process and converted its plate glass works at Moustier for this purpose. Despite the rationalisation that has been a corollary of the mergers in the industry, the distribution pattern has not fundamentally changed, and the largest concentration of plants is still found round Charleroi, where 6 of the 8 Glaverbel works are situated. Indeed this firm opened a second plant in 1971 at Moustier, between Charleroi and Namur, in preference to a site in the north where it runs the works at Mol-Gompel and Zeebrugge. Other firms which have recently opened plants also seem to prefer the Walloon coalfield – an example is the Verlica bottle plant at Ghlin in the Borinage – and of the 27 largest plants at present in operation, some 20 are on or adjacent to the *pays noir*. As a footnote, the glass industry provides a unique example of state ownership in Belgian manufacturing, for the government has bought the ailing Val St. Lambert works from the Société Générale to prevent it from being sold to an American company.

Brewing

The manufacture of beer is an example of a traditional industry undergoing rationalisation into a smaller number of larger plants. For this reason the activity is in decline if the criterion of employment is adopted, and as Table 10 indicates, there was a 15 per cent fall in the combined brewing and soft drinks workforce between 1955 and 1972. However, in contrast to the situation in textiles where employment contraction is being accompanied by an increase in output, beer production has exhibited a long-term downward trend. Despite the consumption in Belgium of more beer per person than in any other country in Western Europe, between 1907 and 1966 there was a 44 per cent reduction in brewery output.[39] However, the development of exports has since allowed production to increase once more. It should be mentioned that the Belgian market for beer is not viewed by breweries elsewhere as a declining proposition. Watney, the British group, have been operating in Belgium since 1967 when they took over the Debruyere plant at Châtelet, Charleroi, and they have subsequently acquired the firm of Vandenheuvel, with three breweries in Brussels and one in Charleroi, and Maes at Mechelen. Bass Charrington, another British firm, has controlled the Lamot brewery at Mechelen since 1970.

The brewing industry does not fit the hypothesis that declining industries tend to be located in Wallonie since it is a market-oriented activity. The locational influence of the three basic raw materials – hops, barley and water – is small. Water accounts for approximately 80 per cent of the weight of beer, and although some water gives beer possessing a particular taste, for example the brown ales of Charleroi and the pale ales of Mechelen, it exerts little pull on breweries since it is effectively everywhere available. The value of beer in relation to its weight means that transport costs account for a relatively high proportion of delivered prices, and beer is seldom moved long distances; in 1947 Olyslager noted that in Belgium it was uneconomic to transport beer more than 70 km by road.[40] The consequence is that breweries are strongly related to their customers. Despite the

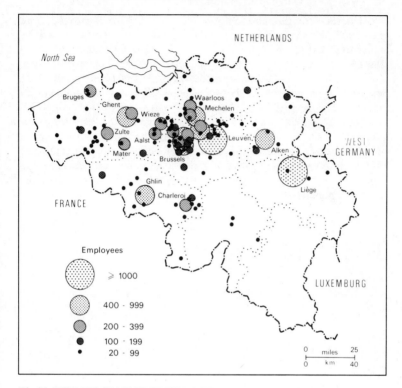

Fig 20. THE BELGIAN BREWING INDUSTRY
SOURCE: W. Vlassenbroeck and L. De Smet, De Lokalisering der Brouwerijen en Aanverwante Bedrijven in België, *De Aardrijkskunde*, 77 (1968) 78

introduction of beer tankers and motorways, beer transport costs are still onerous, and it is no accident that the largest Belgian breweries are in or adjacent to large towns. The situation in 1968 is mapped in Fig 20. That there is a correlation with population may be demonstrated by the use of the Spearman rank correlation technique, the formula for which is

$$R = 1 - \frac{6 \sum d^2}{n^3 - n}$$

where R is the correlation coefficient, d is the difference in ranking between population and employment in brewing and n is the number of frequencies – in this case 9 since the data for the 9 provinces are employed. Where an absolute correlation exists, the coefficient will be equal to 1 and an absolute inverse correlation will be equal to -1[49] In 1960 R was found to be 0.93, and in 1970 to be 0.85, both significant at the 1 per cent level, suggesting that at the provincial level at least, there was a strong correlation between population and employment in brewing. Further evidence for brewing's market-orientation is provided by Table 16 which sets out the location quotients for the industry by province. That the quotients cluster about the value of unity again suggests a positive relationship between brewing and the distribution of population. Thus brewing is a declining industry most well developed in the Belgian growth axis because this region has a large part of the country's population.

Table 16

LOCATION QUOTIENTS FOR THE BREWING INDUSTRY BY PROVINCE, 1972

Brabant	1.67	West-Vlaanderen	0.75
Oost-Vlaanderen	1.05	Antwerpen	0.69
Liège	0.96	Hainaut	0.63
Limburg	0.94	Luxembourg	0.34
Namur	0.93		

Source: Office National de Sécurité Sociale, *Rapport Annuel, 1972*, Brussels (1973)

The reduction in the number of breweries has been made possible by the collapse of breweries unable to compete and by the introduction of more efficient means of transport, allowing large urban breweries to underprice small rural firms. By 1967 there remained but 117 breweries each employing 20 or more workers. Indicative of the downward trend was the closure of a further 10 over the following three years, leaving only 107 in existence at the end of 1970.[42] Mergers have caused some closures, and in one case three firms amalgamated, closed all their old premises, and built a new brewery on the industrial estate at Ghlin. However, a few small breweries have succeeded in remaining in business by virtue of their production of special beers for limited local markets. Some of these plants are run by Trappist monks at rural locations such as Westmalle, east of Antwerp, Chimay and Rochefort, both of which are in the Ardennes.

The existence of rather more brewing employees in Brabant than would be expected (Table 16), may be attributed to the great nodality enjoyed by the province, enabling many parts of the country to be economically served by road from the centre, and to the presence of dynamic brewers who have managed to overcome the disadvantage of a brewery with a restricted local market. Examples of this last factor are breweries in the small towns of Opwijk, Merchtem, Steenhuffel and Boortmeerbeek in the northern part of the province, all now able to market beer in both Brussels and Antwerp. The same may be said of other breweries in small settlements such as Wieze and Waarloos between Brussels and Antwerp; likewise the size of the Artois brewery, the largest in Belgium, in relation to the population of Leuven, owes much to superior management ability. Brussels itself has a small number of breweries which produce *gueuze*, a strong local beer which undergoes a long fermentation period, and which as a consequence is a very distinctive and expensive brew. The price of the beer is high enough to offset the diseconomies of the small size of these breweries.[43] The paucity of breweries in the Antwerp region is puzzling, but as Vlassenbroeck and De Smet remark, the preoccupation of local capital with port activities, coupled with proximity to several breweries further south, may well provide the answer.[44] The second largest brewery is Piedboeuf at Jupille, Liège, a firm which has absorbed a number of smaller plants and which serves a larger market than is locally available. As a consequence the Liège quotient comes close to unity. The low quotient for the province of Luxembourg suggests that the population of the province is now below the threshold level required to justify the existence of more than a small brewing capacity.

The Clothing Industry

Belgium has a well developed clothing industry whose 92,000 employees give it fourth place behind engineering, metallurgy and textiles among the country's manufacturing industries. Not only is output expanding – between 1962 and 1971 the annual value of production more than doubled – but the workforce is growing at the same time. As Table 10 indicates, the increase in numbers employed almost matched the rate of growth for all industries over the period 1955–72, a remarkable achievement in an old established industry. Its outstandingly successful export strategies have resulted in a sixfold increase in foreign sales between 1962 and 1971; exports now account for half the total output. Some firms formerly operating on their own account have switched to contract work for Dutch companies, and in these cases the entire production is exported to the Netherlands. The EEC has certainly made its contribution to this industry.

Although the installation of expensive machinery has caused the manufacture of clothing to become more capital intensive, labour costs continue to play an important role, accounting for between 40 and 45

Table 17

PROVINCIAL EMPLOYMENT IN THE CLOTHING INDUSTRY, 1955 AND 1972, %

	1955	1972		1955	1972
Oost-Vlaanderen	23.1	24.9	Hainaut	10.8	9.5
Brabant	32.9	21.8	Liège	5.8	3.5
West-Vlaanderen	11.6	16.0	Namur	0.8	0.6
Antwerpen	13.8	13.1	Luxembourg	0.2	0.3
Limburg	1.0	10.3	BELGIUM	100.0	100.0

Source: Office National de Sécurité Sociale, *Rapport Annuel, 1955, 1972*, Brussels
(1956, 1973)

per cent of total costs.[45] Materials represent a similar element, but they are of high value and can readily be transported. Labour, on the other hand, is notoriously immobile in the short term, with the consequence that both the supply of labour and labour cost have been powerful influences upon the location decisions. The industry is heavily dependent upon female labour, which constituted 84 per cent of total employment in 1972, and firms are now being drawn almost irrevocably to the development areas by a combination of government financial assistance and cheap female labour. The existence of skilled labour does not seem to be an important locational influence.

Even before the changes of the 1960s, the industry was rather more widely dispersed than textile production, largely because of the importance of Brussels and of a few specialist centres such as Binche in Hainaut. Table 17 illustrates the flight of the industry from Brabant and Brussels and its congregation in Limburg and West-Vlaanderen between 1955 and 1972. The three *arrondissements* in the latter province to exhibit the greatest absolute increase in employment, namely Ieper, Kortrijk and Tielt, all had female wage rates below the national average, Ieper substantially so. The position in Limburg was rather more complex: here the *arrondissements* of Maaseik and Tongeren did have lower wage rates than the national average, but Hasselt did not. The explanation for growth in this province must be seen in the presence of a number of large Dutch-owned plants on new industrial estates: since 1965 some forty Dutch factories have been established in Belgium, almost all of them in Limburg where they may be easily controlled from the Netherlands. The greatest changes between 1960 and 1972 have been in Brussels and Halle-Vilvoorde, whose share of clothing employment fell from 27.1 per cent to 17.4 per cent. This sharp decline has not been due to high industrial wages, but rather to the competition that the specialist *haute couture* of the capital have had to face from ready-to-wear fashions, to rising rents and to problems of expansion in an area of high land values. Fig 21 shows the

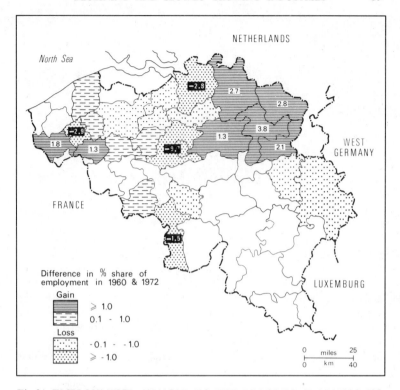

Fig 21. EMPLOYMENT CHANGE IN THE BELGIAN CLOTHING IN-
DUSTRY, 1960–1972
Only those *arrondissements* whose share is greater than 1 % are shaded
SOURCE: Office National de Sécurité Sociale, *Rapport Annuel, 1960, 1972*,
Brussels, 1961, 1973

full picture of changes between 1960 and 1972; the expansion in the
three Limburg districts and in the adjacent areas of Turnhout and
Leuven is quite striking. The map does not illustrate simple percentage
change, for some *arrondissements* had only small numbers in the
industry in 1960 and a small absolute increase in these would cause an
unduly high score to be registered. In order to reflect absolute changes,
differences between the share of employment in clothing in 1960 and
1972 are shown. The industry may be growing more slowly than the
national average, but it has played an important part in the reconversion of the Kempenland and Westhoek. In this way it is similar to
some of the growth industries to be considered in the next chapter.

4

The Growth Industries

THE GROWTH INDUSTRIES whose expansion, whether it be measured by turnover, investment or employment, is superior to that in manufacturing as a whole, are in the main those based on recent technologies and on the increased importance of disposable income. The petrochemical industry dates only from the 1940s; in vehicle manufacturing although the principle of flow production methods was introduced by Henry Ford in Detroit in 1908, the sophisticated techniques currently employed in this industry are of much more youthful origin. The electronic products industry began in the 1950s and is associated with the great strides that have been made in telecommunications and computing in the last two decades. A quickening interest in reading has contributed to the expansion of an old activity, printing, and the introduction of convenience foods has transferred much 'home' cooking from the kitchen to the factory. Table 18 identifies the growth industries on the basis of employment performance between 1955 and 1972.

The locational pattern of the growth industries reflects three factors. Firstly, by virtue of their recent origin they are not restricted to existing manufacturing areas. Areas of low wages, many of them development areas, are therefore attractive to many growth industries. The province of Limburg in particular and the Flemish provinces in general have benefited from this attraction. Secondly, coastal and canal-side locations in Flanders are advantageous for those activities, such as heavy chemicals and oil refining, which process imported raw materials. Their products are for the most part used locally by other activities, not least of which is the manufacture of petrochemicals. Thirdly, a number of activities – paper-making and printing are two – always associated with the capital in the past, still remain so. The city had no less than 39 per cent of all printing workers in 1972 and scored a high location quotient of 3.17. The capital also exercises a compelling attraction for the manufacture of pharmaceuticals and for metalworking. Only the food processing industry appears not to be attracted to the Flemish development areas, to port and canal locations and to Brussels. Rather it is related to the distribution of population, suggested by a rank correlation of +0.9, obtained when using the province as the unit of area.

Table 18

EMPLOYMENT CHANGE IN THE RAPIDLY GROWING INDUSTRIES, 1955-1972

	1955	1972	%Increase
Engineering	187,278	293,272	56
Printing	29,019	41,739	44
Chemicals	51,650	68,044	32
Paper	20,950	26,683	27
Food processing	67,498	81,890	21
Metalworking	52,931	63,429	20
All manufacturing	998,690	1,151,093	15

Source: Office National de Sécurité Sociale, *Rapport Annuel 1955, 1972*, Brussels (1956, 1973)

The preference of the growth industries for the growth axis and for Flanders is their major spatial attribute, but additional characteristics may be added. The first of these is the importance of foreign, particularly American, investment; foreign firms now account for 33 per cent of Belgian manufacturing turnover. Secondly, the growth industries are important exporters, largely because of the selection of Belgium by foreign companies as a suitable location from which serve EEC markets. That subsidiaries of foreign firms now export some 63 per cent of their output is an indication of their marketing strategy.[1] Together with a fast rate of growth and the spatial characteristics described above, these three parameters make up a simple model of Belgian growth industries. The selected examples which follow illustrate many of the facets of the growth industries and allow comparisons to be made with this growth industry model.

The Engineering Industry

Engineering is the largest Belgian industry by an appreciable margin for in 1972 it accounted for 25.5 per cent of manufacturing employment. As Table 18 indicates it is also the most rapidly growing activity in the country. Since both its materials and its products are of considerable value, the industry is by no means restricted by transport costs to particular regions. Although Antwerpen and Brabant have respectively 23 and 22 per cent of Belgian engineering workers, these provinces have not experienced the most rapid growth between 1960 and 1972. Table 19 shows that Limburg, West-Vlaanderen, Luxembourg and Oost-Vlaanderen all exhibited faster expansion. Here a number of *arrondissements* such as Turnhout, Mechelen, Roeslare and Dendermonde, recorded increases of more than 100 per cent, but the three Limburg *arrondissements* of Maaseik (+ 1389 per cent), Hasselt (+ 544 per cent) and Tongeren (+ 440 per cent) were the outstanding performers. The Hasselt *arrondissement* has a quotient of 2.02

Table 19

EMPLOYMENT CHANGES IN THE ENGINEERING INDUSTRY, 1960-1972 '000 workers

	1960	1972	% change	LQ
Limburg	3.7	26.2	601	1.60
W-Vlaanderen	15.5	29.8	93	0.86
Luxembourg	0.6	1.0	73	0.42
O-Vlaanderen	14.4	23.3	61	0.54
Antwerpen	45.2	67.9	50	1.19
Hainaut	27.0	37.4	38	0.94
Namur	4.2	5.1	21	0.73
Brabant	53.7	65.0	21	1.01
Liège	34.0	37.4	10	1.13
BELGIUM	198.4	293.3	48	

Source: Office National de Sécurité Sociale, *Rapport Annuel 1960, 1972*, Brussels (1961, 1973)

compared with scores of 1.39 for Antwerp, 1.36 for Charleroi and 1.21 for Liège. Hasselt exhibits the greatest specialisation in the country, but a second new engineering district, Bruges in West-Vlaanderen, lies close in second place with a quotient of 1.99. Both Limburg and West-Vlaanderen are peripheral regions, and both were formerly largely agricultural; that they have succeeded in attracting engineering firms says much for the influence of unskilled labour upon new investment decisions. The skills and solid industrial environment of Wallonie have made little impact upon recent growth, and only the Flemish provinces expanded faster than the national average between 1960 and 1972.

If Flanders is strong in the newer, lighter branches of engineering such as vehicle assembly, then Wallonie is a specialist in machine tools and the heavier sectors. Of the thirty-eight leading machine tool firms, some eleven are in Liège and six in Charleroi; Brussels with nine firms is the only other area to have more than one.[2] The presence of the three great heavy engineering firms of Ateliers de Constructions Electriques de Charleroi (ACEC) at Marcinelle, Mont-sur-Marchienne and Liège, of Fabrique Nationale (FN) at Herstal (Liège) and of Cockerill at Seraing, also supports this contention. Smaller concerns such as Ateliers de Construction de la Meuse at Liège and Caterpillar at Gosselies manufacture turbines and diesel engines respectively. Flanders, on the other hand, lacks this strength, although there are a few heavy engineering firms, including ACEC and Anglo-Belgian at Ghent, both manufacturing marine diesel engines. The shipbuilding industry is clustered at the largest port, Antwerp, where the Cockerill yards have the greatest capacity. Thus even in Flanders, two of the heavy engineering plants belong to the foremost Walloon trio, which have not made a major attempt at diversification. ACEC is a perfect case in point. In the late 1940s the company was as large as Philips Electric, but ACEC has remained rooted in the heavy end of the electric business and failed to match the performance of Philips. Ultimately it ran into difficulties, and was taken over by the American Westinghouse Corporation in 1969. Cockerill has been rather more successful, but several commentators have compared FN with Rolls Royce, for it is managed by engineers rather than entrepreneurs and in the 1970s engineering excellence is no substitute for managerial expertise.[3] All three are very much part of the past era of Walloon prosperity, although ACEC dates only from 1904 when it was set up through the efforts of Leopold II and Baron Empain. A further common feature is that they are all part of the Société Générale (ACEC until 1969).

Founded in 1822 by William I of the Netherlands, the Société Générale was the world's first industrial development association. It advanced funds to Cockerill and eventually took over his empire. It advanced funds to Cockerill and eventually took over his empire. It has major interests in iron and steel (Cockerill and SIDMAR), non-ferrous metals (Hoboken-Overpelt), coal (Kempense Steenkolenmijnen), electricity (EBES and UCE Linalux-Hainaut), glass (Glaverbel) and cement (CBR), but not in the new industries. La Générale is dominated by traditional financiers rather than industrialists and this has had the effect of imposing conservative strategies upon the companies it runs. Val St. Lambert and ACEC have already been lost and Cockerill and FN continue to pay the penalty of their master's régime; to the extent that diversification is not being effected by La Générale, Wallonie is also suffering.

Vehicle Manufacture

The manufacture of motor vehicles, more particularly cars, displays many of the characteristics of the growth industries. From a level of 200,000 cars in 1960, output rose to 905,000 in 1971. Since there are only 2.3 million cars registered in the country, this is a remarkable performance, for the implication is that export markets are more important than the domestic market; indeed between 80 and 88 per cent of production is exported. Perhaps even more unusual is the fact that not a single car is constructed entirely from Belgian-made materials, for each one is merely assembled from imported components. Belgium is the world's leading automobile assembler by a large margin, the second country, South Africa, turning out only 162,000 cars in 1971. There are no Belgian firms in the industry, and only in the lorry, bus and trailer sector is there indigenous ownership. In 1953 only 31 per cent of vehicle employment was in non-Belgian firms, and such has been the pace of foreign investment that by 1970 the figure had risen to 76 per cent.[4] Vehicle manufacture certainly conforms to the contention that the driving force behind the Belgian growth industries stems from foreign initiative.

Cars may not be produced today by Belgian manufacturers, but in the early years of the century they were manufactured by more than ten firms, three of which, Auto Miesse in Brussels, Brossel at Anderlecht and FN, still exist, although not as automobile makers. One company, Minerva at Antwerp, produced 600 cars and 1500 motor cycles in 1907, and by 1914 they had a workforce of 3000. The demise of this flourishing industry began after World War I, which itself caused a complete cession of production. It became difficult to export vehicles to markets protected by tariffs, while the Belgian market was too small to permit the growth of firms large enough to utilise flow production methods. Governmental economic policy coupled with the desire of the large American firms to penetrate European markets ultimately brought the Belgian industry to the ground. Ford, General Motors and Chrysler all established assembly plants in Antwerp during the 1920s. In this way they were able to reduce the ocean transport costs of shipping complete vehicles. Further incentive to assemble in Belgium was provided by the 1935 agreement with the USA which provided for the import of certain Belgian commodities into America at preferential tariffs in return for the reduction of Belgian duties on imported vehicle components, provided that Belgian labour and components accounted for 25 per cent of the value of the vehicle. Shortly afterwards these terms were applied to other countries, helping to expand the assembly operations of Citroën and Renault which established themselves in Brussels in 1924 and 1926 respectively. In 1948 the tariff on assembled cars was fixed at 24 per cent and that for components other than those, such as glass and upholstery, manufactured in Belgium, was set at 8.5 per cent, greatly stimulating assembly.

Government action after World War II continued to encourage automobile assembly. In 1954 the import of assembled cars from European countries other than the Netherlands was limited to 250 of each make. At the same time imports from the USA were restricted to 3 per cent of the value of the components entering Belgium from that country, and a complete prohibition was placed on the import of vehicles capable of carrying more than ten passengers.[5] This latter regulation certainly helps to account for the strength of Belgian bus manufacturers, for they were thus presented with the entire domestic market for public service vehicles and coaches without any foreign competition. The protection so obtained was not necessarily conducive to high production costs, for two firms, Van Hool at Koningshooikt and the Bus and Car Co at Bruges have been able to develop important export markets. The common external tariff of the EEC has slightly undermined the advantages of the assembly of components by non-member countries, for the component duty is now 14 per cent and that on assembled cars 22 per cent. There were fears that the end of intra-EEC duties in 1968 would see the last of assembly in Belgium by EEC firms, but only Fiat, which had opened a plant at Waterloo in 1957, chose to withdraw.

1. The Distribution of Automobile Production

The distribution of car plants, illustrated in Fig 22, shows a striking concentration in Flanders and Brussels. Were it not for British Leyland at Seneffe, these areas would have a monopoly of this important growth industry. It is also evident that, with the exception of Volvo at Ghent and Ford at Genk, automobile plants exhibit a remarkable clustering within the Brussels-Antwerp axis. Indeed it is arguable that the Seneffe works is in reality an extension of this corridor rather than an outlier in Wallonie. That assembly plants should be established in Flanders is not surprising, for quite apart from lower wages there, the engineering skills of Liège and Charleroi are superfluous to an activity relying upon imported components. Recently, a few plants have begun to carry out some of the early production stages, but the fundamental engineering work is still undertaken outside Belgium. The creation of Ford Europe has caused each of their plants to install specialist production lines, but this has been achieved in the existing plants without recourse to Walloon labour. The Genk works has two automatic lines capable of turning out 15,000 wheels a day and the Antwerp tractor plant has facilities for an annual production of 150,000 rear axles and 112,000 gear boxes.

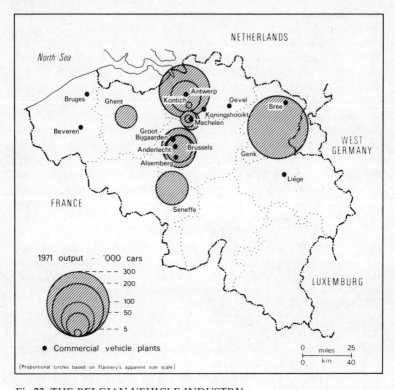

Fig 22. THE BELGIAN VEHICLE INDUSTRY
SOURCE: *Conjoncture*, Paris, June 1971. *The Financial Times*, London, 20th December 1972

A number of other considerations help to explain the rejection of Wallonie by the industry. Firstly, Ford, General Motors and Chrysler selected sites in Antwerp docks, and Volvo in 1963 a site on the Ghent-Terneuzen (Boudewijn) Canal, in order to avoid the cost of moving overland components delivered by sea. Chrysler no longer assemble in Belgium and Ford switched their Antwerp plant to tractors in 1962, but General Motors now have a second factory, opened in 1967, in the Antwerp docks, and clearly the advantages of tidewater and canal-side locations are considerable. Secondly, in the inter-war period Brussels was an attractive assembly point, for the capital was not only the largest market but also an important source of skilled labour. Thus Citroën and Renault selected sites in the Brussels suburbs of Forest and Haren respectively. However, since the 1920s only Volkswagen has used the capital for assembly operations, which began in 1954, also at Forest. Relatively high wages and the attractions of Flanders are the principal causes, but three important factories remain in Brussels. Thirdly, there are the efforts of the city of Mechelen to promote its industrial estates in the 1950s, mentioned in Chapter II. Usines Ragheno began the assembly of Peugeot cars there in 1953, two years later IMA signed an agreement with Mercedes-Benz to set up an assembly line, and in 1956 Triumph (now British Leyland) went into production in the city. Triumph was particularly attracted by the low site costs of 20 BF per metre^2. More recently, in 1973, Saab opened a plant in conjunction with IMA. Fourthly, the unattractiveness of the old industrial areas, largely a result of high wages and militant trade unionism, was underlined by Ford's decision to build Belgium's largest vehicle plant at Genk, an area of agriculture and coalmining. Development grants and low wages were considered by Ford to outweigh the problem of training most of the 11,000-strong workforce. Located in peripheral Limburg, the plant is no great distance from its parent at Cologne.[6]

2. Production of Commercial Vehicles

The output of lorries has remained static over the last decade, but the production of buses has increased tenfold from 100 to 1000 per annum. At the same time the manufacture of tractors has more than doubled. Just as with automobiles, the Brussels-Antwerp axis is responsible for the greater part of production, including as it does Van Hool at Koningshooikt, Ford Tractor, Volvo at Alsemberg, British Leyland at Mechelen and Hocké which assembles MAN, Seddon and Steyr lorries at Groot-Bijgaarden (Fig 22). Of the plants outside the axial belt, only the Van Hool branch plant at Liège and the Bus and Car Co at Bruges may be regarded as being located in engineering areas. The others, Jonckheere at Beveren, DAF at Oevel and LAG at Bree are in rural areas. Protection has, in part, encouraged these companies to burgeon, but that they have done so in Flanders is indicative of the adventurous qualities of the Flemish engineer-entrepreneurs.

The locations of Ford Tractor in Antwerp and the British Leyland bus and heavy truck plant at Mechelen are direct results of the earlier production of cars at these sites. The manufacture of tractors at Antwerp is a result of decisions made by Ford Europe to expand their output of tractors and to centralise output at one of their plants in Western Europe. The importance of tractors in Belgium is therefore purely a consequence of decisions made by the board of a multi-national corporation. British Leyland's bus plant was originally at Anderlecht. The firm had supplied engines and chassis to the Belgian bus firm of Brossel at Anderlecht and eventually took a majority shareholding in Brossel. In 1970, owing to the difficulty of expansion on the Anderlecht site, British Leyland elected to move its bus production to Mechelen where it was already assembling cars. In this sense the location of heavy vehicle manufacture there was predetermined. The third large firm, Van Hool, is unusual in that although it has always used engines and chassis made by Fiat and Volvo, it has remained independent and has proved sufficiently aggressive to expand with impressive speed. Its growth is less a function of its location to the south of Antwerp than of entrepreneurial flair. The first Van Hool coach body was built on a war-surplus military vehicle chassis in 1947 by Bernard Van Hool for his brother who had a coach tour business. A decade later modified flow production methods were introduced to allow two buses to be completed per day, and in 1964 the firm went into the production of specialist lorries and trailers. The Liège works was opened in 1966 and there are subsidiary assembly plants in the Netherlands, France, Spain, Peru and Brazil.[7] The Bus and Car Co at Bruges is a division of the engineering group of La Brugeoise et Nivelles, also at Bruges. The firm has a daily capacity of one bus and exports virtually all its output to the USA.

Although not strictly part of the vehicle industry, cycle and motor cycle manufacture is another sector of transport engineering, and locational trends closely reflect those in both automobile and commercial vehicle production. The growth of car ownership has now removed much of the market for motor cycles, but that Honda should have a plant at Aalst in Oost-Vlaanderen rather than in Wallonie emphasises the northward migration of engineering. Similarly cycle and moped manufacture is entirely a Flemish activity, the major plants being operated by Claeys-Flandria at Zwevezele and Zedelgem in West-Vlaanderen and by Remi-Claeys, also at Zedelgem. The former is responsible for three-quarters of Belgian moped output, and alone among Belgian transport engineering concerns, it designs and builds its own engines.[8] Unlike car and commercial vehicle production, the manufacture of cycles is carried on by Belgian-owned firms, possibly because at present the market is virtually static.

The Electronic Products Industry

In the manufacture of electronic products, as in the vehicle industry, Belgium has come to be regarded by many international companies as a convenient base from which to penetrate the West European market. The level of technology required in this sector is of the highest, but much of the assembly work requires little training of workers, and for the most part the industry is free to establish itself where the investment climate and the labour supply situation are good. Belgium certainly fulfils these requirements. Like the vehicle industry, Belgian firms have only a small share in the manufacture of electronic products. There are a few diversified Belgian firms such as Manufacture Belge des Lampes et de Matériel Electronique (MBLE) and about a dozen smaller firms are specialist radio and television manufacturers; although exports of radios and television equipment account for three-quarters of the total revenue of the industry, there are some very large foreign firms like Philips in this sector. The second half of the 1960s saw a remarkably rapid increase in foreign investment and there were a number of take-overs by American corporations of Belgian firms. Westinghouse acquired ACEC, and ATEA, with plants at Antwerp, Herentals and Frameries, is now part of General Telephone and Electronics. The consequence was that by 1970 a larger part of the industry was controlled by non-Belgian interests than even vehicle production. A mere 12 per cent of employment in the industry was engaged in Belgian plants in 1970, and yet in 1965 the figure had been 51 per cent, eloquent testimony to the sharp upsurge of foreign investment. The same trend is evident in data for turnover, shown in Table 20. The more modest showing of the other engineering branches is indicative of the extent to which international firms see vehicles and electronics as growth areas.

Table 20

THE PROPORTION OF EMPLOYMENT AND TURNOVER IN ENGINEERING IN FOREIGN-OWNED PLANTS 1953-1970 %

	Employment			Turnover		
	1953	1965	1970	1953	1965	1970
Electronic Products	37	49	88	28	46	86
Vehicles	31	64	76	57	70	79
Other Engineering	12	21	33	24	36	56

Source: *Weekly Bulletin of the Kredietbank,* , Brussels (31st March 1972)

Although it is a highly capital-intensive industry, there are now some 20,000 workers employed in the manufacture of electronic products, and the speed with which the industry is growing is impressive. Between 1966 and 1970 the output by value doubled from 7446 to 14,319 million BF, slightly more than half the latter figure coming from telecommunication equipment.[9] During the same period foreign sales of electronic tubes rose fourfold, while those of capacitors and radiological equipment doubled.

Fig 23. THE MAJOR PLANTS OF THE BELGIAN ELECTRONIC
    PRODUCTS INDUSTRY
SOURCE: Trade Directories

The distribution pattern exhibited by the industry, mapped in Fig 23, is of particular interest, for its recent origin makes it possible to judge whether or not Flanders is still as powerfully attractive to new firms as it was in the early and middle 1960s. There is evidence that the Walloon coalfield does not entirely repel the electronic companies, for although twenty-four plants are in the Brussels-Antwerp axial belt, some sixteen are in the *pays noir*, and if Verviers to the east of the coalmining region is included, the figure rises to eighteen. The absence of savings resulting from a tidewater location removes some of the advantages of Antwerp, and although the area had seven plants, including two operated by Bell, the industry is better developed in the Brussels region where there are fifteen plants. Here Philips has a factory, as does MBLE, and other important plants in the region belong to the Electronics Corporation of America at Herent, to SAIT Electronics and to Macq Electronique. On the basis that there appears to be some correlation with the size of settlement, it might be hypothesised that Liège and Charleroi should have similar shares in electronics. This is by no means the case, for Charleroi has only four plants, one owned by ACEC at Mont-sur-Marchienne dating from 1952, two at Gosselies where SA Belge de Constructions Aéronautiques (SABCA) has its aircraft electronics division, and a fourth at Seneffe, the site of one of Burroughs' computer plants. Only the Burroughs plant, which opened in 1966, belongs to the present generation of electronics factories. Liège, on the other hand, has no fewer than ten plants, almost all of them situated on industrial estates and dating from the mid-1960s onward. The multi-national firms, which include Burroughs, Philips, ITT and Radio Corporation of America, clearly have confidence in Belgium's oldest engineering district, in spite of its high wages. At the other end of the coalfield, the Borinage has secured three factories, operated by Bell, Siemens and General Telephone and Electronics, making the unpopularity of Charleroi for this industry even more puzzling. Emphasising the apparent attraction of low cost and untrained labour is the success of the Kempenland where there are ten plants. This itself is not a complete explanation, however, for West-Vlaanderen has only four factories, two of which are not large, and yet the labour situation is not fundamentally different from than in Limburg, nor is the extent of financial assistance. It would seem that proximity to the Netherlands and West Germany is behind the preference of recent investment for Liège and the Kempenland, and that wage levels are not a critical factor. Should the trend be followed by other new activities, present events in electronic products are a favourable augury, at least for Limburg and Liège.

The Chemical Industry

Although it is not one of the largest employers of labour, the chemical industry has both expanded twice as fast as manufacturing as a whole between 1955 and 1972, and has also been able to push its exports up to 70 per cent of total output. At the same time it has become a highly capital-intensive industry. Some 144,100 BF per worker are invested in chemicals compared with only 27,100 BF in metalworking, the second most capital-intensive sector.[10] However, for all its reliance upon modern technologies, the manufacture of low value chemicals is not an outstandingly footloose activity, and many plants are tied to ports, to canal-bank sites and to coalfields. On the other hand chemical plants not concerned with initial processing should possess great mobility, at least in terms of transport costs. It is not surprising, therefore, that Antwerpen has 32.6 per cent of chemical employment, but that Brabant claims 33.1 per cent suggests that late-stage processing is not as mobile in practice as it is in theory, and that it is strongly attracted to the capital. The two provinces of the growth axis have come increasingly to dominate the industry, but between 1960 and 1972 by far the greatest expansion was experienced by Antwerpen, as Table 21 indicates. The national increase amounted to 11,900 jobs of which some 9400, or 79 per cent, were in Antwerpen alone.

Table 21

EMPLOYMENT CHANGE IN THE CHEMICAL INDUSTRY,
1960-1972 '000 WORKERS

	1960	1972	% change	LQ
Antwerpen	12.8	22.2	73	1.70
Namur	1.6	2.5	54	1.60
Limburg	2.0	2.5	23	0.66
Hainaut	4.3	4.9	14	0.54
Brabant	20.6	22.5	10	1.53
O-Vlaanderen	8.5	8.8	3	0.89
W-Vlaanderen	1.8	1.7	−4	0.22
Liège	4.3	2.9	−52	0.38
Luxembourg	0.1	0.04	−276	0.06
BELGIUM	56.1	68.0	21	

Source: Office National de Sécurité Sociale, *Rapport Annuel 1960,
         1972,* Brussels (1961, 1973)

The high degree of localisation exhibited by the chemical industry may also be demonstrated by location quotients, shown in Table 21. Antwerpen and Brabant are joined by Namur as the only provinces revealing specialisation. Much the same pattern comes through at the *arrondissement* level, Antwerp scoring 2.15, Namur 1.93, Brussels-Capital 1.84 and Halle-Vilvoorde 1.46. A small number of *arrondissements* outside the axial belt, including Ostend (2.67), Ath (2.10) and Ghent (1.58), exhibit specialisation, but in the first two cases the high quotients are caused by large plants in otherwise weakly industrialised districts.

Inorganic Chemicals

Manufacture of chemicals in the nineteenth century exhibited three main characteristics. Firstly, it was almost entirely a heavy industry, oriented to its sources of raw materials. Secondly, the industry was inorganic in nature, its products including sulphuric acid, soda, caustic soda, chlorine and the products of coal distillation. Indeed it was a Belgian, Ernest Solvay, who in 1861 invented the method of producing soda by the ammonia process. His works began production at Couillet four years later, and the electrolysis of common salt was first carried out in Belgium there in 1898. Thirdly, the manufacture of chemicals was very strongly associated with the Walloon coalfield, a regionalisation which remained unaltered until the early years of this century when coking plants made their appearance on canal and waterway sites at Zandvoorde, Zelzate, Willebroek, Vilvoorde and Marly in Flanders. The production of nitrogenous fertilisers from coke oven gas after 1923 diversified the range of chemicals made in the north.[11]

The growth of coking plants in Flanders presaged the subsequent establishment of other inorganic chemical works in the same region. The Liège saltpetre and pyrites deposits had long since been exhausted, making imported materials a pre-requisite and a port or canal-side location desirable for processing plants. One of the first of the new generation of plants was the Kuhlmann works at Ertvelde on the Ghent-Terneuzen Canal. It began manufacturing sulphuric acids and superphosphates in 1911. A later addition was Produits Chimiques de Limbourg at Kwaadmechelen, established in 1929 to make potash fertilisers using raw materials from Alsace. Additionally, since the non-ferrous metal plants at Hoboken, Beerse, Balen and Overpelt also produced inorganic chemicals, the first three decades of the present century witnessed a marked locational change in the industry. The events of the last two decades have emphasised the greater attraction of the north, as Fig 24 suggests. Recent additions have included Fison-Union Chimique Belge (UCB) at Ostend, two plants run by FOSAL, a company controlled by UCB and Solvay, at Ostend and Antwerp producing respectively alkalis and polyphosphates, and Limburgse Vinyl making sodium sulphate at Tessenderlo. The two West German firms BASF and Bayer, both in Antwerp docks, are particularly large and produce a variety of chemicals. BASF manufactures 700,000 tonnes of nitrophoska and 325,000 tonnes of nitric acid per annum; Bayer has an annual capacity of 620,000 tonnes of sulphuric acid and 400,000 tonnes of ammonium sulphate. On the other hand there have been no new developments in Wallonie, which can now claim of the larger works only three nigrogenous fertiliser and nitric acid plants at Tertre, Houdeng and Liège, the Prayon non-ferrous chemical works and the two Solvay works at Couillet and Jemeppe-sur-Sambre. It is indicative of the trend that Solvay has plants at Ostend and Antwerp using imported materials, and that fertiliser plants are

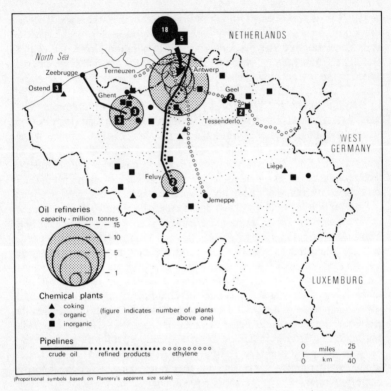

(Proportional symbols based on Flannery's apparent size scale)

Fig 24. THE BELGIAN OIL REFINING AND CHEMICAL INDUSTRIES
Source: Trade Directories

switching to oil and natural gas as their raw materials, further reducing the attraction of the Walloon coalfield.

A curious feature of the manufacture of inorganic chemicals, by no means a slowly growing sector, is the almost complete absence of American investment, representing a distortion of the growth industry model developed above. Witco Chemical has taken over Synthetische Produkten Adjubel at Lembeek, but other than this foreign interest has been provided by West Germany, France and Switzerland. The French group Potasse d'Alsace controls the three plants at Kwaadmechelen and Tessenderlo and has a half share in the Vilvoorde coking plant. Kuhlmann at Ertvelde is a subsidiary of the French Ugine-Kuhlmann group, and the Oelegem nitrogenous derivatives plant is operated by the Swiss Lilachim group. At the same time this is one growth industry in which there are a number of important Belgian companies, the largest of which are Solvay, itself a multi-national corporation, and UCB. Both Solvay and UCB have established research divisions in Brussels; UCB has research establishments at Drogenbos, Forest and Braine l'Alleud while Solvay's is at Neder-over-Heembeek.[12]

Organic Chemicals

The twentieth century has witnessed the increasingly rapid growth of the organic chemicals industry. Until 1962 only UCB manufactured polyethylene, but a dozen firms now do so; similarly Solvic at Jemeppe monopolised the production of PVC until as recently as 1968.[13] Always sensitive to new trends, American firms have invested heavily in Belgium, helping to make the manufacture of organic chemicals conform to the growth industry model. Associated with this expansion has been a switch from coal to oil as the basic material, and although there are still a number of carbochemical plants such as those at Tertre, Zelzate and Vilvoorde, their importance has waned as the cost of coal has risen above that of oil.

1. Oil Refining

Such were the advantages of oilfield-located refineries when the demand for petroleum products was small and specialised, that it was not until 1934 that the first Belgian refineries began operations. They were located at the ports of Antwerp and Ghent and were owned respectively by Raffinerie Belge des Pétroles and Shell. Albatros began refining at Antwerp the following year, but it was not until after World War II that domestic demand began to justify substantial expansion. In 1948 the consumption of products was a mere 1.4 million tonnes and refinery capacity only 0.55 millions, compared with a 1973 capacity of 42 million tonnes. The first large plant, belonging to Société Industrielle Belge des Pétroles (SIBP), a firm controlled by BP and Petrofina, was opened in Antwerp in 1951. Its initial capacity was 1.3 million tonnes, but this has steadily risen until in 1973 it stood at 16.2 million tonnes, making it by far the largest in Belgium. Esso established itself in Antwerp in 1953, but there then followed a lull in the construction of new plants, although those already built grew inexorably.[14] The next flurry of activity took place in 1968 with the opening of the second Albatros refinery in the newly built northern Antwerp docks, and of the Ghent Texaco plant. The Ghent-Terneuzen Canal is capable of handling only 60,000 tonne tankers, and Texaco therefore laid a 55 km pipeline from Zeebrugge which is capable of dealing with 100,000 tonne ships. The ability of Europoort to handle 250,000 tonne tankers, coupled with the cost of improving the Scheldt to accommodate tankers of more than 80,000 tonnes, compared with the cost of a pipeline, resulted in the construction of the Rotterdam-Antwerp pipeline (RAPL). Opened in 1971, RAPL carried 21 million tonnes of crude oil in 1973. Although transmission by RAPL is expensive – about 15 BF per tonne[15] – such are the economies of very large tankers that the price at Antwerp of oil delivered by pipeline is lower than the cost of oil brought up the Scheldt in 80,000 tonne tankers. As a refinery complex Antwerp continues to develop; Esso is raising its capacity from 5 to 13.5 million tonnes and expect the work to be complete in 1975.

Since Antwerp and Ghent are virtually inland refineries dependent upon their crude oil pipelines, it is not surprising that other, more obviously landlocked refineries should be built. Thus Chevron Oil Belgium, a subsidiary of Standard Oil of California, established a 6.5 million tonne plant at Feluy, north-west of Charleroi, in 1971 (Fig 24). Crude oil is transmitted to it from Antwerp by pipeline and there are product pipes from Feluy to Brussels and Antwerp. The plant has broken the previous monopoly of Antwerp and Ghent in this growth industry, and had it not been for the language war, Wallonie would have been able to take a further share in the activity. An agreement was reached in 1972 between the government and the Iranian Oil Company to set up a joint concern, Imbramco, to run a 6 million tonne refinery at Lanaye, north of Liège. Both the Christian Democrats and the Liberals are opposed to governmental participation in industry in any case, but when it emerged that three Socialists had been appointed to direct the company, a minor political crisis ensued in May 1973. This might have been settled, but the Flemish-dominated Christian Democrats objected to the expenditure of 9000 million BF in Wallonie and pointed to the Dutch concern about pollution which would affect Zuid-Limburg. The Shah of Persia saw this intractable wrangle as a signal to withdraw from the whole project, drawn up before he committed himself to bargaining oil supplies in return for industrial investment in Iran. The impossible affair ensured the downfall of the Leburton government which resigned in February 1974.

2.   Petrochemicals

The availability of a large number of oil refinery products at relatively low cost has encouraged the oil companies, and others, to move into the manufacture of petrochemicals. From its introduction in Belgium in 1948, the activity has expanded very rapidly, and since oil refineries are the principal source of materials, petrochemical plants tend to cluster about their supply points, making Antwerp an obvious choice of site. The port exercises a remarkable domination of the industry, not only claiming eighteen of the twenty-nine plants at work, but also some of the largest. BASF employs 2650, Bayer 1900 and Degussa, Monsanto, Petrochim and Union Carbide all employ more than 500 workers. Some Belgian plants are functionally integrated with plants in the Netherlands and West Germany – an example is BASF which is linked with operations at its parent in Ludwigshafen – and others take supplies from specialist producers; the Polysar synthetic rubber plant receives materials from Grangemouth in Scotland. A port location also facilitates exports, especially important since petrochemical capacity is greatly in excess of national demand. No less than 3 million tonnes of chemicals were handled by the quays at BASF in 1970, although inorganic materials account for part of this. As the number of firms rises, the range of products manufactured widens, offering great scope for a fresh round of plants using such products as materials. Thus Polyolefins, Union Carbide, BASF, Badiphil and USI receive ethylene by pipeline from the 500,000 tonne plant operated by Petrochim. The sheer size of this plant, which also pipes ethylene to Tessenderlo, Beek (Netherlands) and Jemeppe, and which has no less than fifteen product/material linkages within the regional complex, ensures large economies of scale. This sophisticated interchange of chemicals gives rise to what Chardonnet has called *un complex à base de pétrole*, which has been mapped in the form of a flow diagram by Wever for the entire Rotterdam-Moerdijk-Vlissingen-Antwerp petrochemical complex.[16] The external economies available to petrochemical firms in Antwerp cannot be matched anywhere else in Belgium, or for that matter, anywhere else in the EEC outside Rotterdam-Europoort.

Advantages similar to Antwerp's, in particular those relating to transport economies, also obtain at Ostend, Zeebrugge and along the Ghent-Terneuzen Canal, giving rise to clusters of petrochemical plants. The Willebroek Canal between Brussels and the Scheldt has made little impression on the industry and the three plants here are coking plants using oil and natural gas for feedstock. Despite the absence of tidewater, Limburg has succeeded in attracting two plants. One of these, Limburgse Vinyl at Tessenderlo, is a subsidiary of two chemical companies already in the area, and receives materials from these sources. It is also located on the Antwerp-Netherlands-Ruhr ethylene pipeline, a form of transport which has partly been responsible for the development of the Solvic works at Jemeppe. A large petrochemical complex headed by Belgochim and Lidechim has arisen adjacent to the Chevron refinery at Feluy. Other sites of the industry in Hainaut include a UCB tar distillation works at Havré, and the coking plants making petrochemicals at Tertre and Houdeng; but the factories in Hainaut and

Limburg pale into insignificance beside the strength of Antwerp and Ghent.[17]

3. Pharmaceuticals

The manufacture of drugs, toiletries and cosmetics is, after the production of plastics and photographic products, the fastest growing chemical sub-sector. Recent annual growth has been of the order of 6 and 7 per cent and the range of goods continues to widen. As with most other growth industries foreign investment has been important and this is reflected in the expansion of exports, which rose from 1200 million BF in 1964 to 4140 million BF in 1970. This performance seems to suggest once more that Belgium has been selected as a manufacturing base within the EEC.

The industry has a number of peculiarities which give rise to a most distinctive location pattern. The size of plant is small, some 66 of the total of 144 factories employing less than twenty persons. Both the materials and the products have a high unit value and the processes require a skilled labour force, one-fifth of which has professional or degree qualifications.[18] For the larger firms research is an essential prerequisite. Consequently this is an industry in which 'staff' outnumber 'workers', and since qualified personnel are most likely to be attracted to, and already inhabit the larger cities, the peripheral areas of low wages exercise no attraction for the pharmaceutical industry. The industry produces goods for consumer rather than for industrial markets, with the result that there are advantages in locations close to major nodal points which are themselves markets and from which goods may be dispatched both nationally and internationally. Predictably Brussels scores heavily as a source of labour, as a market and as a distribution centre. Brabant claims 68 per cent of the national workforce, but since only one plant, at Leuven, is outside the suburban area of the capital, this figure effectively represents Brussels's share of the activity. Of the 12 Belgian plants employing more than 200 workers, some 8 are in the Brussels region. The second largest city, Antwerp, has two of the remaining large plants, and by virtue of the presence of Janssen Pharmaceutica at Beerse, the province of Antwerpen has 20 per cent of the national workforce. The two provinces of the axial belt thus have almost 90 per cent of employment in the industry; only the opening in 1971 of the large Beecham factory at Heppignies, near Charleroi, in any way opposes the view that this is indeed a growth industry belonging to the growth axis.[19]

4. Man-made Fibres

The strength of the Belgian textile industry, coupled with the obstacles placed in the way of the French inventor of the artificial silk process, Hilaire de Chardonnet, by the French natural silk industry, caused artificial silk production in Belgium to commence at an early date. Factories were set up at Tubize in 1900 and at Obourg and Aalst in 1904. By 1913 Belgium was responsible for 17 per cent of world output.[20] With the possible exception of Obourg, near Mons, these plants reflect the distribution of the textile industry, although their siting was influenced by the need for cooling water and by the use of water transport for raw materials.[29] The Obourg, Tubize and Swijnaarde plants constitute the Fabelta Division of UCB, and there has been some functional integration between the Belgian plants. Obourg now merely processes fibres from the other plants, and Zwijnaarde polymerises nylon salt manufactured by UCB at Zandvoorde. These changes and diversification into chemical manufacture have nullified the earlier locational influences, and the foreign investments which have been made since 1965 would suggested that wage rates and development area grants are now critical factors. The Celanese Corporation opened a plant at Lanaken in Limburg in 1965, and the following year Owens Corning Fiberglass established themselves at Battice near Verviers, where Clark-Schwebel also began making fibreglass in 1967. ICI Fibres Division began production at Peruwelz, north-west of the Borinage, in 1971, and Regal Manufacturing have a small fibre plant at Houthalen in Limburg. Curiously enough West-and Oost-Vlaanderen, for all their textile strength, assisted area status and arguable growth image, have not featured in recent developments in the man-made fibres industry. That three of the five recent investments are in Wallonie makes synthetic fibre manufacture something of an exception to the growth industry model.

The Paper Industry

Paper manufacturing exhibits a number of distinctive traits, for although it is a growth industry, it is an old established activity which has experienced no great increase in the number of plants, and as a consequence the location pattern is relatively stable. In spite of the rationalisation which has necessarily accompanied the successful transformation of an old industry into an efficient modern activity, employment rose 27 per cent between 1960 and 1972. During the late 1960s production expanded rapidly from 555,000 tonnes in 1967 to 755,000 tonnes in 1971, a remarkable increase considering that there was actually a reduction in the number of mills from forty to thirty-eight during this time.[22] This sharp upsurge in output follows the recent

interest taken by foreign firms in Belgian companies. No less than half
the annual output of paper is now exported.

Paper-making has, since the middle ages, been associated primarily
with Brabant and with a number of areas of secondary importance in the
pre-Ardennes, such as Verviers, Liège and Huy. One map depicting
paper mills between 1799 and 1808 shows nineteen mills strung out
along the Zenne to the north and south of Brussels, and eleven in the
northern Ardennes between Namur and the present West German
frontier.[23] Water for power and processing was an important site factor,
and while this helps to explain the mills in the hilly areas, it does little to
account for the cluster in Brabant. Brussels was the principal printing
centre, and at a time when transport was inefficient, proximity to the
city would have been helpful. In addition urban areas were the source of
two of the basic raw materials, rags and waste paper. Brussels was thus
at once the largest market and material source, while the waters of the
Zenne were adequate. In 1846 Brabant accounted for 53 per cent of the
national workforce; by 1972 this had fallen to 41 per cent. Both
Antwerpen and Oost-Vlaanderen had a larger paper-making labour
force than Liège by 1937, a trend which accords with the growth
industry model.

The industry was one of the first to exhibit migratory tendencies from
south to north, a change at the root of which was technological
evolution rather than labour cost differentials. The importance of rags in
paper production dwindled throughout the nineteenth century; at the
same time wood pulp came to be the principal raw material. Between
1880 and 1913 the proportion of rags used fell from 30 to 8 per cent
while the proportion of wood pulp rose from 10 to 60 per cent.[24] Since
the bulk of the new material was imported there were advantages in a
location at a port or waterway site in the north. Mills were therefore
opened at Langerbrugge on the Ghent-Terneuzen Canal, Gentbrugge,
Oudegem, St Gillis-bij-Dendermonde, Willebroek and at Duffel on the
Nete. The process was effectively completed during the inter-war
period, and since then the share of the three provinces of Brabant,
Antwerpen and Oost-Vlaanderen has remained at between 72 and 78 per
cent of the national total.

Changes in employment between 1960 and 1972 point to two trends
in the distribution pattern of the industry. The first is the contraction
experienced by Brussels-Capital and Halle-Vilvoorde, and the second is
the growth of the industry in the development areas, both in Flanders
and in Wallonie. The financial attraction of the assisted areas is one
important factor here, but rather more influential is the speed with
which the paper-processing sector has grown. Plants in this sector take
delivery of their paper from the mills and are not therefore bound by the

same locational considerations. Material ties are much less critical and since a third of their output is exported, their market ties are not powerful either. This leaves them free to seek sites with low labour costs in development areas. The expansion recorded by *arrondissements* such as Mons (+ 121 per cent), Soignies (+ 118 per cent), Tournai (+ 104 per cent), Charleroi (+ 91 per cent), and Maaseik, Tongeren and Virton, all three of which had no workers in the industry at all in 1960, is almost entirely the result of expansion in paper-processing rather than paper-making. However, the specialist paper industry areas are, in the main, also the established areas of production. This is supported by the location quotients for *arrondissements* scoring more than 1, shown in Table 22. The extremely high quotient for Virton follows the establishment in 1964 of a pulp mill in this *arrondissement* at Harnoncourt, accounting for three-fifths of the total industrial employment of the area. The presence of Turnhout in the table is the result of historic specialisation in the manufacture of playing cards in the town of Turnhout.

Table 22

LOCATION QUOTIENTS BY *ARRONDISSEMENTS* FOR THE PAPER INDUSTRY, 1972

Virton	16.18	Halle-Vilvoorde	2.30	Soignies	1.33
Nivelles	7.09	Tongeren	2.01	Ghent	1.19
Mechelen	3.44	Tournai	1.82	Brussels-Cap.	1.11
Verviers	2.55	Dendermonde	1.33	Turnhout	1.10

Source: Office Nationale de Sécurité Sociale, *Rapport Annuel, 1972,* Brussels (1975)

The distribution of paper-making mills is mapped in Fig 25. The Cellulose des Ardennes plant at Harnoncourt is the sole specialist pulp mill in the country. This is not surprising since there are economies in the production of both pulp and paper on the same site. The mill, which has an annual capacity of 100,000 tonnes of bleached sulphate pulp, processes deciduous wood from France, Luxemburg and the immediate area. The five other pulp mills are, more conventionally, integrated works. Three are clustered to the south-east of Brussels in Nivelles. Those at Genval and Mont St Guibert are operated by Papeteries de Genval, a firm with some thirty plants in various countries, but only one other, at Tournai, in Belgium. The third in the 'swarm' is the La Hulpe plant of Intermills, a group controlled by US Plywood-Champion, with eight paper-making mills in Belgium. All three integrated works are

well placed to supply pulp and paper to other works within Belgium, but
their presence in Nivelles, rather than further north, closer to imported
pulpwood supplies, is better explained in terms of individual
entrepreneurial success than in the context of favourable locational
influences there. The Denaeyer mill at Willebroek on the canal of the
same name produces 45,000 tonnes of sulphite pulp each year,[25] but the
best theoretical location is that of the Papeteries de Belgique mill at
Langerbrugge. The plant, which has an annual capacity of 100,000
tonnes of mechanical pulp, is able to take delivery of wood supplies
directly from ocean-going vessels, which simply dump their cargo into
an old branch of the Ghent-Terneuzen Canal. As Fig 25 illustrates, the
great concentration of paper-making mills is in the Brussels region, with
sixteen of the thirty-eight mills. Secondary clusters are found along the

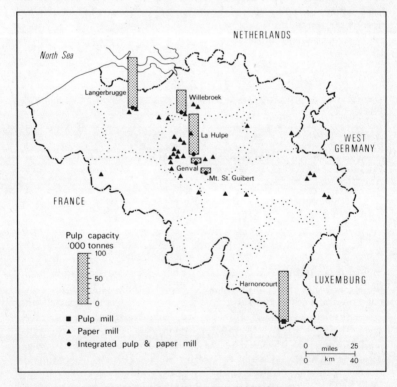

Fig 25. THE BELGIAN PULP AND PAPER INDUSTRY
SOURCE: Pulp, Paper and Paperboard in Belgium, *Belgium Economy and Technique*, 27 1971, II–VI

line of the lower Scheldt between Ghent and Antwerp, in the Meuse valley and in the pre-Ardennes above Liège.

Although the 1960s saw few changes in the distribution of the industry, the advent of foreign interest caused a reduction in the number of firms. The most spectacular merger was the creation of the Intermills group in 1963 from five firms with plants at La Hulpe, Andenne, Fleury, Malmédy, St. Servais and Brussels. The group now operates two plants producing corrugated cardboard in conjunction with the American Weyerhauser company, and it has integrated forwards into wholesale distribution through its control of Scaldia Paper at Wilrijk, an Antwerp suburb. The driving force behind this reorganisation was US Plywood-Champion. More muted was the acquisition by Papeteries de Belgique of two firms at Lembeek and Halen, but this was in reality the tip of the iceberg, for not only has this firm a French subsidiary, but in 1966 a merger was effected with the West German firm of Feldmühle, and a joint mill opened in the Netherlands. Wiggins Teape, a British group, controls mills at Nivelles and Virginal, where it is in association with the Mead Corporation, an American firm. By the end of the 1960s the Belgian paper industry had become an integral part of a West European industry, exhibiting all the characteristics of the growth industry model, even though not all its capacity is in Flanders.

5
The Brussels—Antwerp
Axial Belt

CONSIDERABLE EVIDENCE WAS advanced in Chapter II to support the proposition that the provinces of Brabant and Antwerpen constitute the most rapidly expanding area of Belgium, and although there is some justification for excluding the Turnhout *arrondissement,* for the purposes of this Chapter the axial belt is defined as the two provinces in their entirety. The capital, Brussels, and Antwerp, the national port, are respectively the first and second largest Belgian cities, with populations of 1,071,194 and 673,111 in 1970 (the figure for Brussels excludes those *communes* peripheral to Brussels-Capital.) On the basis of the size of their populations, it is predictable that the two areas should also be the leading industrial districts. In 1972 Brabant could claim 21.6 per cent, and Antwerpen 19.1 per cent of industrial employment, and five of the ten most populous industrial *arrondissements* are located in the two provinces. These are: Brussels-Capital, Antwerp, Halle-Vilvoorde, Turnhout and Mechelen. The use of other measures indicates that two provinces possess about two-fifths of Belgian industrial capacity. Thus Brabant was responsible for 20.6 per cent and Antwerpen for 20.7 per cent of the value of manufactured goods sold in 1968,[1] and in 1971 their share of the national value added by manufacture was 19.7 per cent and 19.8 per cent respectively.[2]

The similarity between the size of the manufacturing sector in both provinces contrasts with difference between them in their total working population figures. Brabant has an employed population of 863,502, very much larger than the 489,274 registered in Antwerpen. Manufacturing is proportionately much more important in Antwerpen than in Brabant, and is increasing its significance within the province,

114

THE BRUSSELS—ANTWERP AXIAL BELT

whereas Brabant shows no such upward trend. Table 23 indicates that industry is responsible for 39.8 per cent of the value added in Antwerpen, but for only 27.2 per cent in Brabant. The position is even more extreme if Brussels-Capital is taken on its own, for in 1971 only 20.3 per cent of the value added there was contributed by manufacturing. In Antwerpen industrial activity is more than twice as important as commerce, but in Brussels the figure for value added by commercial activities is very nearly twice as large as the figure for manufacturing.

Table 23

VALUE ADDED BY THE PRINCIPAL ECONOMIC SECTORS IN ANTWERPEN, BRABANT AND BRUSSELS-CAPITAL, 1966-1971

	Antwerpen		Brabant		Brussels-Capital	
	1966	1971	1966	1971	1966	1971
Manufacturing	36.1	39.8	27.2	27.2	21.5	20.3
Commerce	21.7	18.6	30.7	29.8	36.5	36.7
Services	40.3	40.6	40.7	42.6	42.0	43.0

Source: Institut National de Statistique, *Bulletin de Statistique*, no 5 (1973)

In the light of the growing capital-intensiveness of industrial processes, it is not surprising that if manufacturing's share of value added is static or declining, the industrial labour force should follow suit. Thus between 1965 and 1972 manufacturing employment in Brabant declined by 8.5 per cent, entirely the result of the contraction of industry in Brussels itself, where a decline of 19.0 per cent was registered (Table 24). Even when Halle-Vilvoorde, which largely comprises suburban areas of the capital, is taken together with Brussels, the two districts still return a drop of 11 per cent in industrial employment over the same period. The province of Antwerpen, on the other hand, expanded its workforce in manufacturing by 10 per cent. There is here an apparent paradox: one of the two provinces which, by those criteria used in Chapter II, is unequivocally part of the national growth axis, is nevertheless witnessing a decline in its manufacturing workforce. The explanation is that Brabant is dominated by Brussels where the tertiary and quaternary sectors are eroding the importance of manufacturing. The city is moving into the stage in which growth is achieved by the accumulation of office workers rather than factory workers. Manufacturing concerns are loath not to have a presence in the capital, even if their plant is located elsewhere, and in this way industry itself contributes to the growth of white collar jobs in Brussels. Between 1970 and 1972, for example, of the fifty-eight new foreign industrial investments in Brussels no less than forty-seven were merely offices of plants established outside the region.[3]

Lest it be thought that employment trends in both provinces are heavily influenced by their capital cities, it should be observed that although Brussels is responsible for contraction in Brabant, Antwerp is not the cause of recent expansion in Antwerpen. Industrial employment in the latter city has grown sluggishly since 1960, as Table 24 shows, while the peripheral *arrondissements* of Turnhout and Mechelen have exhibited notable dynamism. It will be recalled that Turnhout (Fig 26) was excluded from the national growth zone on the basis of its indifferent net migration balance, but should its industrial performance since 1960 continue, it may achieve a net migration inflow in the not too distant future. Halle-Vilvoorde has exhibited the most rapid growth in Brabant, and this, coupled with the performance of Turnhout and Mechelen, certainly undermine the frequent equation of the Belgian industrial growth axis with the two largest Belgian cities.

Table 24

MANUFACTURING EMPLOYMENT CHANGE IN ANTWERPEN AND BRABANT, 1960-1972

	1960	1965	1972	1960-72 %	1965-72 %
Antwerp	127,092	132,724	135,410	6.5	2.0
Mechelen	25,070	31,810	36,965	47.4	16.2
Turnhout	28,974	35,659	47,879	65.2	34.3
ANTWERPEN	181,136	200,193	220,254	21.6	10.0
Brussels-Capital	198,705	168,289	141,393	−1.1	−19.0
Halle-Vilvoorde		50,084*	55,061		9.9
Nivelles	21,464	24,627	25,357	18.1	3.0
Leuven	24,297	26,529	26,591	9.4	0.2
BRABANT	244,466	269,529	248,402	1.6	−8.5

* Includes data for the *randarrondissements*

Source: Office National de Sécurité Sociale *Rapport Annuel 1960, 1965, 1972*, Brussels (1961, 1966, 1973)

The Influences on the Trends in Manufacturing Employment

Four trends are apparent from Table 24: the rapidity of the expansion in Turnhout and Mechelen, the more modest growth of the districts which encircle Brussels, the slow development of Antwerp and the decline of Brussels as a manufacturing centre. The four trends are interconnected and are influenced by a number of common factors, the first of which is regional policy. Until the 1950s there was a pronounced dichotomy between the urban and rural working populace. The former

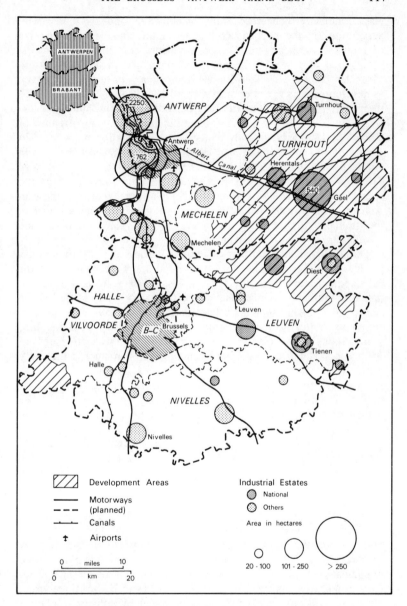

Fig 26. THE PROVINCES OF ANTWERPEN AND BRABANT: LOCATION
MAP

was principally concerned with manufacture and the latter with
agriculture, but the mechanisation of agriculture and the increasing size
of farm caused heavy rural unemployment. This in turn led to the
designation of much of Turnhout, a number of *communes* in eastern
Mechelen and the Hageland-Zuider-Kempen area of north-east Leuven
as development areas under the 1959 and 1966 regional legislation. To
the resulting financial benefits may be added a second influence, low
wage levels in the rural areas stemming from abundant supplies of
labour. In 1960 average daily industrial wage rates for males were 24
per cent lower in Turnhout, and 19 per cent lower in Mechelen than in
Antwerp. By 1970 the differential had narrowed, but they still give
Turnhout and Mechelen very real advantages over Antwerp. Although
wage levels in Halle-Vilvoorde and Nivelles are lower than those in
Antwerp and Brussels, the differentials with these cities are less than in
the case of Turnhout and Mechelen. Further, Halle-Vilvoorde and
Nivelles are not development areas.

   Thirdly, as an integral part of regional policy, the government has
funded a number of industrial estates, and many are naturally in the
development areas (Fig 26). Three kinds of estates have been set up:
national, regional and local. National estates are entirely funded by the
central government, regional estates receive 65 per cent of their funds
from this source, and local estates are supported by municipalities.
Some estates such as Geel-Punt and Herentals, with respective areas of
540 ha and 230 ha, are large, but it is not their size so much as their very
presence in formerly non-industrial regions, helping to polarise
factories at particular points, which is important. There are forty-eight
publicly-owned estates in the two provinces, and apart from those
associated with Antwerp docks, they are all located outside the two
principal cities, providing incentive for peripheral development by new
plants and by those quitting the congested urban areas alike. Industrial
estates have also been established by municipalities, many of which
have been very active in their promotion and in adopting lenient
financial policies towards incoming firms. Mechelen is a case in point.
Sensing the danger of placing too many expectations on the old
established furniture industry, which accounted for 36 per cent of the
manufacturing workforce in 1947, the municipality decided in 1951,
long before the initiation of regional policy, to encourage new
manufacturing. Sites were sold at well below market prices, and
municipal taxes on power plant, such as electric motors and diesel
engines and on labour employed were waived for the first three years,
although firms profess not to have been especially influenced by these
concessions.[4] By 1960 the city numbered such firms as Procter and
Gamble, du Pont de Nemours (chemicals), Burndy Electra and

Standard-Triumph among its captures, and could point to the creation of 2000 jobs as the reward.[5] A fourth factor has been government investment in motorways which greatly reduce the friction of distance in rural areas. It is no accident that industrial estates are strung out along these transport axes, as Fig 26 indicates.

Those factors favourable to the growth of manufacturing in the newer industrial areas exercise no mean pull on new employment, but there are also powerful push influences at work in the large urban areas. Traffic congestion is irksome, outdated premises are inconvenient, but the cost of land is critical. In 1971 the average cost of building-land in Brussels was 1365 BF per square metre (m²), nearly seven times higher than the figure for Turnhout of 205 BF per m². Even Halle-Vilvoorde had a value of only 375 BF per m². Other *arrondissements* returned the following figures: Antwerp 340, Leuven 289, Mechelen 272 and Nivelles 265 BF per m²[6]. It is not unusual to find plots near the centre of Brussels fetching 100,000 BF per m², and manufacturing firms find it extremely difficult, if not impossible, to secure the capital to purchase contiguous blocks of land for expansion in such locations. Indeed many concerns find that their property has become so valuable that it is highly profitable to sell and move out. This phenomenon of plants moving down the rent gradient is a general feature of urban manufacturing, but it has been accentuated in Brussels by the recent demand for offices which has greatly increased land values. The city not only houses the EEC Commission, but also the EEC Council of Ministers, the European Investment Bank, the headquarters of NATO and certain branches of Supreme Headquarters Allied Powers in Europe (SHAPE). Some 90 countries have diplomatic representation with Belgium and the EEC, and a growing number – at present 375 – of international firms have offices in the city. Faced with high site rents, industry is showing a distinct tendency to concentrate on high value adding plants, that is, those which greatly add to the value of materials during manufacture, which are frequently compact rather than space-extensive. At the same time industrial white collar jobs are increasing, and now account for 33 per cent of the manufacturing labour force of Brussels, contrasting with the national figure of 20 per cent.[7] Notwithstanding the ability of some sectors to adapt to the changing situation, the decline in manufacturing employment in the capital is very much across the board, and of the growth industries, only printing lived up to this classification between 1965 and 1972.

Whatever the disadvantages of major urban areas for manufacturing, the fact remains that Antwerp is continuing to grow, albeit slowly. The most important reason is the construction of new docks and industrial estates in the port. A number of industries related to the movement of goods through the port had developed during the nineteenth century and oil refining had begun on a small scale in the inter-war period, but major expansion dates from 1956 when the port authorities inaugurated a ten-year plan. The boom in the chemical industry, based largely on imported materials, coincided with dock extension work, and by the completion of the scheme in 1967 Antwerp had become one of the leading chemical and petrochemical complexes in Western Europe. In addition to 1848 ha of industrial land on the right bank of the Scheldt are 274 ha on the left bank at Zwijndrecht, providing respectively 23,954 and 5019 jobs in 1971.[8] It is not unreasonable to suppose that Antwerp will shortly outstrip the capital in respect of its industrial labour force.

Table 25

MANUFACTURING EMPLOYMENT AND COEFFICIENT OF SPECIALISATION IN ANTWERPEN AND BRABANT, 1955 AND 1972

	Antwerpen			Brabant	
	1955 %	1972 %		1955 %	1972 %
Engineering	24.5	30.8	Engineering	19.9	26.2
Chemicals	6.2	10.1	Chemicals	7.5	9.1
Food processing	10.2	8.1	Food processing	8.9	8.5
Base metals	6.4	6.2	Clothing	10.9	8.1
Metalworking	4.7	6.2	Printing	5.0	7.6
Clothing	6.8	5.5	Metalworking	7.7	7.4
Art & précision	6.1	5.3	Base metals	4.9	5.7
Non-met. minerals	8.9	5.2	Paper	4.2	4.4
Coefficient of specialisation	31.7	21.0		27.6	19.6

Source: Office National de Sécurité Sociale, *Rapport Annuel 1955, 1972,* Brussels (1956, 1973)

The Industries of the Axial Belt

Table 25 illustrates that at present, engineering, chemicals and food processing are the leading industries in both Antwerpen and Brabant. All three are growth industries, and although food processing has suffered a reduction in its relative importance since 1955, the engineering and chemical industries have improved their position. Since 1955 chemicals have exhibited dramatic expansion and engineering has moved even further ahead of the field. The manufacture of clothing, more important in Brabant than in Antwerpen, is contracting in relative terms, as are metalworking in Brabant and base metals, *art et précision* and non-metallic minerals in Antwerpen. The trend is towards increased diversification, and with its unique mix of older craft industries and neotechnic manufacturing, it is to be expected that Brussels, and therefore Brabant, should be the least specialised. The Lorenz curve was used in Chapter II to measure industrial diversification, but the coefficient of specialisation may also be employed. This relates the percentage distribution of workers in industries in the provinces to the national employment structure. A large deviation from the national situation, which is one of diversification, will result in a high coefficient. The formula is expressed as

$$C_s = \tfrac{1}{2} \sum_{i=1}^{n} \left| \frac{100X_i}{X_t} - \frac{100y_i}{Y_t} \right|$$

where X_i is the number of workers in industry i in province X, X_t is the total industrial employment in province X, Y_i is the national employment in industry i, and Y_t is the total national industrial workforce. The coefficients shown in Table 25 indicate the extent to which both provinces have become specialised; it is noticeable that Antwerpen has become almost as diversified as Brabant.

Engineering

One in every four industrial workers in Belgium is employed in engineering and the industry is even more important in the axial belt, where some 28.4 per cent of the labour force works in the activity. While Brabant experienced a decline of 1.4 per cent between 1965 and 1972, Antwerpen expanded handsomely by 30.0 per cent, and in so doing overtook Brabant which had 13,700 more workers in the industry in 1965. In absolute terms Antwerpen's increase in engineering employment of 15,600 was the largest returned by any industry at the provincial level during the period 1965–72, and caused this activity to increase its domination in the province. No fewer than 30.8 per cent of workers in Antwerpen are now in engineering compared with 26.1 per cent in 1965. The industry dominates the employment situation in six of the seven *arrondissements* of the province; Nivelles is the exception because of somewhat anomalous presence there of iron and steel plants at Clabecq and Court St. Etienne.

The industry has in some cases gained considerable ground over other activities. In 1960 food processing was the leading industry in Leuven, furniture had more workers than engineering in Mechelen, and in

Turnhout industries based on non-metallic minerals, food processing and clothing were all numerically superior to engineering. As Fig 27 suggests, Turnhout's performance has been particularly impressive: between 1965 and 1972 the district registered an increase of 6200 workplaces, some 100 more than Antwerp, and this is an area without specific skills. As is usual with the Belgian growth industries, foreign firms have been in the van. The arrival of Philips at Turnhout has generated 2700 jobs alone, while Bell Telephone at Geel and the DAF lorry plant at Oevel had added employment increments of 1900 and 500 respectively. Mechelen has not been able to match Turnhout's record, although employment in engineering more than doubled between 1960 and 1972, making it the second fastest expanding district. The two industrial estates at Mechelen itself, and the dynamic qualities of the municipality noted above have been especially attractive. Firms on these estates include Friden (calculators) employing 1000, Burndy Electra, British Leyland and the MacCulloch outboard motor plant. Both Mercedes-Benz and Peugeot are established in the city and the Van Hool bus plant is at Koningshooikt to the north-east. Despite their recent growth neither Turnhout nor Mechelen have location quotients greater than unity, although Mechelen with 0.96 almost achieves this distinction.

Antwerp may not contrive to register a high growth rate, but unlike Brussels it is expanding and is the largest engineering district in Belgium (Fig 27). In fact the 49,000 engineering workers in the *arrondissement* constitute the largest concentration of labour in a single industry in any of the 43 administrative districts. That specialisation occurs is reflected in the *arrondissement's* location quotient of 1.40; more than one-third of the industrial labour force is engaged in engineering. Two of the three principal engineering sectors, vehicles and electronic products, have already been referred to in Chapter IV. Suffice it to say here that the plants operated by Ford Tractor and General Motors have a combined workforce of 10,000, and that some of the electronics plants such as Bell Telephone, have more than 1000 employees. The third sector, shipbuilding and shiprepair, is well developed, as befits a port of the standing of Antwerp. Some 80 per cent of the national employment in this industry is located in the Antwerp region and three of the four major yards are also in the area: Beliard Murdoch, Mercantile Marine Engineering and Graving Docks, both of which are in the docks, and Cockerill at Hoboken on the Scheldt above the city. Together these yards employ 8000 workers, of which Cockerill has 3300.[9] The physical restrictions placed upon the Cockerill yard by the depth of water available is a main reason for its specialisation in medium sized vessels such as container ships, tankers for chemicals,

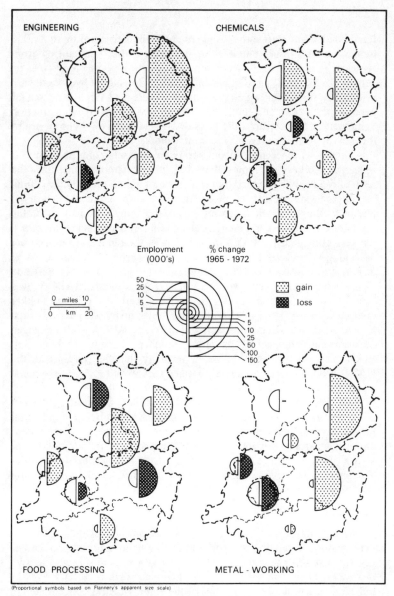

ENGINEERING

CHEMICALS

Employment (000's)

% change 1965 - 1972

50
25
10
5
1

1
5
10
25
50
100
150

gain

loss

0 miles 10
0   km   20

FOOD PROCESSING

METAL - WORKING

(Proportional symbols based on Flannery's apparent size scale)

Fig 27. EMPLOYMENT IN 1972 AND CHANGES BETWEEN 1965 AND 1972 IN THE LEADING INDUSTRIES OF ANTWERPEN AND BRABANT

SOURCE: Office National de Sécurité Sociale, *Rapport Annuel 1965, 1972*, Brussels, 1966, 1973

123

ferry boats and cargo ships. Tankers and bulk carriers of up to 80,000 tonnes can be built, but it is in this sphere that competition from Japanese yards is extremely fierce,[10] so that specialisation has an economic as well as a physical basis. The other two yards are principally ship repairing establishments. There are a number of smaller yards in the docks and lining the Scheldt involved in the construction and repair of barges, tugs, dredgers and other small craft. The largest of these is Scheepswerven St. Pieter at Hemiksem.

Although engineering is contracting in Brussels, one in every 3.7 industrial workers is employed in the activity, almost three times the ratio of the capital's second industry, printing. Until recently the capital had a larger engineering workforce than Antwerp, and it did so without any of the huge vehicle assembly plants and shipyards that exist in the northern city. The average engineering plant in Brussels employs 29.5 workers compared with 53.8 in Antwerp. Although heavy engineering is lacking, vehicle assembly is present in the shape of Citroën and VW at Forest and Renault at Haren, where the aircraft firm of SA Belge de ⸱nstructions Aéronautiques (SABCA) is located. SABCA was established in 1920; since 1966 it has been part of the Dutch Fokker company, carrying out work on designs drawn up by outside firms such as Sud Aviation, Bréguet as well as Fokker.[11] SABCA is also engaged in electronic engineering as are a number of firms such as Sait Electronics, MBLE and Philips. It is likely that the presence of the NATO headquarters has helped to make the city attractive to specialist electronic, aeronautic and weaponry producers.[12]

Halle-Vilvoorde is the third most important engineering district within the axial belt, and has benefited from the opening up of industrial estates around the capital at towns such as Diegem, Grimbergen, Groot-Bijgaarden, Lot and Zaventem. These estates are of modest size, as are the firms located on them. Two of the larger firms, Caterpillar Tractor at Grimbergen and Waterbury Farrel at Lot, each muster only 300 employees, and the largest, IBM at Diegem, has but 400.

Chemicals

The manufacture of chemicals is the second largest industry in the axial region, occupying 9.5 per cent of the manufacturing population, yet because of the strength of the activity's localisation, the two provinces have two-thirds of the national workforce. As Fig 27 indicates, the bulk (72.7 per cent) of the employment is concentrated in Antwerp and Brussels which account for 47.7 per cent of Belgian workers in the industry. This is reflected in the location quotients of 2.15 for Antwerp and 1.84 for Brussels. With the exception of Halle-Vilvoorde, which returns a quotient of 1.46, all the remaining *arrondissements* have scores close to unity, suggesting that the manufacture of chemicals is nowhere undeveloped in relation to the size of the working population. In Halle-Vilvoorde chemical production is the third largest industry after engineering and metalworking. Paint and varnish manufacture is especially well developed. Some fifteen of the national total of sixty-six paint and varnish plants are found in the district, including the largest, Levis at Vilvoorde.[13] Halle-Vilvoorde also has one-fifth of Belgian employment in the rubber transforming industry, achieving a location quotient of 4.45, and possessing the largest works in the country, Michelin at Sint Pieters-Leeuw.[14] Elsewhere employment in chemicals is less important; its existence can in most cases be explained by the presence of a few large plants. Janssen employ nearly one-third of the chemical workers of Turnhout in its pharmaceutical plant at Beerse, and the addition of the Amoco and Kanegafuchi petrochemical plants at Geel accounts for half the chemical workforce in the district.

Recent employment trends in chemical production have been dominated by the switch in the positions of Brussels and Antwerp. In 1965 there were 6000 more chemical workers in Brussels than in Antwerp, yet by 1972 Antwerp led Brussels by 2000. While chemical firms were abandoning the capital they were clustering in Antwerp to a truly remarkable degree, more particularly during the late 1960s. Between 1960 and 1965 employment in the Antwerp district rose by 1502, but in the following 7-year period the increase was 5608. The greater part of this new employment was accounted for by the construction of some eighteen large plants in the dock area. The mean size of plant is 195 workers, as against only 65 in Brussels, indicative of the concentration of the later stages of manufacture and research in the capital. Some firms with large plants at Antwerp, for instance Union Carbide and Monsanto with payrolls of 900 and 500 respectively, nevertheless have set up their very much smaller research divisions in Brussels, a trend noted in Chapter IV. The absence of serious constraints on space in the recently constructed dock area has encouraged the purchase of sufficient land to permit subsequent expansion. Such a case is BASF which has a 570 ha site at the northern extremity of Kanaaldok. Since 1967 the firm has gradually extended its facilities and now employs 2650 workers on this site.[15]

The arrival of new plants on the Kanaaldok industrial estate and on the left bank of the Scheldt has brought diversification to the port. Moreover, the availability of a wider range of chemicals has attracted further plants desirous of using the new chemicals as raw materials. In 1970 there were thirty-nine pipelines, of which five crossed the Scheldt, moving some sixteen different chemicals – a veritable spaghetti bowl.

The interplant flows, which can be reversed if necessary, include those of ammonia from BASF to Bayer, ethylene from Petrochim to USI, Union Carbide, Polyolefins and BASF, and nitrogen from Union Carbide to SIBP, Albatros and Monsanto. As the size of the chemical complex reaches particular thresholds, further specialist services become available. For instance, BASF initially received its liquid oxygen supplies from the Air Liquide plant at Mons, but by 1972 demand from BASF and other plants had reached a level sufficient to justify the commencement of oxygen-making on the BASF site. The existence of such a multiplicity of plants inevitably gives rise to considerable quantities of waste material. Some is removed into the North Sea by a special vessel, but by 1972 there was sufficient waste to justify the opening of a chemical incinerator by Haltermann.[16] Problems of space and the increasing resistance to pollution on the part of Rotterdammers are slowing down the pace of expansion in Europoort, and this has been to the benefit of Antwerp which is now the second largest chemical, oil refining and petrochemical complex in Western Europe.

Food Processing

Although this industry has almost as many workers as the chemical industry it exhibits neither the speed of change nor the degree of regional specialisation characteristic of the latter activity. The distribution of food processing is closely correlated with the distribution of population, with the consequence that Brussels and Antwerp have the largest share of employment, and Nivelles the smallest. For the same reason the location quotients for five of the seven *arrondissements* are close to unity. The two least industrialised districts of Turnhout and Leuven exhibit specialisation, the former having a quotient of 1.51 and the latter the much higher score of 2.69. For an activity which is market-oriented this is a high quotient, and is the highest in the industry of any Belgian *arrondissement*. The existence of the largest Belgian beet sugar refinery at Tienen and of a smaller plant at Hoegaarden[17] helps to explain the importance of the industry, which at present claims 19.2 per cent of industrial employment in Leuven, but which as recently as 1960 accounted for 30.0 per cent. More important, however, is the strength of factories processing market garden produce cultivated in the central and western areas of the *arrondissement*. Two such factories are located at Wespelaar and Wilsele near Leuven. Vegetable canning is important in Turnhout with plants at Westmeerbeek, Hulshout and Grobbendonk. Fig 27 indicates that Leuven, Antwerp and Brussels have a common characteristic, namely that employment in food processing is falling. This contraction has been greatest in Leuven, where the workforce declined by 34.2 per cent between 1965 and 1972, largely as a result of rationalisation, and has been least in Brussels.

Related to food processing are the drink and tobacco industries. Neither is an important employer in absolute terms, but the axial belt has a substantial proportion of the national workforce in both industries. Brabant has 35.9 per cent of Belgian workers engaged in production of drinks, Brussels and Leuven being the leading districts with respective location quotients of 1.28 and 5.86. Belgium's largest brewery, Artois, is located in the city of Leuven and 12 per cent of the *arrondissement's* workforce is involved in drink manufacture. The manufacture of tobacco is even more localised than that of drink, for the two provinces making up the axial belt account for 69.3 per cent of Belgian employment in the making of cigars and cigarettes. Some 33.6 per cent work in Turnhout alone, and the district has a location quotient of 8.19, indicative of a very high degree of specialisation. There are factories at Arendonk, Dessel, Geel, Herentals, Rijkevorsel and in the town of Turnhout, making the industry the sixth largest in the *arrondissement*. Brussels has 18.7 per cent of the national labour force, but a much lower quotient of 1.52, and virtually all the remaining employment is in the cities of Antwerp and Leuven. The strength of Turnhout is a result of retaliatory measures taken by Dutch firms in Noord-Brabant, immediately to the north, against the imposition of high import tariffs by the Belgian government: they built factories in Belgium, behind the tariff wall. Low female wages in Turnhout were an added incentive for the establishment of branch plants, particularly those making cigars, where labour represents 35 per cent of total costs. The five cigarette factories in Brussels owe their existence to the expensive nature of early hand-made cigarettes, causing them to become *articles de luxe*, and therefore especially saleable in the capital. Some 95 per cent of the tobacco used is imported, through Antwerp, and this has contributed to the existence of manufacturing at Merksem, adjacent to the old docks.[18]

Metalworking and Base Metal Production

These two industries are respectively the fourth and sixth largest in the axial belt. Both concerned with metals, they nevertheless have distinctively different location patterns, largely stemming from the economies of scale to be obtained from large plants at the early production stages. Production of base metals is carried on in plants large enough to allow a degree of independence from the immediate economic environment. On the other hand metalworking plants are much smaller, most of them are close to their markets and rely upon the external economies of larger towns. The average base metal enterprise in the two provinces employs 175.8 workers as against 21.2 in metalworking, which is clustered in the four core *arrondissements* of Brussels, Halle-Vilvoorde, Mechelen and Antwerp (Fig 27). In spite of the continuing contraction of metalworking in Brussels, the capital is still the most important district in the country, scoring a location quotient of 1.34. In relative terms the industry is even more strongly developed in Halle-Vilvoorde, which has a quotient of 1.89, and Mechelen with a score of 1.75 also exhibits considerable specialisation. Antwerp is second to Brussels in respect of numbers employed, but the quotient of 1.11 indicates only a slight concentration in the activity. Base metal production is dominated by the presence of a number of large works, many of which lie outside the core district. This is best exemplified by Nivelles, whose high quotient of 2.84 is a result of the large integrated iron and steelworks at Clabecq, a steelworks at Court St. Etienne and a rolling mill at Nivelles. The second highest quotient of 1.00 is returned by Turnhout with its non-ferrous metal works at Beerse, Balen and Olen.

Clothing and Textiles

The distribution pattern of clothing manufacture is heavily influenced by the importance of Brussels, which has 43 per cent of the regional workforce in this industry, and at the same time by the sharp decline of the activity in the capital, contrasted with expansion in the peripheral *arrondissements* of Turnhout and Leuven. As recently as 1965 clothing was the second largest industry behind engineering in Brussels, but it now lies in fourth place. Some of the firms are highly specialised, but the forces making for migration have taken their toll on an activity often installed in old, small premises. The average size of factory in the capital is only 15.1 workers, compared with 36.3 in Turnhout, which registered a 73.7 per cent increase in employment between 1965 and 1972, and where several large plants have been set up by Dutch and American firms. The activity is now the second largest in this *arrondissement*, which has a location quotient of 1.46. Rather more modest expansion has been made by Leuven, but here the quotient is 1.60, making the district the most specialised clothing area in the region. By contrast the textile industry is characterised by decline in urban and rural areas alike. It has practically disappeared from the province of Antwerpen, and even Nivelles, which has the highest quotient of 0.72, suffered a 73.7 per cent decline in employment between 1965 and 1972.

Printing and Paper Production

These two industries are respectively the seventh and eighth largest in the region, which dominates the national output of both. Within the region both activities display considerable localisation. Brussels has 38.9 per cent of the national employment in printing, and the activity has the highest location quotient – 3.17 – of all the capital's industries. Not only is it in second place behind engineering, but printing is one of the three industries which actually increased their labour force in the capital between 1965 and 1972. There is, however, some evidence of dispersal from the urban centre, for the *arrondissements* of Halle-Vilvoorde and Nivelles tripled their employment over this period. The paper and pulp industry is rather more widely distributed throughout the region, five of the seven districts returned a quotient greater than unity. The high quotients for Mechelen (3.44) and Nivelles (7.09) are directly attributable to the existence of large plants at Willebroek in Mechelen and at Genval, La Hulpe and Mont St. Guibert in Nivelles. The paper industry ranks third in Nivelles and its location quotient there is the highest scored by the district.

Other Industries

There remain several industries whose numerical significance is not great but which exhibit market localisation within the axial belt. The existence of clays suitable for brick-making is the basic cause of the importance of non-metallic mineral production in Turnhout, giving rise to a location quotient for this industry of 1.85. The strength of furniture manufacture in Mechelen, itself largely due to chance factors, coupled with the development of external economies in the city, causes the *arrondissement* of Mechelen to register a woodworking quotient of 1.81. One industry, termed *art et précision* by the Office National de Sécurité Sociale, exhibits a high degree of localisation, and in Mechelen, where it has a quotient of 6.93, it has sufficient workers to rank third in importance. Turnhout has a score of 3.36 and Antwerp one of 3.21; yet in Brussels, where the presence of these craft-like activities might be predicted, *art et précision* is under-represented with a quotient of 0.73. The most important contributor to this industry is diamond processing. Belgium has slightly less than one-third of the world employment in the manufacture of diamonds, an extraordinary situation stemming from the supply of uncut stones from the Belgian Congo and other African areas towards the end of the nineteenth century, and from the migration after World War I of many dealers from Amsterdam to Antwerp, where they found the social climate more attractive and wages lower.[19] The cutting of small diamonds became a domestic industry in rural areas since the capital equipment need was small, but was restricted to the Antwerp hinterland by the presence of the four specialist diamond exchanges, and therefore dealers, in the city. Clusters exist at Nijlen and Berlaar in eastern Mechelen and at

Vorselaar, Herenthout and Grobbendonk in western Turnhout. Processing of the larger stones is carried out within Antwerp itself at Deurne and Borgerhout. Industrial diamonds are becoming increasingly important, but the major firm, Diamant Boart, is located not in the Antwerp region, but in Brussels. The concentration of production into fewer, larger factories following severe competition from Israel has caused a sharp reduction in diamond processing employment, and there seems little prospect of improvement. The manufacture of jewels is related only in part to diamond cutting, for both Brussels and Kortrijk have a greater number engaged in the activity than Antwerp, although these three centres have 80 per cent of the total workplaces. The importance of market outlets in Brussels is an obviously important location factor.[20]

6

The Brussels and Antwerp Industrial Regions

ALTHOUGH BRUSSELS AND Antwerp have frequently been referred to in the foregoing comment, the approach has largely been systematic and the treatment of the two leading Belgian industrial regions has been consequently rather fragmentary. Further, no attempt has been made to transform the administrative areas represented by the Brussels-Capital and Antwerp *arrondissements* into geographical industrial areas. It is to this task we must now turn.

The Brussels Industrial Region

Using population density as the criterion, Gourou has shown the way in which Brussels has spread along three corridors terminating at Tubize, Braine l'Alleud and Ottignies, deep in central Nivelles.[1] The first of these three corridors he recognised as the industrial axis of the Senne valley, although strictly the line of the Charleroi-Brussels Canal would have been preferable since the Senne valley is not industrialised south of Huizingen. The first study to concern itself specifically with manufacturing around Brussels was that by Bauwin and Annaert, who isolated an industrial region comprising the nineteen *communes* of Brussels-Capital and seventeen others outside it by regarding 500 manufacturing workers per *commune* as the minimum delimiting criterion.[2] The result of this exercise appears in Fig 28. Gourou's Tubize axis stands out strongly, but the northward extension of the Senne valley, utilised above Vilvoorde by the Willebroek Canal, is also apparent, as are the smaller axes in the north-west, formed by Zellik and Groot-Bijgaarden, and in the north-east by Diegem and Zaventem. Within Brussels-Capital, the *communes* with more than 30 per cent of

131

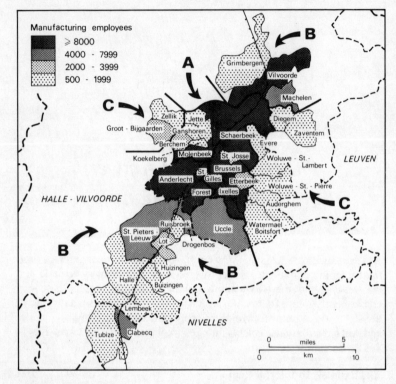

Fig 28. THE BRUSSELS INDUSTRIAL REGION
The Sub-Regions are:
A. Central Brussels
B. The Upper and Lower Senne valley
C. Eastern Brussels-Capital and Outgrowths
SOURCE: E. Bauwin and J. Annaert, 'La Région Industrielle Bruxelloise', *La Géographie*, 97 (1973 116

their working population in manufacturing extend in an almost unbroken line through the west of the city linking St. Pieters-Leeuw and Drogenbos, the northernmost districts of the Tubize axis, with Grimbergen and Vilvoorde to the north of the city. Without exception, the *communes* in the central and eastern sectors of the capital have less than 30 per cent of their workforce in manufacture, emphasising the south-west-north-east trend of the industrial region along the Senne valley.

The region as defined by Bauwin and Annaert has some 197,260 workers engaged in manufacturing, representing 17 per cent of the total so employed in Belgium. As such the region is much the most important in the country and yet it occupies only 1.1 per cent of the area of Belgium. Brussels-Capital accounts for 75.5 per cent of the total manufacturing employment in the region as defined, and of the six *communes* with more than 10,000 industrial workers (Brussels, Anderlecht, Forest, Vilvoorde, Ixelles and Molenbeek), only Vilvoorde lies outside the *arrondissement*. To these six may be added a further three – St. Gilles, Schaerbeek and Uccle – with more than 6000 operatives, to give an industrial core from Anderlecht in the south-west, through the *commune* of Brussels to Vilvoorde in the north-east, accounting for 74 per cent of the regional workforce. The remaining eleven *communes* in Brussels-Capital and the three outgrowths together share the remainder.

The Sub-Regions

Three industrial sub-regions may be recognised; their boundaries are mapped in Fig 28. The first comprises the *communes* in central Brussels-Capital, headed by Brussels itself with 45,300 workers, a total only slightly smaller than that of the entire Turnhout *arrondissement*. Other *communes* include Ixelles, Molenbeek, St. Gilles and Schaerbeek. Factory employment accounts for less than 20 per cent of all workplaces in the *commune* of Brussels, and for less than 30 per cent in Ixelles and Schaerbeek and the large plants typical of the Walloon coalfield are seldom found. Here are localised the *industries de grande ville*, that is printing, food processing, the manufacture of jewellery, furniture, musical instruments, clothing and a diversity of engineering products. Data provided by the 1961 Industrial and Commercial Census, published in 1967, enable local location quotients to be computed for four industries: food and drink, textiles, shoes and clothing and metalworking and engineering.[3] Here we are using location quotients to relate employment in a *commune* to that in an *arrondissement*, in this case Brussels, which in 1961 included what is now Brussels-Capital and Halle-Vilvoorde. The two central *communes* of Koekelberg and Molenbeek had quotients of 4.15 and 2.32 respectively for food and drink. Clothing manufacture is a universal element in the central sub-region, and the local quotients for shoes and clothing both demonstrate this and also show that the activity is important in only one other *commune*, Halle. The textile industry, with its larger factories, is localised only in St. Gilles, but not a single *commune* in the central area returns a metalworking and engineering quotient greater than unity. Old-established industries, small in scale and frequently exhibiting a high degree of craftsmanship, typify the central area. However, such activities find it difficult to resist central area redevelopment and they consequently contribute much to the strength of industrial migration to the suburbs. Neotechnic industries such as aircraft production, electronic engineering and pharmaceuticals, do exist, but it is noticeable that the plants have a high proportion of white collar jobs.

The second sub-region is that which lies immediately to the north and south of the central area, continuing the Senne axis in these directions. Straddling the Willebroek Canal, which contributed greatly to their industrial growth, lie Vilvoorde, Machelen and Grimbergen. To the south of the central area, astride the Charleroi-Brussels Canal, but within the city boundary, are Anderlecht, Forest and Uccle. Beyond the city the Tubize axis stretches away to the south-west. Anderlecht with 25,200 workers and Vilvoorde with 13,700 are numerically the most important *communes*, but apart from Uccle and Clabecq, the remaining areas have fewer than 5000 manufacturing workplaces. At the same time they are more industrialised than the *communes* in the central area in the sense that all have at least one worker in two in manufacturing. White-collar jobs are in the main insignificant, for this is an area of relatively heavy industry in which research and development plays but a small part. Vilvoorde, Grimbergen and Machelen have many of the characteristics of a port consequent upon the existence of the Willebroek Canal, which links Brussels directly with the Rupel, by-passing Mechelen. The canal is navigable for vessels of 4500 tonnes, which makes the capital an inland port, but when the 7 km section north of Ruisbroek, giving directly into the Scheldt, is complete, ocean-going vessels of 10,000 tonnes will be able to reach the capital. In 1970 3.2 million tonnes of goods were handled by the port, mostly raw materials for about fifty factories, including coking plants, paper mills, oilseed crushing plants, heavy chemical factories, cement works and the 380 MW power station at Grimbergen, that line the bank between Saincteletteplein in Brussels and Grimbergen 12.5 km further north.[4]

The influence of the Charleroi-Brussels Canal traversing the southern sector of this sub-region has been somewhat circumscribed, not least because until 1922 it could handle nothing larger than an 80 tonne barge; not until 1968 when the Ronquières inclined plane was opened was the canal brought to the standard EEC capacity of 1350 tonnes. Manufacturing here is rather more diversified than in the northern sector. Engineering and metalworking are important, particularly in Buizingen, and both Citroen and VW have assembly plants in Forest, while ACEC has a branch plant at Ruisbroek. Fabelta has its large man-made fibre plant at Tubize, giving the *commune* an exceptionally high local chemical quotient of 26.6. Major diversification has been effected through the industrial estate at Lot, which is especially strong in metal fabrication, precision engineering, electronic products and paper packaging. Anderlecht and Uccle even have a number of textile mills to add to the diversity of their activities. Ironically enough, the plant that 'ought' to be on the Willebroek Canal in the northern sector, the integrated iron and steelworks, Forges de Clabecq, is tucked away in remote Clabecq as though to demonstrate that navigable waterways are not always powerful locational influences.

The third and final sub-region comprises the lightly industrialised *communes* of eastern Brussels-Capital from Evere in the north-east to Watermael-Boitsfort in the south-east, and the two zones extraneous to the city, Zellik and Groot-Bijgaarden in the north-west and Diegem and Zaventem in the north-east. The five Brussels *communes* have less than 30 per cent of their working population in manufacturing, and in Woluwe-St-Pierre, Auderghem and Watermael-Boitsfort there is a very high proportion of administrative to shop floor workers. A number of head offices and research divisions of firms such as Glaverbel, CBR the cement group, MBLE, Sinclair and Singer-Friden have recently been established in Watermael-Boitsfort, and the same trend is evident in the other four Brussels *communes*. As Bauwin and Annaert remark, were these jobs officially regarded as falling within the tertiary sector, not only would there be very little industrial employment, but also the proportion of administrative labour would approach the general level of the capital.[5] The development of the two outgrowths may be attributed to the attraction of suburban sites proximate to motorways. Groot-Bijgaarden and Zellik are served by the E5, and both have modern industrial estates. Similarly Diegem and Zaventem make use of the motorway linking Brussels National airport at Zaventem with the city, and the Diegem industrial estate has been patronised by IBM, Goodyear, Coles pharmaceuticals, Esso research division, the Scaldia-Volga technical centre and Broomwade compressors – a cameo of neotechnic industrial activity. Zaventem is dominated by aircraft support industries.

Although they lie outside the Brussels industrial region as defined, the industrial estates at Mollem, Ternat, Braine l'Alleud, Wavre and Erps Kwerps exert an important influence on it, for they assist the suburbanisation process, as do motorway links with Brussels. The estate at Ottignies is unusual in that its origins owe much to the linguistic problem. Ottignies was chosen as the site for the French-speaking faculties of Leuven university following the schism of 1966, and the university conceived the idea of establishing an industrial estate to be used by research organisations which would feed on and at the same time contribute to the university's scientific expertise. The first firm to begin work at Louvain-la-Neuve, as the estate is known, was Monsanto whose staff of ninety are researching into rubber chemistry and plasticisers. The growth of manufacturing on the peripheral estates, and of research centres on a more dispersed basis, is the counterpart of the contraction in the centre which has characterised the industrial geography of Brussels-Capital during the last decade. The pace of development will doubtless accelerate as the very comprehensive motorway building programme is completed. By the end of the 1970s there will be an outer ring road and no less than ten radial motorways, of which six are already open, as Fig 28 shows. It is conceivable that decentralisation will also be assisted when regional planning bodies are more effective. Dr Herman Baeyens, director of the Mens en Ruimte planning group, has suggested that Aalst, Mechelen, Leuven and Nivelles be officially recognised as countermagnets to Brussels, and that Mechelen might become the Flemish capital. To some extent the former is happening spontaneously, but were both to receive official sanction, the decentralisation of manufacturing would receive additional impetus.[6]

The Antwerp Industrial Region

Although there is a plethora of studies concerning the port of Antwerp, few comprehensive analyses of the broader industrial region have been undertaken. One attempt to delimit the region, by Dupon in 1956, provides a starting point, but the criteria on which her region is based are not stated and the rationale is not always clear.[7] Using data from the Industrial and Commercial census of 1961, unfortunately the latest available, and selecting contiguous *communes* with more than 500 industrial workpeople, the region mapped in Fig 29 is derived. From the basic semicircular shape of the city four sub-regions radiate. That to the north results from the extension of the nineteenth century dock system towards the Dutch frontier; it lies almost entirely in the large *commune* of Antwerp which benefited from extensions in 1929 and 1958. Fringing the docks is a ring of suburbs from Kapellen in the north to Wilrijk and Aartselaar in the south, forming the second sub-region. A third sub-region has developed in a southerly direction, extending through the Mechelen *communes* of Willebroek and Tisselt and terminating in Kapelle-op-den-Bos in Halle-Vilvoorde. The growth of this corridor has been heavily influenced by the Scheldt, by its tributary the Rupel and by the Willebroek Canal. The fourth sub-region is a south-easterly extension from Antwerp through Boechout and Lier to Berlaar, where it meets a line of *communes* including Rumst and Duffel which straddle the Nete. The Antwerp industrial region thus comes very close to incorporating the city of Mechelen. As defined, the Antwerp

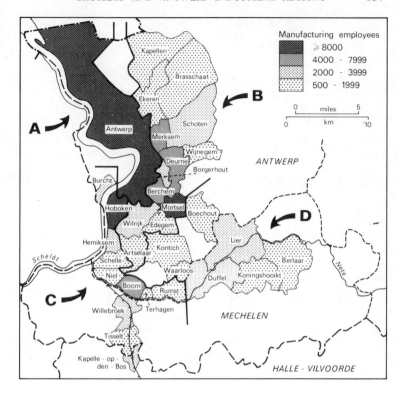

Fig 29. THE ANTWERP INDUSTRIAL REGION
The Sub-Regions are:
A. Dock Area
B. The Eastern Suburbs
C. The Southern Riverine Axis
D. The South-Eastern Extension

industrial district had some 139,468 workers in 1961, 40.9 per cent of whom were employed in the Antwerp *commune*. With the addition of those districts immediately outside the old city walls, including Merksem, Deurne, Berchem, Mortsel, Wilrijk and Hoboken, the proportion becomes 72.6 per cent, a fact which highlights the importance of the port at the core of the region.

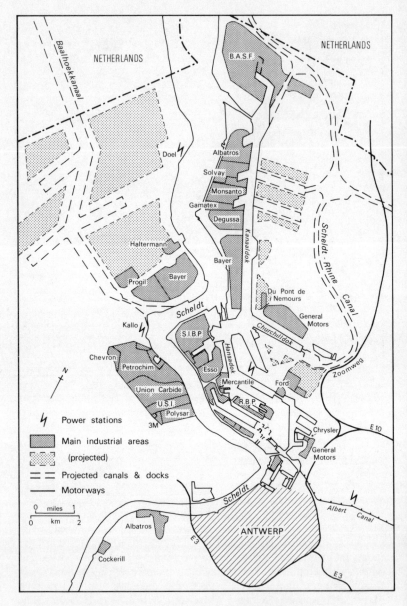

Fig 30. THE INDUSTRIES OF THE PORT OF ANTWERP
SOURCE: Maps published by the General Management of the Port

The Port Area

The establishment of a port on a major river at a location which was adjacent to, and even part of prosperous medieval Flanders, whose wealth was largely based on trade, and which was also a sheltered, deepwater anchorage, was in many ways inevitable. The silting up of Antwerp's great medieval competitor, Bruges, coupled with the later development of an industrial complex of the first order in Wallonie, the need for a national port following the creation of the state of Belgium in 1830, and the purchase from the Dutch in 1863 of their right to levy tolls on shipping using the Scheldt, combined to encourage the growth of the city. The smallest docks, Bonaparte and Willem, were the earliest, dating from 1811 and 1813, although Hout, Kempisch and Asia, completed by the early 1870s, were not much bigger. Kattendijdok is also of this period, but is larger and its western side is now occupied by dry docks owned by the port authority. Lefebvre and Amerika docks were opened in 1887, but it was not until the construction of Albertdok in 1914 that the northward march of the port, now the most remarkable feature of the entire industrial region, became apparent.[8] The present day extent of the docks is mapped in Fig 30.

Albertdok is also significant in another sense, for in the 1920s and 1930s it became the scene of American automobile investment by Ford, General Motors and Chrysler, marking the beginning of the trend towards the recognition of major ports as industrial areas in their own right. Subsequently dock building was increasingly associated with industrial development. Leopolddock and Hansadok, with direct access to the Scheldt 10 km below the city, were opened in 1928, and four years later No 4 Havendok, connected to Hansadok, followed. Beliard Murdoch, the shipbuilding and shiprepair firm, now occupy the eastern end of No 4 Havendok, and Raffinerie Belge des Pétroles has been installed on the south side since 1934. Mercantile Marine Engineering and Graving Docks have their premises on the western side of Hansadok. Marshalldok was completed in 1951 and was quickly surrounded by the SIBP refinery, the largest in Belgium, the Esso refinery and two petrochemical plants operated by Union Carbide and Petrochim. 1960 saw the completion of No 5 Havendok, but meanwhile the 1956–1966 plan, which called for the digging of the 10 km-long Kanaaldok with direct access to the Scheldt via the Zandvliet locks, and the construction of specialist container berths in Churchilldok, had begun. The building programme incorporated lavish provision of industrial land in the hope that firms desirous of operating at sites with deepwater access would be attracted, and the principle of the integrated port realized.

The scale and success of the ten-year plan can only be compared with that of Rotterdam-Europoort in Western Europe. By 1970 an uninterrupted line of oil refineries, petrochemical plants, heavy chemical works and chemical storage companies extended the length of the western side of Kanaaldok (Fig 30). The presence of General Motors does not initially square with the port authority's declared policy of allowing only those industries requiring access to deepwater to set up in the dock area. However, components are imported and assembled cars exported by sea; it is estimated that 1000 vehicles are handled daily, adding substantially to the revenue of the port. The plan made some 1700 ha of industrial land available, a figure which must be related to the total area of 230 ha existing in 1953, and indeed to the mere 80 ha of 1945. The total expenditure involved, 80 billion BF, was more than Antwerp was able to meet, with the consequence that the project was heavily subsidised by the central government, presumably on the grounds that the multiplier effect of the new manufacturing capacity would work through the entire Belgian economy. The 1960s also saw the colonisation by chemical firms of the western bank of the Scheldt in the *commune* of Zwijndrecht. Pipelines are not inconvenienced by the river and plants can lock into the grid without difficulty; thus Union Carbide pipes nitrogenous chemicals to SIBP adjacent to Marshalldok. By 1971 industrial land on both sides of the Scheldt totalled 2660 ha, of which 2123 ha had been rented or sold. Chemicals and petrochemicals accounted for 54 per cent of the area, oil refining for 23 per cent, vehicle manufacture for 11 per cent and shipbuilding and repair for 3 per cent. Electric power stations took 6 per cent, largely because of the 127 ha allocated to the nuclear plant at Doel on the left bank.[9] However, plants which make great demands on space are not always labour intensive, and as Table 26 shows, for all their striking advances, oil refining and chemicals employ fewer than engineering. Of particular importance in terms of its multiplier effect within Antwerp is the 12,000 strong dock labour force, a highly paid body of men.

Unable to expand beyond Zandvliet into the Netherlands, despite the existence of Benelux and the EEC, the port authority has plans for the construction of two further Havendoks, as Fig 30 indicates. It is likely that the area to the east of Kanaaldok will benefit handsomely from the completion of the Scheldt-Rhine Canal which will join the existing dock system at the northern end of Kanaaldok. There will also be a Verbindingskanaal or Junction Canal looping round Antwerp to join the Albert Canal at Oelegem, capable of taking 9000 tonne push-barge convoys. The whole scheme is scheduled to be finished in 1977. Even more ambitious plans have been drawn up for the land to the west of the Scheldt, outside the existing industrial area. The basis of the project is

Table 26

INDUSTRIAL EMPLOYMENT IN THE ANTWERP DOCK AREA, 1971

	Workers	%	Investment per worker, million BF
Vehicles	11,440	39.7	0.80
Chemicals & Petrochemicals	6,742	23.4	5.19
Shiprepair	4,468	15.5	0.45
Shipbuilding	4,000	13.9	not available
Oil refining	2,184	7.5	8.13
	28,838		

Source: R. Op De Beeck, 'L'Industrie du Port d'Anvers', *Hommes et Terres du Nord* (1971), 19, 26

the construction of a 125,000 tonne canal from Baalhoek in the Netherlands to Kallo, to feed an industrial area at least as large as that on the east bank. One estimate puts the amount of land likely to be made available at 3740 ha[10] The problem here is the difficulty of negotiating an agreement with the Dutch who have little to gain from the scheme, and the Belgians have gone ahead with an 80,000 tonne lock at Kallo, at least to ensure that the commencement of the scheme is not entirely left to the capricious whim of the politicians. Should agreement not be forthcoming, the plan to cut out the navigational hazard of the 'Bath Bend' in the Scheldt in Dutch territory, by shortening the main channel by 4 km, may be sufficient to justify the use of the Kallo locks by all shipping destined for the west bank industrial areas.

The proportion of the port's traffic destined for and originating from the industries of the dock area amounts to 40 per cent, so that the port's transit function, more properly a tertiary than a secondary activity, is obviously of great importance. Between 1948 and 1958 traffic increased from 21.1 to 35.2 million tonnes, but by 1968 this had more than doubled to 72.4 million tonnes, reaching a peak of 80.7 million tonnes in 1970. Principally because of the opening of the Rotterdam-Antwerp pipeline, imports fell from 57.1 to 39.1 million tonnes between 1970 and 1971, and for the same reason the tonnage of traffic handled in 1972 was restricted to 67.2 million. Some measure of compensation may be extracted from the rise in exports which, after hovering in the 24 million tonne range during the late 1960s, stood at 28.1 million tonnes in 1972. The composition of the traffic of the port is shown in Table 27. The importance of oil imports, despite a drop from 26.8 million tonnes in 1970, is evident; the large inward cargoes of mineral ores and shipments of steel, oils, fertilisers, chemicals and engineering products reflect the basic transforming nature of the Belgian manufacturing

142 BELGIUM

Table 27

TRAFFIC HANDLED BY THE PORT OF ANTWERP, 1972

	Imports million tonnes	%		Exports million tonnes	%
Crude oil	10.5	26.9	Steel	8.2	29.2
Ores	10.1	25.8	Oil products	7.3	26.0
Oil products	2.3	5.9	Fertilisers	3.6	12.8
Fertilisers	2.0	5.1	Chemicals	3.0	10.7
Steel	1.7	4.3	Crude minerals	1.5	5.3
Chemicals	1.3	3.3	Metal products	0.4	1.4
Coal	1.1	2.8	Non-ferrous metals	0.4	1.4
Grain	0.7	1.8	Motor vehicles	0.4	1.4
Non-ferrous metals	0.6	1.5	Machinery	0.3	1.1
Pulp and paper	0.5	1.3	Glass	0.3	1.1
Textile fibres	0.4	1.0			
	39.1			28.1	

Source: Fédération Maritime d'Anvers, *Rapport Annuel 1972*, Antwerp (1972)

economy. Extensions to the Rotterdam-Antwerp pipeline will not affect this latter characteristic, only reduce seaborne imports through the port still further.

The Other Sub-Regions

The other industrial sub-regions may not be able to match the publicity attaching to the outstandingly rapid expansion of the dock area, but their albeit secondary role is nevertheless an important one. The *communes* ringing the old city have many old established industries associated with the port, and some are highly industrialised areas. For instance Mortsel had 84.0 per cent of its working population in manufacturing in 1961, while the inner suburbs of Schoten (63.0 per cent), Merksem (57.8 per cent), Deurne (50.5 per cent), Wilrijk (49.8 per cent) and Berchem (49.4 per cent) had a substantial industrial workforce. The most distinctive activity is food processing. Local location quotients computed for 1961 indicate that six *communes* are specialist food and drink producers. Of these, Merksem (4.13) with flour mills, vegetable oil plants, a biscuit factory and a chocolate works adjacent to the Albert Canal, and Schoten (3.41), have very high scores. Diamond processing is related to the port, but less typical are the shoe and clothing industries of Borgerhout, Wilrijk and Deurne. The presence of the Agfa-Gevaert photographic works at Mortsel employing 6000 is quite unrelated to the port. Engineering and metalworking are localised in the districts to the south of the city, even though one of the largest and earliest plants, Bell Telephone, employing 10,000 and dating from 1882, is within the old city. These two activities are most well developed in Aartselaar, whose quotient is 1.99, at the southern tip of the suburban ring. This is in part because of space restrictions in the inner area, but more important because the expansion of the Antwerp industrial region, outside the docks, is in a southerly direction towards Brussels. A study of the birth and death of plants in the Antwerpen province covering the period 1955–1964 indicated that, the *commune* of Antwerp apart, by far the most attractive districts were Aartselaar and Wilrijk. Both registered a balance of twenty new factories, and the next best performance was registered by Kontich, adjacent to Aartselaar, with a balance of four plants. Antwerp itself had a balance of only twenty-eight factories, for although forty-eight opened, some twenty closed, supporting the hypothesis of a southward suburbanisation process.[71] Many of the new plants are of medium size, but three are particularly large: Atlas Copco Airpower and Werkhuizen furniture at Wilrijk, and Electro-Navale, a firm which has decentralised from the dock area, at Aartselaar.

Predictably the third sub-region, that based on the Scheldt, Rupel and Willebroek Canal, is characterised by transport-oriented plants and shipyards. Because many of these are large and are in lightly populated districts, the *communes* in this sub-region have a very high proportion of their workpeople in manufacturing. On the Scheldt the *communes* of Hemiksem, Hoboken and Schelle all have more than 60 per cent of their working population in industry, the figure for Hemiksem rising to 81.3 per cent. Not a single *commune* on the Rupel has less than 68 per cent of its total employment in manufacturing, while Kapelle-op-den-Bos and Tisselt on the Willebroek Canal have respective shares of 89.5 and 84.0 per cent. A common feature of the four Scheldt waterfront *communes* is their shipbuilding and repair yards, of which there are eight all told.[12] The largest is Cockerill at Hoboken; this firm has almost completed an investment programme which will allow the construction of 250,000 tonne bulk carriers. Other yards are very much smaller and can accommodate small vessels of less than 4000 tonnes. Scheepswerven St-Pieter at Hemiksem is typical in specialising in inland waterway barges, small tankers, pusher units and ocean-going tugs. Boelwerf at Temse, just outside the confines of the Antwerp industrial region, is the third largest Belgian yard, and specialises in methane tankers. Also on riverside locations are a number of construction engineering firms such as Titan at Hemiksem, which manufactures heavy duty cranes, Fansteel Metals at Hoboken, and the large Hoboken-Overpelt non-ferrous metal complex. The Cockerill wire drawing mill is sited at Hemiksem.

Hoboken is the location of Antwerp's original oil refinery, now operated by Albatros, with a capacity of 1.75 million tonnes. Belgium's largest thermal power station, operated by Interescaut, with a capacity of 525 MW, is sited on the Scheldt at Schelle. The industrial pattern is similar in nature if not in scale along the Rupel with its small shipyards and metal fabricating plants, but additionally between Niel and Rumst there are no less than thirty brickworks which make full use of the river for the dispatch of their products. Local clays which reach a thickness of 40 m at Boom provide the basis for the industry. Perhaps as a result of the paucity of alternative industrial employment for women, the clothing industry is important in the Rupel-side *communes*. The Willebroek Canal, with a coking plant and an integrated paper mill at Willebroek, extends this sub-region of riverine functions south into Brabant.[13]

The southern expansion of Antwerp has caused the Rupel valley towns to become entangled in its web, and similarly the Mechelen *arrondissement* towns of Lier and Duffel have now been engulfed. This fourth sub-region thus gives the Antwerp industrial region a pronounced eastern bulge at its southern extremity. Some of the *communes* are only lightly industrialised, although Kontich has its BMW plant and Boechout its steelworks, and it is only in the older settlements of Duffel and Lier, which have 73.5 per cent and 49.8 per cent of their respective working population in manufacturing, that industry becomes important. Duffel is dominated by Sidal, the aluminium fabricating company, and by paper mills, but Lier has a relatively diversified structure. Employment in Koningshooikt, to the east of Duffel, is almost entirely in the Van Hool bus and truck assembly plant. It is possible that this sub-region may extend further east in the near future, since it is the only part of the Antwerp industrial area to have a contiguous boundary with a development area. If present trends continue, however, and if the lavish provision of industrial land astride the Willebroek Canal and on the south bank of the Rupel envisaged by the Mens en Ruimte planning group is translated into reality, there seems little doubt that the Brussels-Antwerp axis will receive substantial reinforcement. Certainly the opening of trading estates at Ruisbroek, Bornem, Puurs, Willebroek and Tisselt within 10 km of each other is likely to act as a bridge between the two leading Belgian manufacturing regions. As it is, two-thirds of employment on estates in the province of Antwerpen is in the Antwerp *arrondissement*.[14]

7

Flanders: Oost-and West-Vlaanderen and Limburg

FOR LONG ASSOCIATED with agriculture and with a manufacturing sector largely related to textiles, the provinces of Oost-and West-Vlaanderen now compare in terms of size with those twin seat of the Belgian industrial revolution, Hainaut and Liège. In 1972 Oost-Vlaanderen had 13,000 more industrial workers than Hainaut, and West-Vlaanderen could claim 6000 more than Liège. Oost-Vlaanderen now has 14.4 per cent, and West-Vlaanderen 11.7 per cent of the national labour force in industry. At the same time Ghent and Kortrijk are respectively the fifth and seventh largest industrial *arrondissements* in terms of employed population. Limburg, however, presents another story. The province has fewer industrial workers than the number employed in engineering alone in Brabant or Antwerpen, and can lay claim to only 5.5 per cent of Belgian industrial employment. Until recently its strength was coalmining, an activity in which it still has more than half the national workforce. Indeed the rationalisation of production in the collieries has been the principal reason for much of the industrialisation that has taken place in Limburg during the last two decades. For many towns the industrial revolution did not begin until the 1950s when factories, usually emblazoned with foreign names, sprang up in rural surroundings to end what was for many the traditional way of life. The process was also witnessed in West-Vlaanderen, although here its impact was less. As Table 28 indicates, manufacturing now occupies a comparable position in West-Vlaanderen and Limburg, despite the importance of coalmining in the latter, while they play a larger role and have grown more slowly in Oost-Vlaanderen.

146 BELGIUM

Table 28

VALUE ADDED BY SECTOR IN LIMBURG, OOST- AND WEST-VLAANDEREN,
1966-1971 %

| | Oost-Vlaanderen | | West-Vlaanderen | | Limburg | |
	1966	1971	1966	1971	1966	1971
Agriculture	7.3	5.4	10.4	8.6	7.4	5.9
Mining	—	—	—	—	13.3	9.5
Manufacturing	40.1	43.4	32.7	37.4	28.6	37.3
Commerce	18.8	17.0	18.0	15.8	14.4	12.7
Transport and Services	33.8	34.2	38.9	38.2	36.3	34.6

Source: Institut National de Statistique, *Bulletin de Statistique*, no 5 (1973)

Table 29

MANUFACTURING EMPLOYMENT CHANGE IN OOST- AND
WEST-VLAANDEREN AND LIMBURG, 1960-1972

	1960	1972	%
Aalst	24,570	27,019	9.9
Dendermonde	19,966	21,960	10.0
Eeklo	7,253	6,252	−16.0
Ghent	63,131	66,652	5.6
Oudenaarde	17,428	17,190	−1.4
St. Niklaas	24,151	27,293	13.0
O-VLAANDEREN	156,499	166,366	5.2
Hasselt	9,973	37,578	276.8
Maaseik	5,260	16,364	211.1
Tongeren	4,031	9,415	133.5
LIMBURG	19,264	63,357	228.9
Bruges	17,900	28,175	57.4
Diksmuide	1,359	2,349	72.8
Ieper	4,697	8,143	73.3
Kortrijk	52,653	53,266	1.2
Ostend	4,692	5,589	19.1
Roeslare	20,240	24,547	21.3
Tielt	5,942	10,205	71.7
Veurne	1,483	2,300	55.1
W-VLAANDEREN	108,966	134,574	23.5

Source: Office National de Sécurité Sociale, *Rapport Annuel*,
1960, 1972, Brussels (1961, 1973)

Precisely because manufacturing has developed late in West-Vlaanderen and Limburg, it is to be expected that the rate of expansion would be more rapid than in Oost-Vlaanderen. The changes in manufacturing employment between 1960 and 1972 shown in Table 29 indicate that this is so, but growth in Limburg, which returned a truly remarkable increase of 229 per cent, far outpaced that in West-Vlaanderen. Only in some of the formerly most rural districts in West-Vlaanderen have there been large increases in employment, although they are hardly commensurate with those in Limburg. By comparison areas such as Kortrijk and Ghent exhibited only modest expansion. On the other hand the manufacturing workforce in Bruges rose by 10,300 between 1960 and 1972, not far short of the 11,100 increase in Maaseik, although appreciably behind Hasselt's 27,600. With the exception of Ghent, the *arrondissements* recording the largest absolute increases are all located in Limburg and West-Vlaanderen, the two peripheral provinces (Fig 31).

Factors in the Recent Expansion of Manufacturing

The absence from Oost- and West Vlaanderen of major mineral deposits, above all of coal which was such a powerful contributory ingredient in the industrialisation of French Nord to the west and Wallonie to the south, and the late date of the exploitation of Kempen coal, were important negative industrial location factors. Given this situation the peripheral nature of West-Vlaanderen and Limburg within Belgium became a critical issue in the distribution of manufacturing in the nineteen century. The Netherlands flanks Limburg on two sides while West-Vlaanderen has France to the west, the English Channel to the north, and a short frontier with the Netherlands to the east. The national road, canal and rail transport systems were not well developed in such frontier regions, inhibiting the rise of manufacturing, with the exception of the Kortrijk district. In Limburg the only major international transport link until the 1950s was the Zuid-Willems Canal, branching off the Bocholt-Herentals Canal into the Netherlands. In both provinces large areas fell under the sphere of influence of important extra-territorial settlements such as Maastricht in the Netherlands and Lille in France. The contiguous Belgian areas became sources of labour supply and between 1850 and 1890 there was a heavy migration flow into French Nord. After 1890 daily and weekly commuting took the place of migration consequent upon the construction of light railways, and by 1910 there were 21,800 *frontaliers,* whose number rose to 100,000 in the years 1926–8.[1] This was a manifestation of the limited employment opportunities in West-Vlaanderen, and therefore of the very slow speed of industrial growth. Commuting assured Belgian

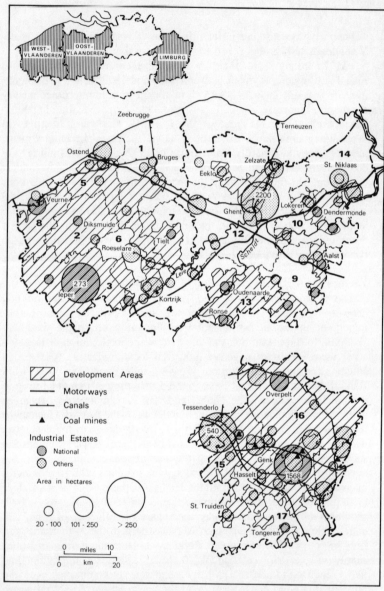

Fig 31. THE PROVINCES OF OOST- AND WEST-VLAANDEREN AND
LIMBURG: LOCATION MAP

The numbers refer to *arrondissements* as follows:

1. Bruges   2. Diksmuide   3. Ieper   4. Kortrijk   5. Ostend
6. Roeslare   7. Tielt   8. Veurne   9. Aalst   10. Dendermonde
11. Eeklo   12. Ghent   13. Oudenaarde   14. St. Niklaas   15. Hasselt
16. Maaseik   17. Tongeren

families of an income, but the value added by manufacture accrued to French rather than Belgian entrepreneurs.

Similar problems existed in Limburg, but here an additional disincentive for the growth of industry was the unsuitability of much of the region for intensive agriculture until the 1890s, when modern techniques were introduced.[2] The resulting scanty population represented both a small demand for manufactured goods and a paltry supply of labour. As it was, surplus labour first migrated and then commuted to Maastricht, Aachen and Liège. Prior to World War I 65 per cent of the working population was engaged in agriculture, and there was an almost complete absence of an indigenous industrial tradition. Although local enterprise was lacking, a number of large firms began to erect plants in the comparative wilds of the Kempen, adjacent to the Bocholt-Herentals and Beverlo Canals. They were highly specialised and fell into three categories: non-ferrous metal, chemical and explosive factories. Monkhouse maps the nine largest plants existing in 1939, and of these 5 were in non-ferrous metals, 2 in chemicals and 2 in explosives.[3] The attraction of the area was its sparse population which helped to reduce the effect of toxic fumes, low land values and canals for water and transport. Like the collieries, these plants were operated by companies located outside the province, thus inhibiting local capital formation and the birth of small enterprises; in 1937 some 60 per cent of Limburg industrial employment was found in plants and mines of more than 500 workers, a very high proportion.[4] This dichotomy between agriculture and large industrial plants was by no means so clearly defined in Oost-and West-Vlaanderen, largely on account of the strength of the textile industry there. Nor was industry in the hands of extra-territorial owners; indeed two important factories, the Picanol loom manufacturing concern at Ieper and the Claeys cycle and light engineering firm at Zedelgem, are classic instances of local entrepreneurs making good in their home towns. Nevertheless, west of a line between Zeebrugge, Roeselare and Menen, West-Vlaanderen employment was almost entirely in agriculture.

The diminishing demand for agricultural labour (consequent upon mechanisation) in all three provinces, and the contraction of the main source of industrial employment in Oost-and West-Vlaanderen, the textile industry, which still accounted for 49 and 42 per cent of the respective workforces in 1955, caused unemployment to rise and incomes to fall. In March 1951, for instance, five of the eight West-Vlaanderen *arrondissements* had unemployment rates in excess of 10 per cent; Diksmuide, with 41 per cent, was a notable victim of the inter-war depression, and Ostend with 27 per cent and Veurne with 25 per cent were not much better off.[5] Because of this parlous economic situation, large parts of the provinces were declared development areas, as Fig 31 illustrates.

During the 1960s a total of 91 industrial estates were set up to encourage new investment. Not only have they provided much new employment, but their existence has ensured that even small towns such as Poperinge, Diksmuide, Veurne and Torhout in West-Vlaanderen have had the opportunity to industrialise. Predictably those estates close to motorways, for instance Aalter, Ottergem and Erembodegem on the E5 in Oost-Vlaanderen, and Tessenderlo-Paal, Zolder-Lummen and Genk-Zuid on the E39 (Boudewijnweg) in Limburg have proved attractive. However, by far the largest estates, with the exception of Genk-Zuid which has an area of 1568 ha, are those associated with the ports of Ghent (2200 ha), Zeebrugge-Bruges (2200 ha) and Antwerp where it spills over into St. Niklaas (3740 ha). The last two estates are still at the planning stage. Regional development associations have been active in persuading firms, especially those of foreign origin, to open premises in their respective areas. Municipalities have also been at work, none more so than Bruges. Long before regional legislation was enacted, the city was able to obtain financial support from the government for the construction of industrial estates. Land was sold or rented at a price commensurate with the anticipated employment rather than at a price reflecting the intrinsic value of the land. Additionally, municipal taxes on labour and power installed were waived for five years, and assistance was given with the repayment of interest on borrowed capital. Even the Belgian Home Secretary declared himself uneasy about some of the methods used to lure firms to Bruges.[6]

Quite apart from the assistance given by local, regional and central authorities, the market values of land are relatively favourable, and are for the most part below the going prices in Halle-Vilvoorde and Antwerp. With the exception of Ostend (471 BF per m^2), the values for Oost-and West-Vlaanderen range from 105 to 371, with a mean of 271 BF per m^2. The values for Limburg, however, range from 157 to 175 BF per m^2, giving the province a marked advantage in this respect.[7] The advent of the EEC, of motorways and of good access roads, coupled with proximity to both the Netherlands and West Germany, have endowed the province with a degree of centrality which it formerly lacked, and help to explain its rapid expansion.

For firms in many industries labour costs are frequently as high as material costs, and areas of low wages are an enticing proposition for branch plants. Table 30 illustrates that wages in the three provinces have been consistently below the national average since 1955, and that male earnings have been lowest in West-Vlaanderen while Limburg has had the lowest female rates. A number of commentators have suggested

Table 30

AVERAGE DAILY WAGES IN OOST- AND WEST-VLAANDEREN AND LIMBURG, 1955-1970. BF

		O-Vlaanderen	W-Vlaanderen	Limburg	Belgium
1955	Male	179	137	189	202
	Female	110	111	99	115
1960	Male	220	217	229	249
	Female	139	137	127	142
1965	Male	332	324	344	358
	Female	222	217	205	223
1970	Male	495	471	499	521
	Female	332	331	342	335

Source: Office National de Sécurité Sociale, *Rapport Annuel 1955-70*, Brussels
(1956-71)

that in Belgium labour supply has been a more important factor than either financial assistance or infrastructural developments such as the provision of roads and technical eduction.[8] This is a difficult case to prove, but it cannot be denied that the excellent labour supply situation, especially in West-Vlaanderen and Limburg, has played an important role in the growth of manufacturing. Liekens and Goossens found that Ford at Genk were able to recruit 5100 workers, and Philips at Hasselt 2300 workers from within a 20 km radius.[9]

That labour has been so readily available is a result of three main considerations. Firstly, not only has there been a high level of unemployment, but also there has been an element of disguised unemployment. Veurne is such a case; here only a mere 11 per cent of women are employed, providing a valuable labour potential. Secondly, the three provinces have a higher rate of natural population increase than the national average, although in this respect Limburg is in a class of its own. Between 1960 and 1970 Limburg's population grew 2.5 times more rapidly than that of West-Vlaanderen and 5 times more quickly than Oost-Vlaanderen's. Thirdly, with improved employment opportunities in their home areas, *frontaliers* gladly forsook their jobs abroad. The number of Belgians working in France during the harvesting season fell from 12,000 in 1954, when they represented 40 per cent of all seasonal workers, to 2700 in 1965. An average of 70 per cent came from West-Vlaanderen and 20 per cent from Oost-Vlaanderen.[10] In 1962 some 22,750 Limburgers were classified as commuters.[11] However, despite the growth of manufacturing, the high rate of natural population increase has caused commuting to remain a feature of Limburg's economic life, and at present commuters number

24,000.[12] Approximately 35,000 people commuted from West-Vlaanderen to France in 1960, but their numbers diminished sharply in the 1960s, falling to 8200 in 1967. It is anticipated that the phenomenon will virtually die out by the mid-1970s, despite the existence of a number of dormitory towns such as Wervik on the Belgian side of the border. The sum of West-Vlaanderen seasonal workers, *frontaliers* and commuters to areas in Belgium, was estimated at 30,000 in 1965, representing a substantial labour reserve.[13] In contrast, cross-frontier commuting has never been important in Oost-Vlaanderen, and since 63 per cent of commuters in the province work in Brabant, with a smaller number from St. Niklaas travelling to Antwerp, there seems to be limited scope for attracting them to work in their own province.[14]

Whatever the disadvantages of a Flemish location might once have been, it may be asserted that such disadvantages are no more. The case of Limburg comprehensively supports this. Between 1960 and 1973 a total of 132 foreign plants generating 31,498 jobs, or 50 per cent of the provincial manufacturing workforce, were established in the province. That Limburg is truly a part of what De Vries has termed the Benelux central region is suggested by the arrival of no less than eighty-eight Dutch plants employing 12,284 people. Since 12 West German plants, providing 12,776 jobs, also appeared, it is arguable that Limburg also possesses some degree of centrality within the EEC.[15]

The Progress of Diversification

The growth of industrial employment, above all in Limburg, where there were only 15,647 workers in manufacturing in 1955, has inevitably resulted in a greater diversity of industrial activities. The remarkable former domination of Oost-and West-Vlaanderen by textiles and of Limburg by mining has been eroded by a contraction of employment in these two industries, and by the rise of the engineering industry in all its forms (Table 31). The West-Vlaanderen engineering industry has almost cut back textile's lead, but it is in Limburg that engineering has proved to be the architect of regional renovation, transforming the province from one unquestionably dominated by coalmining to one with a much broader base. The importance of textiles in the two western Flemish provinces virtually ensures that the manufacture of ready-made clothing should be well represented, and this activity is now also the third largest industry in Limburg. Food processing has universally improved its position, and the SIDMAR iron and steel plant is responsible for the rise of base metals in Oost-Vlaanderen. The absence of chemical manufacturing from the leading industries in all but Oost-Vlaanderen reflects the need for skilled labour for the late stage processes and research work, and the

Table 31

INDUSTRIAL EMPLOYMENT AND COEFFICIENT OF SPECIALISATION IN OOST- AND WEST-VLAANDEREN AND LIMBURG, 1955-1972

	Oost-Vlaanderen			West-Vlaanderen			Limburg	
	1955 %	1972 %		1955 %	1972 %		1955 %	1972 %
Textiles	48.9	30.9	Textiles	42.5	24.2	Engineering	2.6	30.9
Engineering	9.0	14.0	Engineering	11.0	22.2	Mining	71.5	25.3
Clothing	12.1	13.8	Clothing	9.7	11.0	Clothing	1.4	11.2
Food	4.5	7.0	Furniture	8.5	10.2	Furniture	2.8	5.0
Base metals	1.5	5.3	Food	5.4	6.6	Food	2.5	4.2
Chemicals	4.7	5.3	Base metals	2.9	6.3	Base metals	5.6	3.9
Coefficient of specialisation	41.4	33.3		33.9	23.4		57.5	32.7

Source: Office National de Sécurité Sociale, *Rapport Annuel, 1955, 1972*, Brussels (1956, 1973)

attraction of ports for many of the initial production stages. It may be observed from the coefficients of specialisation (see p.121) computed for 1955 and 1972 in Table 31 that all three regions have become more diversified during the period. Limburg was the least diversified in 1955, following the importance of mining, but the multiplicity of manufacturing in Kortrijk, Roeselare and Bruges combined to give West-Vlaanderen appreciably greater diversity than the more traditionally industrial Oost-Vlaanderen. Despite the unimportance of chemicals, West-Vlaanderen still has the most diversified structure, but Limburg now returns a lower value than Oost-Vlaanderen, where textiles continue to loom large and engineering has not grown as it has in the other two provinces.

The Major Industries

In terms of employment, textile manufacture is the most important activity in the three provinces taken together. However, such is the extent of the localisation of the activity in Belgium within Oost-and West-Vlaanderen, that a complete regional examination of the industry has already been undertaken in Chapter III.

Engineering

This, the second largest industry, has 20.6 per cent of the total industrial workforce of the three provinces. It is most well developed in West-Vlaanderen, where there are 29,800 workers, and least well developed in Oost-Vlaanderen (23,300 workers); Limburg lies between the two with 26,600. This represents a fundamental change from the situation in 1955 when Oost-Vlaanderen led West-Vlaanderen; then Limburg was barely involved in the industry. Although Oost-Vlaanderen has suffered a striking reversal, this was not entirely unexpected, for the problems associated with the peripheral nature of both West-Vlaanderen and Limburg, as we have seen, enabled these provinces to supply cheap labour when this became important in the 1960s. Even so, the much slower rate of growth experienced by Oost-Vlaanderen should not obscure the fact that engineering in the province did expand by 60 per cent between 1955 and 1972.

Three centres, one in each of the provinces, dominate the industry. Hasselt is the most important, claiming 19,600 workers, or 75 per cent of the Limburg engineering workforce. This is reflected in a high location quotient of 2.02. Some 11,000 of the total work in the 178 ha Ford plant in the Genk-Zuid industrial estate. The factory began production in 1964 and was originally a branch plant of Ford Werke at Cologne. Proximity to West Germany was thus a factor, as were labour costs compared with those in Cologne, site costs and the proximity of the Boudewijnweg to the estate, for 60 per cent of output is delivered by road.[16] Smaller than Ford, but an important employer nevertheless, is Philips, which has a plant and research division at Hasselt where 5000 are engaged in the manufacture of record players and amplifiers. In West-Vlaanderen, Bruges is the leading district with 14,500 workers, representing 48 per cent of the provincial engineering sector, and giving a location quotient of 2.02. A number of important factories have chosen to succumb to the temptations offered by the city of Bruges and have established themselves on the dock estate. A substantial contribution to engineering in the district has been made by the Claeys family who started making bicycles in 1896 at Zedelgem and who now employ 2600 in the town in the production of cycles, scooters, mowers and agricultural machinery.[17] Ghent is the third large engineering district, and although there are only 11,400 workers, they represent 48 per cent of the engineers in the province. The industry is under-represented in the *arrondissement*, with a location quotient of only 0.67. Only two other *arrondissements*, St. Niklaas and Roeselare, have more than 5000 workers in the industry; the former is heavily influenced by the 2500 workers in the Boelwerf shipyard at Temse on the Scheldt, but the latter has several medium-sized firms including Jonckheere and MBLE.

Clothing

The manufacture of ready-made clothing accounts for 12.3 per cent of the industrial workforce in the three provinces, for although once an adjunct of the textile industry, it has expanded rapidly in Limburg since the province has been a development area. There are now 9500 clothing workers in Limburg, compared with 14,800 in West-Vlaanderen and 23,000 in Oost-Vlaanderen. The industry has been exhibiting sluggish growth or even decline in many of the older textile districts within the three provinces, and the most rapid increases in the workforce have been registered in formerly highly agricultural areas. Some of these areas now exhibit considerable specialisation: Ieper's location quotient is 3.09, Maaseik's 2.26 and Tongeren's 3.03. Aalst, the old establish specialist centre, has a quotient only slightly in excess of these, namely 3.30. A feature of the expansion of the industry in Limburg has been the virtual colonisation of the province by Dutch interests. They have been responsible for sixty-one out of the eighty-nine plants opening between 1960 and 1973, and for 6677 of the 9286 jobs so created. One plant, Mac België, has even been set up in a disused church at Zolder.[18] These Dutch branch plants are effectively managed from the Netherlands and their products are sent to the parent factories to be distributed through Dutch marketing channels. This is a means of reducing administrative costs, at the same time taking advantage of low production costs in Limburg.[19]

Furniture and Wood

Because of its labour-intensiveness, this industry has exhibited similar locational changes to those in clothing. The districts returning the greatest increases in employment since 1965 have been Hasselt, Eeklo and Tielt, where competition for labour has not yet forced its price up unduly. Both Kortrijk and Ghent are undergoing contraction and of the more important and older centres only Roeselare is expanding, causing its location quotient to reach 3.58. The industry is also growing in the *arrondissement* of Bruges, but in rural areas such as Torhout rather than in the city itself. Similarly in Hasselt the most important concentration of factories is at Opglabbeek in the far north of the *arrondissement*, although the largest plant, operated by Recor, is in the town of Hasselt itself.[20]

Food Processing

Like the manufacture of clothing and furniture, this industry is attracted by low cost of unskilled labour, but in contrast with those activities, food processing is expanding rapidly in urban areas such as Kortrijk and Ghent as well as in rural districts. Predictably the more rural *arrondissements* including St. Niklaas, Aalst and Dendermonde, exhibit high growth rates. However, if the numbers employed in food processing are related to total employment, the industry does not seem to have favoured particular rural areas, and location quotients tend to be close to unity.

Coal Mining

In the space of two decades the Limburg collieries have seen their share of the provincial workforce slip from three-quarters to one-quarter. The decline in mining jobs between 1951 and 1971 was 20,600, a figure equal to the number working in the pits in 1971; many of those who lost their positions were foreigners, and some of these went home. The measures to protect the Kempen mines by guaranteeing markets at power stations and by subsidising coking coal deliveries to steelworks have slowed contraction, as have the efforts of the unions who managed to secure a reprieve for Eisden, which was scheduled for closure in 1971, but which was remained open.[21] Although the workforce has been halved, coal production has not been cut back quite so sharply. From a peak of 10.5 million tonnes in 1956, output fell to 7.3 million tonnes in 1972, a contraction of 44 per cent, and it is conceivable that the fourfold increase in crude oil prices during 1973 and 1974 will cause production to rise once more, and that the three reserve concessions will be exploited.

Base Metals

Two areas dominate this activity: Ghent, by virtue of SADACEM, which manufactures alloy steels at Langerbrugge, and of the arrival of SIDMAR in the mid-1960s; and Kortrijk, by virtue of a number of firms of medium size, the largest of which is the wire drawing concern of Bekaert with plants at Zwevegem and Deerlijk. The two non-ferrous metal refineries run by Hoboken-Overpelt at Lommel and Overpelt are responsible for the 2300 workers in the industry in Maaseik.

The Principal Industrial Regions

The Ghent Industrial Region

It was in the Ghent region that the Flemish industrial revolution was inaugurated, and inevitably the greater part of factory employment in Oost-Vlaanderen has long been located in the city. As recently as 1960 the Ghent *arrondissement* accounted for 43 per cent of industrial employment in the province, and of the thirty plants of more than 1000 workers, fifteen were in the city region. Perhaps because of its historic associations, Ghent is not often seen as an industrial city, but a greater proportion of its working population is engaged in manufacturing than in either Liège or Antwerp. Although the Ghent-Terneuzen Canal was opened in 1827, the city was slow to become a port, but rather an industrial complex with a maritime canal link. This was reflected in the circumscribed dock building programme of the last century, for Handelsdok (1828), Tolhuisdok (1880) and Voorhaven (1881) were effectively only improvements to the southern end of the Terneuzen Canal. Not until Grootdok was completed in 1930, the canal improved to accommodate 60,000 tonne vessels (1968) and Sifferdok opened in 1968 could Ghent really claim to be a major port. The traffic handled in 1972 amounted to 13.7 million tonnes. By the end of the nineteenth century, Ghent had established itself as an important industrial complex based on textiles rather than on port activities, and only in the inter-war period did appreciable diversification take place. Because of the importance of textiles early diversification efforts did little to help the regional economy, for contraction in textile employment was more rapid than the expansion of new industry. In 1952 there were 25,600 unemployed in the region, some 10.4 per cent of the national total, but between 1937 and 1960 employment increased by a mere 9 per cent, compared with 56 per cent for Antwerp.[22] The textile industry has continued to contract, a process which has been accelerated by mergers such as that between the three large UCO, Loutex and Hanus groups. However, during the 1950s and 1960s the arrival of new manufacturing, above all in the canal zone, has put the region on a much sounder footing.

Vlassenbroeck and Regniers recognise four distinct sub-regions.[23] Firstly, the central area which is characterised by clothing, printing, brewing, food processing, furniture and metal fabricating plants. Secondly, the southern periphery includes several large mills and factories, such as ARBED (wire drawing) at Gentbrugge, Monsanto Chemicals, SIDAC (plastic packaging) and the Fabelta synthetic fibre plant at Zwijnaarde. There are 109 plants employing 9830 in this sub-region.[24] Thirdly, the northern part of the city is the site of the early factories, many of which are clustered along the Verbindingskanaal, Handelsdock and Tolhuisdok. They include a multiplicity of textile mills and a sprinkling of large engineering plants belonging to firms like Bell Telephone, Anglo-Belgian, ACEC and Vynckier. The fourth sub-region, termed the canal zone, which is mapped in Fig 32, has been the scene of important recent industrialisation, and plants now extend 12 km along the canal almost to the Dutch border. Between 1957 and 1962 older plants on the west bank of the canal added 1200 workplaces through expansion, and nine new plants arrived, creating some 8800 jobs.[25] By 1972 the canal zone had 14,720 workers employed in fifty-five plants, and the east bank had been almost completely occupied between Ghent and Zelzate. The plants on the west bank form three clusters. The Kleinendries-Wondelgem group includes the 0.5 million tonne Shell oil refinery, UCB and a superphosphate works. At Evergem-Langerbrugge there is a 335 MW power station, SADACEM, Electrochim, a cement works and a pulp and paper mill. To the north at Rieme, forming the third group, are six chemical plants. Developed during the 1960s, the east bank is host to some twenty-two factories, the biggest of which is SIDMAR with a payroll of 5000, the 5.6 million tonne Texaco oil refinery, Johns Manville and Volvo. The 423 MW Rodenhuize power station uses blast furnace gas from SIDMAR, and the CBR cement works in the course of construction will consume 0.5 million tonnes of blast furnace slag, also from SIDMAR. Impressive though these developments may be, by no means all the 2200 ha earmarked for industrialisation has been taken up, and the port authorities hope to attract new investment by digging Rodenhuizedok, and by supporting the proposal to link Zeebrugge with Antwerp via Ghent by a 125,000 tonne ship canal.[26]

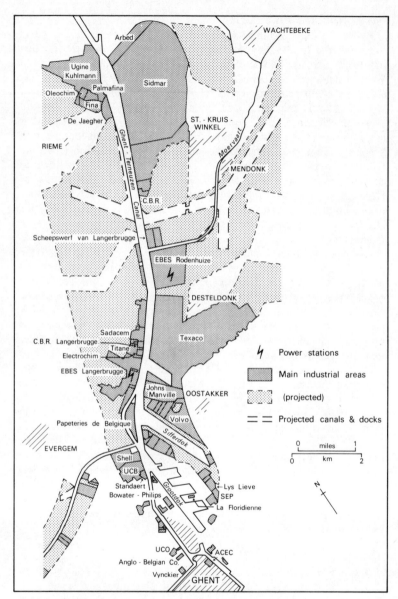

Fig 32. THE INDUSTRIES OF THE PORT OF GHENT
SOURCE: maps published by the Port Authority

The Kortrijk Industrial Region

Extending some 25 km between the French frontier and Zulte, its axis following the Leie valley, with its core in the city of Kortrijk, this industrial region has some 39 per cent of manufacturing employees in West-Vlaanderen. Not being a port, it has not developed the large plants associated with maritime break of bulk points, and indeed a main characteristic is the small size of plant. Nowhere else in Oost-and West-Vlaanderen is the small family business so important, and it represents an instance of self-induced industrialisation, in contrast with Limburg. Some ten industrial estates have been established by the regional development association Leiedal, but there is nothing to compare with the Ghent canal zone, the Antwerp Kanaaldok or Genk-Zuid. Manufacturing sprang initially from the switch by textiles from a domestic to a factory industry, and has slowly evolved from this start point. Textile production called for the maintenance and later the manufacture of machinery, and an engineering industry was created. Out of flax and cotton came the manufacture of carpets, which led to the production of upholstery fabrics, an activity localised at the eastern end of the axis at Vichte, Deerlijk and Waregem. Furniture production provided an outlet for the local labour supply in Kortrijk in the nineteen century, and it was not until the 1950s that the industry was thoroughly organised on a factory basis. Other than at Kortrijk, the activity is important in the west at Wervik, Ledegem and Menen. Another industry which has retained its craft structure even more than has furniture is jewellery-making, whose success may be attributed to the genius of the Beheyt family. Brick and tile production was and is an important activity, but that base metals are now second to textiles is the result of the remarkable growth of the Bekaert wire drawing firm at Zwevegem and Deerlijk.[27] Even engineering, that most rapidly expanding industry in Belgium, has not been able to overtake the manufacture of base metals in the Kortrijk region. The relative importance of the region's leading industries in 1972 is as follows (data are percentages of total employment): textiles 43.6, base metals 11.5, engineering 9.0, clothing 8.6, furniture 7.6 and non-metallic minerals 4.6. Textiles, it should be mentioned, accounted for 58.8 per cent of employment in 1960.

The Zeebrugge-Bruges Industrial Axis

The industrial revolution brought few factories to the medieval city of Bruges and it was avoided by the otherwise ubiquitous textile industry. Fortunately the absence of an industrial tradition is no longer an obstacle to the growth of manufacturing, and with the assistance of the municipality, the West-Vlaanderen development association (WIER)

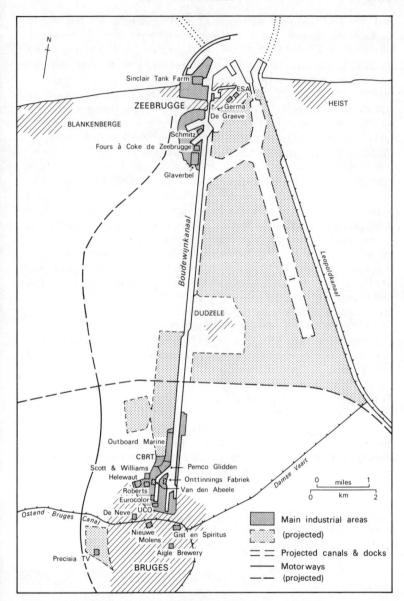

Fig 33. THE ZEEBRUGGE-BRUGES INDUSTRIAL AXIS AND
    PROPOSED EXTENSIONS
SOURCE: maps published by the Bruges Port Authority

and the contemporary attraction of port locations, the region has become the growth point of West-Vlaanderen. Kortrijk remained virtually static between 1960 and 1972, registering a mere 1 per cent increase in employment, but Bruges expanded by 57 per cent. The city contains some small-scale industries such as printing, brewing and food processing, but although some larger plants, including Gist en Spiritusfabriek making yeast and industrial alcohols, dating from 1897, and the engineering firm La Brugeoise (1902), were set up prior to 1914, industrialisation there did not gather speed until the interwar era. At this time FN opened a plant which was employing 1100 workers by 1939, and a variety of furniture, paint, cigar and textile firms began operations in the city. Development was also taking place at Zeebrugge, where the port facilities had been greatly improved in 1907. A coking plant was erected in 1902 and a glassworks followed in 1925. The first attempt at planned industrialisation was the opening of a 49 ha industrial estate based on the new Nijverheidsdok at Bruges in 1952. This was a great success and by 1960 there were 3000 jobs on the estate, mostly in engineering plants such as CBRT, Scott and Williams, Amsco and Outboard Marine. Industrial estates were also established at St. Andries and Oostkamp, where Siemens employ 2000. The growth of La Brugeoise, which spawned the Bus and Car Co. in 1960, should also be noted.[28] When Clark Automotive (transmissions) at St. Michiels and Schmitz-Söhne (heavy engineering) at Zeebrugge are added to the list, it is not surprising that engineering now accounts for 51.6 per cent of industrial employment in the region. Furniture takes second place with a mere 8.0 per cent, and non-metallic minerals (6.9 per cent) are third. It is possible that the impressive plan for a dock and for a 1300–2200 ha industrial estate, adopted by the government for Zeebrugge and shown in Fig 33, will result in the modification of the present industrial structure to give chemicals a greater role. At present Zeebrugge acts merely as the maritime terminal for the oil pipeline to Ghent, and this is reflected in the rapid rise in tonnage handled by the port from 2.1 to 10.5 million tonnes between 1967 and 1972. Several proposals for offshore tanker terminals are under consideration,[29] but one authoritative commentator, P.R. Odell, believes that there is only limited scope for new oil refining complexes in North-West Europe.[30]

8

The Coalfield Provinces:
Hainaut, Namur and Liège

THE PROVINCES OF Hainaut, Namur and Liège include the Belgian *pays noir*, a region whose characteristics originate in the steam industrialism of the late eighteenth and nineteenth centuries, and one which is suffering from the intractable problems of old coalfield areas. The relative importance of these provinces rooted in the industrial revolution is declining in favour of the axial belt and Flanders. Hainaut, once the largest industrial province in the country, is now fourth behind Brabant, Antwerpen and Oost-Vlaanderen in terms of employment, while Liège is in sixth place after West-Vlaanderen. However, Liège and Charleroi, the origins of so many industrial innovations, remain the nation's second and third largest industrial districts, although both are contracting.

Table 32 illustrates the importance of manufacturing in Hainaut (only West-Vlaanderen has a higher percentage) and Liège, and its unimportance in Namur where agriculture still predominates. Rationalisation in the Hainaut and Liège coal industry is reflected in the dwindling significance of mining in these provinces; the continuation of large-scale quarrying is responsible for the slight increase in the importance of mining in Namur, where the coal industry no longer exists. It is noticeable that the tertiary sector in Liège is now responsible for 54.5 per cent of the value added, compared with 50.6 per cent in Hainaut, and that manufacturing has a larger contribution in Hainaut than Liège, despite an analogous situation in 1966. Since in mature economies the secondary sector declines relatively in favour of the tertiary, it would seem that Liège is more 'advanced' than Hainaut,

Table 32

VALUE ADDED BY EMPLOYMENT SECTOR IN HAINAUT, NAMUR AND LIÈGE, 1966-1971, %

	Hainaut		Namur		Liège	
	1966	1971	1966	1971	1966	1971
Agriculture	4.9	3.9	11.7	8.5	5.5	4.1
Mining	6.6	3.5	2.7	2.8	3.0	2.1
Manufacturing	38.8	42.0	25.5	29.2	38.1	39.3
Commerce	16.9	15.6	17.5	15.5	18.8	17.3
Transport & Services	32.8	35.0	42.6	44.0	34.6	37.2

Source: Institut National de Statistique, *Bulletin de Statistique*, no 5 (1973)

parts of which are indeed still typical of the last century in their occupational structure.

Table 33

MANUFACTURING EMPLOYMENT CHANGE IN HAINAUT, NAMUR AND LIÈGE, 1960-1972

	1960	1972	%		1960	1972	%
Ath	4,107	5,003	19.3	Dinant	3.140	3,558	13.3
Charleroi	74,213	73,185	—1.4	Namur	19,473	19,123	—1.8
Mons	16,375	22,405	36.8	Philippeville	4,274	4,030	—6.0
Mouscron	—	12,188	—	NAMUR	26,887	26,711	—0.6
Soignies	14,534	15,917	9.5				
Thuin	10,462	9,060	—15.5	Huy	6,597	5,879	—12.2
Tournai	14,419	15,722	9.0	Liège	102,899	93,642	—9.9
HAINAUT	134,209	153,533	14.4	Verviers	27,899	26,316	—6.0
				Waremme	2,003	2,401	19.9
				LIEGE	139,398	128,238	—8.8

Source: Office National de Sécurité Sociale, *Rapport Annuel 1960, 1972*, Brussels (1961, 1973)

The limited prospects for manufacturing caused downward employment trends in Liège and Namur between 1960 and 1972, as Table 33 indicates, while the 14.4 per cent increase returned by Hainaut is in large part due to the acquisition of Mouscron during that period. When Mouscron is excluded, the increase falls to 5.3 per cent. It is a sobering thought that half the *arrondissements* of the three provinces recorded a contraction between 1960 and 1972, and that apart from Mons, where there was a substantial shift from coalmining to manufacturing, no district expanded by more than 20 per cent. It would appear that mining areas are repellant rather than attractive to industry, yet they nevertheless dominate the employment picture. Liège, Charleroi, Verviers and Mons have 70 per cent of the manufacturing labour force in the three provinces, and when Namur, Soignies and Tournai are included the figure rises to 86 per cent. The *arrondissements* to the north and south of the old industrial district are for the most part rural with weakly developed industrial sectors. Monscron is an exception here for it is economically, but not of course culturally, part of the Flemish textile district, and has a number of sizeable mills. The administrative divisions may be located on Fig 34.

The aura of decline which pervades the Walloon coalfield is supported by several economic indicators other than employment trends, some of which have already been discussed in Chapter II, but it is useful to recapitulate with particular reference to this region.[1] Of the four core industrial districts, three, that is Liège, Mons and Verviers, had unemployment rates well above the national average in 1972. Charleroi was fractionally below the national level. The availability of female labour, such an attractive feature of the Limburg mining districts, does not seem to have assisted Mons and Liège, which were saddled with respective female unemployment rates of 13.2 and 13.0 per cent in 1972. By comparison the Limburg mining districts of Maaseik and Hasselt had figures of 6.9 and 7.3 per cent respectively.[2] Mons, Verviers, Tournai and Namur had lower male industrial wage rates than the national average in 1972, a result of the demand for labour and the influence of slowly growing or declining industries which usually do not offer high wages. Liège and Charleroi benefited from wages above the national average, but the iron and steel industry which is at the root of this is not expanding its labour force. The per capita product in all three provinces in 1971 was below the national average, and Hainaut was in the unenviable position of finding only the rural province of Luxembourg and recently industrialised Limburg below it.[3] This must be regarded as an indication of an inefficient use of labour, heavily influenced by the importance of older industries. Employment opportunities are not considered to be especially outstanding by the inhabitants judging by the number who left for other districts in the 1960s. Liège, Mons and Charleroi had the most unfavourable net migration balance of all the Belgian *arrondissements* save Brussels-Capital between 1967 and 1971, all losing upwards of 3400 inhabitants. The short distances involved and the favourable prices charged by Belgian Railways for season tickets, have allowed many people to commute to Brussels from all the principal coalfield towns. To take one

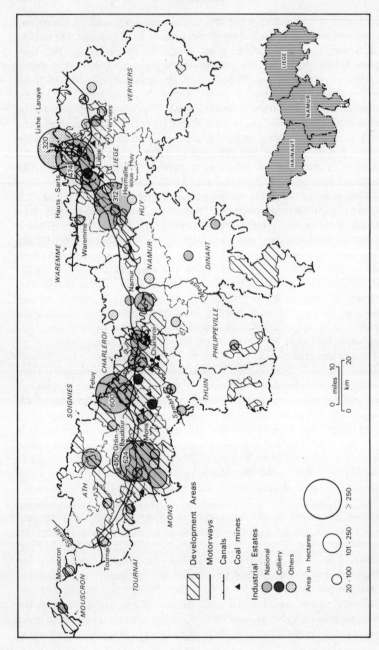

Fig 34. THE PROVINCES OF HAINAUT, NAMUR AND LIÈGE: LOCATION MAP

example, the number of season tickets issued for the La Louvière district in the Centre coalfield for travel to Brussels, increased from 2981 (67 per cent of all season tickets issued) in 1961 to 5391 (82 per cent) in 1970.[4]

Foreign investment in new factories is a useful index of how entrepreneurs with views unclouded by local ties see the potential of the region. Between 1959 and 1968, Hainaut, Liège and Namur took a mere 15.2 per cent of overseas investment in Belgium, the individual shares being 12.1, 3.0 and 0.1 per cent respectively. Between the same dates Limburg, lacking the external economies of established industrial areas, took 21.4 per cent of the total. Liège, for all its impeccable pedigree, was clearly held in no kind of esteem at all. On the other hand investment by Belgian sources showed Wallonie in a different light, for Hainaut took 26.0 per cent and Liège 24.0 per cent of the total, a situation flavouring of former eras. However, much of this investment was made by Wallonie-based firms setting up branch plants in their own region.[5] Since 1968 there has been a swing in favour of the Walloon provinces, causing their share of foreign investment to rise to 25.1 per cent, Hainaut taking 18.2, Liège 5.5 and Namur 1.4 per cent of the total between 1959 and 1973. Hainaut is now fractionally behind Limburg, but Liège continues to trail badly and to rely on Belgian funds for growth. The employment generated by foreign investment is approximately proportional to that investment. Between 1959 and 1973, 15,719 jobs were created in Hainaut, and 7634 were generated in Liège. It says much for the strength of foreign capital in Hainaut, if not in Liège, that more employment resulted than was generated by domestic capital, which gave rise to 10,924 workplaces in Hainaut in the fifteen year period.[6]

The very fact that the coalfield districts are old industrial areas is sufficient to make many firms wary of Wallonie, for it is difficult to engender an image of cleanliness, modernity, spaciousness and efficiency in the congested, grimy and outworn districts fashioned in the last century. It is possible to find perfectly satisfactory conditions in the new peripheral industrial estates, but for many entrepreneurs the ambience of the old core areas is perceived to spill over into the new locations. In Liège, for instance, estates such as Alleur, Loncin and Grâce-Hollogne are sited in the pleasant Hesbaye countryside from which the spoil heaps and blast furnaces of the Meuse valley are invisible. Perhaps the worst depredations from spoil heaps are in the Centre and the Borinage. The latter has 130 heaps covering 618 ha; interspersed between them are small mining villages, while barracks for foreign miners have been hastily erected at the foot of many of the old tips, as at Flénu. Some heaps have been deliberately afforested, a few are cultivated as allotments and enterprising Italians have even established vineyards on some at Quaregnon.[7] The general impression is, however, unpleasant, even though a start has been made on their removal. The severe contraction of coalmining in the Borinage has caused many dwellings to become derelict, adding to the air of depression. The average age of housing in the Borinage is 74 years compared with the national average of 59 years.[8] Clearly the coalfield is still suffering from its nineteenth century legacy, and much rebuilding and landscaping remains to be done before it is possible to compete with the many areas in Flanders where the old industrial artefacts are absent.

The Industrial Structure

Throughout this book the paleotechnic nature of so many of the coalfield industries has been a recurrent theme, and the injection of neotechnic manufacturing has been advanced as the obvious solution to the problem. The real reconversion effort did not come until the 1960s, so that the 1955 industrial structure shown in Table 34 reflects that of previous decades. Mining, base metals, engineering and non-metallic minerals accounted for 77.7 per cent of industrial employment in Hainaut, and save for the substitution of metalworking for base metals, the same activities had 64.1 per cent of the Namur industrial labour force. Three industries, base metals, engineering and mining, accounted for 62.8 per cent of industrial labour in Liège. The virtual demise of coalmining during the last decade and a half has not prevented some of the old staples, such as non-metallic minerals in Hainaut and Namur and base metals in Hainaut and Liège, from increasing their share of employment between 1955 and 1972. Engineering improved its position in all three provinces, but this is a desirable trend for it is a growth industry. However, engineering does not have the clear lead it enjoys in Antwerpen and Brabant; indeed in Namur it lies second to non-metallic minerals. That other important growth activity, chemicals, features only in Namur. Another growth industry, food processing, now makes a greater contribution in Liège and Namur than in 1955, and metalworking has developed in Liège.

The impression that this is a region reliant on the old industries is confirmed by investigating the extent to which the six growth industries share in total employment. During the years 1955 to 1972, the growth industries increased their share of employment in Hainaut from 24.3 to 35.1 per cent, in Liège from 34.2 to 47.7 per cent and in Namur from 36.8 to 51.2 per cent. As a guideline, the data for Antwerpen moved from 51.6 to 61.5 per cent. In terms of growth activities, not one of the Walloon industrial provinces has yet reached Antwerpen's position of 1955, while Hainaut is still very far from it. The coefficients of

Table 34

INDUSTRIAL EMPLOYMENT AND COEFFICIENT OF SPECIALISATION IN HAINAUT, LIÈGE AND NAMUR, 1955 AND 1972

	Hainaut			Liège			Namur	
	1955 %	1972 %		1955 %	1972 %		1955 %	1972 %
Engineering	14.1	22.4	Engineering	19.5	27.6	Non-met. min	17.3	21.8
Base metals	15.9	20.9	Base Metals	24.7	26.4	Engineering	11.2	17.6
Non-met. mins	10.1	12.7	Metalworking	5.7	7.6	Metalworking	11.3	10.8
Textiles	3.6	9.8	Food	3.8	6.7	Chemicals	4.8	8.7
Mining	37.6	8.1	Textiles	8.7	5.5	Food	5.2	8.4
Clothing	4.1	5.2	Mining	18.6	5.2	Mining	24.3	7.7
Coefficient of specialisation	34.5	22.4		25.6	23.0		32.9	33.9

Source: Office National de Sécurité Sociale, *Rapport Annuel 1955, 1972*, Brussels (1956, 1973)

specialisation (see p.121) indicate that both Hainaut and Liège deviate
only modestly from the national employment situation, and may
therefore be regarded as diversified provinces, but they unquestionably
lack an adequate growth sector. Namur is the least diversified of the
eight provinces for which a coefficient has been computed, registering
an increase rather than a decrease in specialisation between 1955 and
1972.

Nowhere in Belgium was the need for diversification greater than in
the Walloon coalfield areas in the late 1950s and early 1960s. Prior to
its contraction coalmining bulked large at the provincial level, but the
pits were restricted to a small number of *arrondissements*, Charleroi and
Liège had well developed manufacturing sectors, but Mons, which is
synonymous with the Borinage, Thuin and Soignies, collectively the
Centre field, lacked this diversity. Some 45 per cent of industrial
workers in Mons were miners, and the situation in Thuin and Soignies
was not very different. Employment in Borinage collieries declined
from 24,030 in 1957 to 11,825 in 1960, and in the Centre the pits
contracted their employment from 20,036 to 10,427 over the same
period. The social problems caused by this extremely sharp contraction
were immense, and subsequent rationalisation was more attenuated, but
nevertheless by 1970 there were only 1,900 miners left in the Borinage
and 1,000 in the Centre. Although the regional impact of pit closures
was less in Charleroi and Liège, this should not disguise the large
number of workplaces lost. Between 1957 and 1970 32,655 jobs were
lost in the Charleroi field and 24,588 in the Liège basin, giving a grand
total of 98,409 lost workplaces in the four fields.[9] Coupled with the
contraction of many of the other old industries, it is understandable that
so many socio-economic indicators show Wallonie in such a poor light.
One study has demonstrated that the loss of one miner's job causes a
reduction in regional employment by a factor of 2.6 and a decrease in
regional income by a factor of 2.3.[10]

Apart from improvements to the social infrastructure, and the
construction of motorways such as the E41, the principal vehicle of
diversification has been the industrial estate, backed by financial
incentives at various levels. Some twenty national estates, funded by
the central government, in some cases in conjunction with the ECSC,
have been established on or adjacent to the coalfield (Fig 34). Six of the
estates have an area of 300 ha or more, and some of these, such as
Hauts-Sarts at Liège, and Feluy and Ghlin-Baudour in the Borinage
have formed the spearhead of the coalfield's reconversion endeavours.
The regional estates, those funded in part by the development
associations, are less numerous and smaller. There are sixteen local
estates, funded entirely by municipalities, all but four of which are in

the Liège region; one such site, Chertal, is host to the recently built
Cockerill steelworks. All the estates mentioned, irrespective of the
origin of their funding, are managed by the development associations.
In addition, sixteen small estates are operated by the Fédération
Charbonnière de Belgique (FEDECHAR) on privately owned colliery
land, thus ensuring that not all pits become the scene of dereliction.[11] In
suitable cases the development associations support firms wishing to
open up outside the estates. The SPl at Liège, for instance, has assisted
twenty-one factories which have set up outside estates; they include
General Electric Medical at Loncin, Liège, and the electronic firms of
Société Générale de Constructions Electroniques at Herve and Münck
Continental at Esneux.[12]

In the decade after 1959 when regional policies were first introduced,
11,748 jobs in new factories were created in Hainaut, no less than 6060
of these being in engineering and 1440 in non-metallic minerals. Liège
did not do nearly so well, for only 4489 workplaces were created, of
which 2122 were in engineering and 679 in non-metallic minerals.
Namur secured 839 jobs in new plants. When this total of 17,076 is
added to the number of new jobs made available in existing firms, about
30,000, the resulting figure of 47,000 is substantial, but is poor
compensation for the loss of 98,409 workplaces in coalmining alone.[13]
In fact, between 1960 and 1972 only seven industries recorded increases
in employment: engineering (14,701), food processing (3511), metalworking (2460), paper (1183), printing (888), furniture and wood (279)
and chemicals (20), giving a total of 23,042. Decline in the other
sectors caused a net loss of 4200 jobs when Mouscron is excluded from
the calculations. Additionally a further 2330 coalmining jobs were lost
by the end of 1972, causing the contraction of employment in this
industry since 1957 to top the 100,000 mark. It is difficult to resist the
conclusion that, despite the performance of the engineering industry,
the Walloon coalfield provinces are unlikely to regain their employment
strength of the later 1950s for many decades to come. Indeed some
commentators convincingly argue that the panacea would be to
encourage the growth of tertiary rather than secondary employment.[14]

Curiously enough the one ray of light in this otherwise gloomy
atmosphere is found in arguably the most unlikely district, the
Borinage. The manufacturing sector here was formerly rooted in
pottery, porcelain, glass, refractory products, steel rolling, mine
equipment, footwear and carbochemicals,[15] in fact industries incapable
of absorbing redundant miners. The single pit still working at the end of
1972, Hensies, employs a mere 1038 miners, the residue of the 24,000
of 1957. Yet in spite of the unattractive milieu and the run-down
infrastructure, Borinage industry has grown more rapidly since 1960

than industry anywhere else in the three provinces. (Table 33). Some 8000 jobs have been generated in 48 factories built since 1960,[16] mostly on the six industrial estates managed by IDEA. The largest estate, Ghlin-Baudour Sud, 624 ha, was developed with the aid of a 121 million BF loan from the ECSC,[17] and other important estates are at Ghlin-Baudour Nord (450 ha) and Dour (203 ha). The junction of the Paris-Brussels and Tournai-Liège-Cologne motorways on the coalfield has been an important location factor, and the high unemployment makes for a favourable labour supply. Several firms have secured low rents by utilising old factories, and one of the largest plants, Bell Telephone, uses the buildings of the former Crachet coalmine at Frameries. Non-metallic minerals is still the leading manufacturing sector; the largest plant, the Verlica bottle works employing 800 at Ghlin-Baudour, is the most recent arrival. Engineering has benefited from the operations of Bell Telephone, Siemens, General Telephone and Electronics and Gleason, a gear-cutting firm. The chemical sector has been helped by the switch to ethylene from coal at Tertre, and by the presence of Pirelli and Chicopharma pharmaceuticals.

The Major Industries of the Coalfield Provinces

Engineering and Base Metals

Between them these two activities dominate industrial employment, accounting for 47.7 per cent of the workforce, engineering being slightly the more important. Manufacture of base metals is, in Belgium, a slowly growing sector, but here it is contracting at some speed, and has lost 14,000 jobs between 1960 and 1972. The concentration of the industry in Liège and Charleroi has been noted in Chapter III; these districts respectively account for 46.5 and 35.0 per cent of the workforce in the three provinces. Of the other *arrondissements* only Soignies, with the Boël integrated iron and steel works at La Louvière, and Mons, host to Forges et Laminoirs de Jemappes, have more than 2000 workers in the industry. During the period mentioned, engineering expanded by 14,700 jobs and yet, symptomatic of the problems facing the coalfield, the leading district, Liège, has been contracting since 1965, despite the newly important electronic products industry. The best performance has come from Mons, but the greatest absolute increase has been recorded by Charleroi, where transport engineering has made some progress. Gosselies appears to be developing into an aircraft construction and repair centre, while Seneffe-Manage is becoming an important vehicle complex. The latter activity has also taken root in Ath (Cibié-Hainaut at Ghislenghien), and the proximity of Brussels suggests that plants in northern Charleroi and Ath lie within the influence of the capital. In addition Champion Spark Plugs have been attracted to Bray in Soignies, and Renault make components at Tournai. Nevertheless the industry is underrepresented in all districts save Charleroi and Liège, which score location quotients of 1.37 and 1.22 respectively. Even Mons has a quotient of only 0.69.

Non-Metallic Minerals

Although this industry accounts for a mere 9.9 per cent of industrial employment in the coalfield provinces, it is as strongly characteristic of the Walloon coalfield as base metals. Unlike the manufacture of base metals, it extends into the peripheral districts of Tournai and Verviers, and only in Huy is it not well developed. The greatest degree of specialisation is exhibited by Namur, which has a location quotient of 5.17, almost entirely the result of important glassworks at Jemeppe, Franière, Auvelais and Moustier. Soignies has a quotient of 4.42, and in addition to pottery and porcelain works at Houdeng and La Louvière, refractory brick-making at La Louvière and a cement plant at Thieu, there are also glassworks at Houdeng and Ville-sur-Haine. The pottery industry of St. Ghislain, Baudour and Hautrage, the two cement works at Obourg and the Ghlin bottle works combine to give Mons a quotient of 4.35. Other districts with high quotients are Thuin, which has a large bottle works at Momignies, Tournai where there are cement plants at Vaulx, Gaurain-Ramecroix and Antoing, and Charleroi with its nine glass-works. Unfortunately this activity, in which the coalfield is such a specialist, is in decline, and between 1960 and 1972 3700 jobs were lost.

Textiles and Clothing

The manufacture of textiles is also a contracting activity, exhibiting a loss of 6000 jobs between 1965 and 1972. The activity accounted for 7.5 per cent of industrial employment in the region in 1972, and is clustered into four districts, three of which are southern appendages of the Flemish textile area. Mouscron, Verviers and Tournai are responsible for 86 per cent of the total employment, and score location quotients of 7.30, 2.42 and 3.11 respectively. Ath is the fourth most important *arrondissement*, where specialisation in knitwear continues, as it does in Tournai.[18] There seems to be no shortage of new entrants to the industry in Mouscron where eight of the twenty-three factories on the industrial estate in the town of Mouscron are in textiles, and of these eight, four employ more than 100 workers.[19] Mouscron barely contracted between 1965 and 1972, but the other areas lost from a quarter to a third of their textile operatives. In contrast the clothing industry showed a slight increase in employment. Thuin, with its well established cluster at Binche, is losing its former importance, although its location quotient is 4.28, and the greatest increase has been experienced by the Borinage, which now has more jobs than Thuin.

Metalworking

Predictably the leading centres are Liège and Charleroi which have 40.7 and 13.6 per cent respectively of workers in the industry. Since 1965 both have exhibited contraction, as has the activity on the coalfield as a whole, but the industry persists in several rural areas. Examples are Couvin in Philippeville,[20] which has a location quotient of 7.24, and the Namur town of Gembloux, where the ancient art of cutlery-making has been modified to form the basis of surgical instrument manufacture.[21]

Chemicals

It is arguably an indictment of the recent industrial performance of Wallonie that this industry, so important in the growth belt, should be able to claim only 3.2 per cent of regional employment. The oil refining and petrochemical complex at Feluy and Solvay at Jemeppe are the high points in a generally disappointing performance.

Coalmining

Not two decades ago the leading industry, coalmining employed 10,000, or 3.1 per cent of the industrial workforce, at the end of 1972. At this time the Borinage had one pit left open, as did the Centre; there were seven in the Charleroi basin and six in the Liège field. Rationalisation relentlessly continues, and following further closures there were in mid-1974 only four pits in the Liège basin. There seems little chance of a reprieve. In the 1950s Romus could write 'le Borinage, c'est le charbon'[22] but today such a comment could hardly have less relevance to the Borinage or to any other region of Wallonie.

The Principal Industrial Regions

The Liège Industrial Region

Although the city of Liège dominates manufacturing in the province of Liège, with three-quarters of the latter's industrial employment, perhaps a more trenchant characteristic is its slow but relentless decline. Between 1960 and 1972, manufacturing lost 9257 jobs, and when coalmining redundancies are added, the loss becomes 23,810. Unlike Antwerp, Ghent and Kortrijk, Liège was an outstandingly powerful centre of the industrial revolution from whose legacy the region is now trying to extricate itself. Doubtless a new equilibrium will be reached when the older industries have completed their rationalisation and contraction, but in the meantime a shrinking labour force and high unemployment testify to the pains of reconversion. In the 1950s, just as in the nineteenth century, the major plants were based on coal, metals and engineering technology. Of those firms employing more than 1500, 5 were in iron and steel manufacture, 3 were non-ferrous metal producers, 2 were engineers, and 1 was a carbochemical firm. Only one, Englebert, the rubber tyre firm, could not be said to fit the model.[23] Rationalisation and mergers in the iron and steel industry caused the base metal sector alone to lose 10,000 jobs between 1960 and 1972. In the absence of initiatives by petrochemical companies, chemical plants lost 1000 workplaces, as did rubber manufacture. Non-metallic minerals exhibited only a slight contraction, for cement production in the plants below the city is a profitable activity, and the large Val St. Lambert glassworks continues with government backing. In this saga of contraction, two of the established sectors, engineering and metalworking, managed a slight expansion. The bankruptcy of engineering firms has been more than replaced by the growth of the electronic products industry in the city, led by Burroughs, Radio Corporation of America, MBLE and Mémorex. None of these plants is large, but collectively they have been the main agents of expansion in engineering. However, when measured against the performance of Bruges, Ghent and Antwerp, the expansion of engineering in Liège is of modest proportions. Food processing and clothing are two other growing industries, although employment has risen by less than 800 in both cases. The establishment of Müller-Wipperfürth, an unusually large clothing factory employing 600 on the Alleur industrial estate, has helped the development of this activity.

The core of the industrial region, which is mapped in Fig 35, lies upstream of the city centre at Seraing, Ougrée, Flémalle and Jemeppe, where all the district's blast furnaces, the majority of the steelworks, the Val St. Lambert glassworks and the nitrogenous fertiliser plant are located. It is palpably an area of heavy industry, with one-third of the industrial employment of the region, and formerly an important coalmining area. The lower valleys of the Vesdre and Ourthe bear some resemblance to the industrial core, for here are non-ferrous metal works, some steelworks and the Société des Conduits d'Eau (steel pipes), but the works are neither as large as those in the core nor are they engaged in primary processing. The central area of the city has a wide variety of manufacturing, ranging from engineering and small metalworking firms to printers, publishers, brewers (Piedboeuf), tobacco firms (Jubilé) and clothing manufacturers. Below the city, at Herstal and Wandre, is an area which, until the construction of the Cockerill steelworks on the Chertal industrial estate in 1963 and the

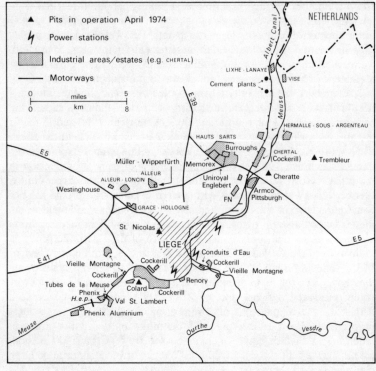

Fig 35. THE LIÈGE INDUSTRIAL REGION

Armco-Pittsburgh works at Wandre in 1966, specialised in engineering, with FN and ACEC very much at its centre. Further diversification has been provided by the opening in 1965 of the region's largest industrial estate at Hauts-Sarts, where at present 474 ha are occupied. In 1972 twenty-seven firms were in residence, employing 3936 workers, very largely in engineering and metalworking; among the largest are the electronic products firms of Burroughs and Mémorex, although the leading plant in terms of employment is Uniroyal-Englebert, relocated from central Liège.[24] To the east and west of the central area are the former specialist coal mining areas, unattractive to other industries by virtue of steep slopes. Beyond the western mining region lies the edge of the Hesbaye plateau, and it is here, adjacent to the Brussels motorway, that three industrial estates have recently been opened. Alleur has attracted 780 jobs, Alleur-Loncin 400 and Grâce-Hollogne

225; Westinghouse, formerly in central Liège and now on its own site on the motorway at Awans, employs 1000.[25] The establishment of other peripheral estates at Ivoz-Ramet, Hermalle, Lixhe and Visé points to the continuation of the decentralisation process, but the massive inertia of the heavy industrial sector will ensure the domination of Seraing and Ougrée for some time to come.[26]

The Charleroi Industrial Region

Rooted in engineering and base metals, which together accounted for 69 per cent of its manufacturing population in 1972, and the fourth Belgian industrial region, Charleroi has managed to undergo reconversion without undue contraction. Between 1960 and 1972 the industrial workforce declined by a mere 1 per cent, thanks largely to the expansion of engineering by 6500 workers. Rationalisation by the iron and steel groups Hainaut-Sambre and Thy-Marcinelle et Monceau, and the growth of engineering have allowed the latter to become the leading activity. ACEC is the largest engineering firm, but Caterpillar at Gosselies now employ 3600, and other recent arrivals include Dassault and Aviation Spare Parts to join SABCA and Fairey Aviation on the Gosselies II estate, Baldwin Lima Hamilton (earth moving equipment) at Mont-sur-Marchienne, Quinton Hazell (vehicle components) at Jumet, and an ACEC branch plant also at Jumet. The Seneffe-Manage estate has a vehicle component firm and one making brake linings in addition to the British Leyland plant; Burroughs make electronic calculators on the same site. Non-metallic minerals are represented by the heavy clay goods sector at a number of sites south of the city, and by the important local glass industry. Printing, food processing and chemicals exhibited modest growth between 1960 and 1972, the performance of the latter industry being consequent upon the presence of Solvay at Couillet, Beecham at Heppignies and the capital-intensive Chevron oil refinery and adjacent petrochemical plants at Feluy.

Conclusion

THE MAIN THEME developed in this book has been the striking concentration of manufacturing during the last decade and a half in regions which were, at the end of the nineteenth century, not especially attractive to industry. Brussels and Antwerp were exceptions, for at the end of the century the capital and the national port were profitable locations for certain activities, although they could hardly match the importance of the vibrant coal-furrow in Wallonie. The 1950s and 1960s have witnessed a reversal of the fortunes of Wallonie and Flanders. The Brussels-Antwerp axial belt has replaced the Haine-Sambre-Meuse coalfield as the economic core of the country, while the Flemish provinces of Oost-and West-Vlaanderen and Limburg have made remarkable strides, considering their poorly developed industrial tradition and infrastructure. It is as though virtually everything that took place in Wallonie in the era of steam industrialism now counts for very little, or indeed for nothing, for the manufacturing industries stemming from the current technological advances tend not only to shun the old industrial districts in favour of newly developing regions, but also appear to have little use for the external economies of established manufacturing areas. That many Flemish towns have effectively moved from an agricultural to a late twentieth century manufacturing economy seems to have posed problems neither for entrepreneurs nor for their inhabitants. Given the advantages of spacious industrial estates, the provision of motorways, cheap and cooperative labour and a pleasant environment, it is hardly surprising that so many firms have chosen Flanders. It is small comfort to the Walloon working population that some of their industries have managed, through the adoption of new techniques, to increase output, for these increases are achieved by a decreased labour force.

Unlike the French and the British, the Belgians have unequivocally sought to attract foreign investment as a major plank in their economic development platform. Once again this has favoured the north since foreign firms have overwhelmingly preferred Flanders to Wallonie. It is difficult to deny that the many financial concessions made to attract foreign firms to Flanders have been eminently successful, and with the assistance of the government, Antwerp and Ghent have become major industrial port complexes. Zeebrugge-Bruges may similarly develop in the near future. In line with the anti-authoritarian spirit with which the country is imbued, much recent industrialisation has been virtually the result of individual efforts by development associations, *intercommunales*, municipalities and presssure groups, and the central government has not played an influential role. Regional policy legislation did, of course, emanate from Brussels, but this is only one weapon among many which have been employed to ensure economic growth at, it would appear, virtually any cost.

The Belgian philosophy of self-interest is inimical to planning and the ordering of society in the best interests of its members. This, coupled with the uniquely thorny linguistic problem, was the principal cause of the late introduction of regional policies in 1959, and equally of the belated enactment of planning legislation in 1962. However the 1962 law failed to lay down clear national and regional goals and concentrated upon the details of planning at the local scale. There were no statements of policy on such matters as industrial estates, the height of buildings, motorways, public transport systems and central area development, with the result that any coordination between *arrondissements*, the basic and overly small planning unit, has been quite fortuitous. Since 1946 some twenty plans at a more realistic, regional scale have been drawn up by a variety of academic and private bodies,[1] but none has been approved because a succession of governments has always regarded the whole issue as very delicate and has lamely equated *arrondissements* with planning regions. Perhaps politicians have been unduly cautious in their unwillingness to interfere with the activities of entrepreneurs for recently there has been an increasing awareness of the need to control manufacturing industry, as an integral part of the environment, in order to improve the quality of life. The Bond Beter Leefmilieu–Inter-Environnement was set up in 1971 to fight pollution, to protect wild life and to prevent the destruction of important urban buildings by the developers. It is a step in the right direction, but it may be some time before the movement gathers sufficient strength to persuade the legislature that it is not always in the public interest to allow manufacturing industry to remain totally preoccupied by profitability.

Notes and References

CHAPTER 1

The Physical and Human Background   pages 1-25

1   There are a number of useful maps of mineral resources in *Atlas de Belgique*, plates 37-39.
2   Vlassenbroeck, *Geografisch Tijdschrift*, 6 (1972), 461-8.
3   *Weekly Bulletin of the Kredietbank*, Brussels, 26 May 1972, 227.
4   Melkin, *Actes de la Journée Economique et Sociale*, (22 April 1972), 70.
5   Christians, (1965), 96-7.
6   Mols, *Population*, 27 (1972), 998.
7   Institut National de Statistique, *Statistiques Demographiques*, No 1 (1973).
8   Van der Haegen, *Bulletin de la Société Belge d'Etudes Géographiques*, 33 (1964) 175-8.
9   For a useful article covering the whole linguistic issue see Stephenson, *Geographical Review*, 62 (1972), 501-23.
10   *Cartactual*, no 38 (1972), fig 13.
11   Mérenne, *Colloqué International de Géographie Appliquée*, Université de Liège (1968), 210-11.
12   Modern Railways, October 1970, 460.

CHAPTER 2

The Development of the Economy   pages 26-54

1   Rostow, *Economic Journal 66 (1956), 25-48.*
2   Malburny, *Bulletin de la Société Belge d'Etudes Géographiques, 20* 258-9.

3   Pounds and Parker (1957), 45.
4   Riley, (1973), 70, 78.
5   Dechesne, (1932), 438.
6   Michotte, *Bulletin de la Société Belge d'Etudes Géographiques*, 8 (1938), 62.
7   Vlassenbroeck, *De Aardrijkskunde*, (1972), 167-71.
8   Mingret, *Revue de Géographie de Lyon, 37 (1962), 18.*
9   Coppé, (1940), 26.
10 Michotte, *Annales de Géographie*, (1929), 58.
11 Riley, *Economic Geography*, 43 (1967), 261-2.
12 International Labour Office, (1954, 1972).
13 Institut National de Statistique, *Bulletin de Statistique*, nos 10-11 (1972).
14 International Labour Office, (1972).
15 The method of construction is given in Yates, (1968), 90-2.
16 Mingret, *Revue de Géographie de Lyon*, 45 (1970), 255.
17 Ministère des Affaires Economiques, *Rapport 1971*, (1972).
18 Mingret, *Revue de Géographie de Lyon*, 45 (1970), 248.
19 Office National de Sécurité Sociale, *Rapport Annuel 1955*, (1956).
20 Office National de Sécurité Sociale, *Rapport Annuel 1972*, (1973).
21 Banque de Bruxelles, (1972), 14-21.
22 Organisation for Economic Cooperation and Development, (1971), 146.
23 *Weekly Bulletin of the Kredietbank*, 5th March 1971.
24 Evalenko, (1968), 219-20.
25 Organisation for Economic Cooperation and Development, *Manpower in Belgium*, (1971), 149.
26 Organisation for Economic Cooperation and Development, *Economic Surveys, BLEU* (June 1972), 38.
27 Vinck, *Tijdschrift voor Economische en Sociale Geografie*, 60 (1969), 9.
28 Warntz, *Geographical Review*, 54 (1964), 171.
29 Nadasdi, *Bulletin de la Société Belge d'Etudes Géographiques*, 40 (1971), 237-46.

CHAPTER 3

The Declining and Slowly Growing Industries   pages 55-89

1   Riley, *Geography*, 228 (1965), 263-4.
2   European Coal and Steel Community, High Authority, *Ninth General Report, (1961).*

3 *Annuaire Statistique de la Belgique*, 92 (1975).
4 *Petroleum Times*, 8th September 1971.
5 Dechesne, (1932), 437.
6 Olyslager, (1947), 176.
7 Vanex, *Bulletin de la Société Royale de Géographie d'Anvers*, 53 (1933), 262.
8 Sporck, *Bulletin de la Société Belge d'Etudes Géographiques*, 17 (1948), 156.
9 Vanex, op cit, 264-5.
10 Beekers, (1972), 134-8.
11 Olyslager, op cit, 79.
12 De Smet, *Bulletin de la Société Belge d'Etudes Géographiques*, 21 (1952), 126-31.
13 Kredietbank, Bibliothèque d'Economie d'Entreprise, (1966), 29-32.
14 Vlassenbroeck, (1972), 395.
15 Ibid.
16 Institut National de Statistique, *Statistiques Industrielles*, No 10 (1972).
17 Institut National de Statistique, *Statistiques Industrielles*, No 3/4 (1973).
18 Kredietbank, Bibliothèque d'Economie d'Entreprise, (1967), 45.
19 Institut National de Statistique, *Statistiques Industrielles*, No 1/2 (1973).
20 De Smet, *Natuurwetenschappelijk Tijdschrift*, 41 (1959), 79.
21 Pounds and Parker, (1957), 45.
22 *Metal Bulletin*, 20th July 1971.
23 Doyen, *Bulletin de la Société Royale Belge de Géographie*, 79 (1959), 30.
24 Olyslager, op cit, 130.
25 *Metal Bulletin*, 11th December 1970.
26 Comhaire, *Tijdschrift voor Economische en Sociale Geografie*, 46 (1955), 125.
27 *Belgium, Economy and Technique*, 24 (1970), 39.
28 *Metal Bulletin*, 16th October 1970.
29 *British Steel* (Spring 1973), 15.
30 Mangelinckx, *Revue Belge de Géographie*, 87 (1963), 269.
31 Duby, *Bulletin de la Société Royale Belge de Géographie*, 79 (1955) III-IV, 45.
32 Mangelinckx, op cit, 290-307.
33 Vlassenbroeck, *Geografisch Tijdschrift*, 7, (1973), 301.
34 Vlassenbroeck, *Hommes et Terres du Nord*, (1969), 88.
35 *Belgium, Economy and Technique*, 33 (1973), 22-3.

36   Ibid, 29 (1972), xi.
37   Olyslager, op cit, 32.
38   Ibid, 147.
39   Vlassenbroeck and De Smet, *De Aardrijkskunde*, 77 (1968), 81.
40   Olyslager, op cit, 168-9.
41   For an explanation of the technique see Cole and King, (1968), 136-8.
42   Institut National de Statistique, *Statistiques Industrielles,* No 1/2 (1973).
43   'Concentration and Rationalisation in the Belgian Brewing Industry' *Belgium, Economy and Technique*, 37 (1974), 44.
44   Vlassenbroeck and De Smet, op cit, 87.
45   *Weekly Bulletin of the Kredietbank*, Brussels, 16th February 1973, 78.

CHAPTER 4

The Growth Industries   pages 90-113

1   Sheaf, *European Community* (January/February 1974), 16.
2   'The Machine Tool in Belgium', *Belgium, Economy and Technique*, 18 (1969), 36.
3   Lefournier, *L'Expansion,* (May 1971), 122.
4   *Weekly Bulletin of the Kredietbank*, 31 July 1973.
5   Kaisin, *Revue Universelle des Mines*, 13 (1957), 424.
6   'The Belgian Car Industry', *Belgium, Economy and Technique*, 18 (1969) 8-12.
7   'Van Hool', *Belgium, Economy and Technique*, 33 (1973), 33-6.
8   'Bicycles, Motor Cycles Made in Belgium', *Belgium, Economy and Technique*, 29 (1972), 33.
9   'Belgian Electronics are Present Everywhere', *Belgium, Economy and Technique*, 26 (1971), II.
10   'Capital Investments and Research in the Chemical Industry', *Weekly Bulletin of the Kredietbank*, 27th October 1972.
11   Deboeuf, *De Aardrijkskunde*, 60 (1964), 7.
12   A useful summary of the industry is given in Kredietbank, *The Belgian Chemical Industry*, Part I, (1969).
13   'New Initiatives in the Plastics Materials Sector', *Weekly Bulletin of the Kredietbank*, 21st March 1969.
14   Evalenko, *Régime Economique de la Belgique,* (1968), 369-74.
15   Delwaide, 'L'Axe Liège-Anvers', *Revue de la Société d'Etudes et d'Expansion*, 228 (1967), 759.
16   Wever, *Tijdschrift voor Economische en Sociale Geografie*, 65 (1974), 8.

17 'The Petrochemical Industry in Belgium', *Belgium, Economy and Technique, 25 (1971), I-XIV.*
18 'The Belgian Pharmaceutical Industry', *Weekly Bulletin of the Kredietbank*, 2nd April 1966.
19 Vlassenbroeck, *De Aardrijkskunde*, 87 (1970), 255-63.
20 Kredietbank, *L'Industrie Textile II, Les Fibres Artificielles et Divers Secteurs*, (1967), 11-12.
21 Vlassenbroeck, *Wetenschappelijke Tijdingen*, 29 (1970), 175-181.
22 Institut National de Statistique, *Statistiques Industrielles*, no 10 (1972).
23 Olyslager, (1947), 34.
24 Ibid, 161.
25 *Weekly Bulletin of the Kredietbank*, 30th May 1969.

CHAPTER 5

The Brussels-Antwerp Axial Belt   pages 114-130

1 Institut National de Statistique, *Bulletin de Statistique*, no 1 (1971).
2 Institut National de Statistique, *Bulletin de Statistique*, no 5 (1973).
3 Ministère des Affaires Economiques et de l'Energie, *Rapport 1970, 1971, 1972*, (1971-3).
4 Malevez, *Bulletin de la Société Géographique de Liège*, 8 (1972), 88.
5 Dereyer, *Revue du Conseil Economique Wallon*, 42 (1960), 33-4.
6 'Investing in Building Land', *Weekly Bulletin of the Kredietbank*, Brussels, 22nd February 1974.
7 Bauwin and Annaert, *La Géographie*, 97 (1973), 127.
8 Kredietbank, *Antwerp as a Growth Pole*, (1971), 90.
9 Fabrimetal, Brussels (1971).
10 Riley, *European Studies*, 14 (1972), 1-4.
11 'The Aircraft Industry in Belgium', *Weekly Bulletin of the Kredietbank*, 2nd March 1968.
12 Linarde de Guertechin, *Bulletin de la Société Géographique de Liège*, 7 (1971), 118.
13 Moerman, (1973), 55-8.
14 Vlassenbroeck, *Wetenschappelijke Tijdingen*, 29 (1970) 186.
15 City of Antwerp, (1973).
16 Op De Beeck, *Hommes et Terres du Nord* (1971), 23, 25.
17 Vlassenbroeck, *De Aardrijkskunde*, 81 (1969), 98.

18 Vlassenbroeck, *De Aardrijkskunde*, 80 (1969), 5-22.
19 Berman, *Annals of the Association of American Geographers*, 61 (1971), 322.
20 Vlassenbroeck, *De Aardrijkskunde*, 88 (1971), 29-34.

CHAPTER 6

The Brussels and Antwerp Industrial Regions pages 131-144

1 Gourou, *Bulletin de la Société Royale Belge de Géographie*, 82 (1958), 12.
2 Bauwin and Annaert, *La Géographie*, 97 (1973), 113-27.
3 Ministère des Affaires Economiques, *Recensement de l'Industrie et du Commerce 13-12-1961*, 3, (1967).
4 Rooryck, *Revue de la Société d'Etudes et d'Expansion*, 225 (1967), 193.
5 Bauwin and Annaert, op cit, 120-1.
6 Baeyens, Mens en Ruimte, (1969), 23.
7 Dupon, *Bulletin de la Société Royale Géographique d'Anvers*, 68 (1956), 60-142.
8 Alexandersson and Norstrom, (1963), 169.
9 Op De Beeck, (1971), 16.
10 Kredietbank, (1971), 28.
11 Meganck, *Economische en Sociale Tijdschrift van Antwerpen*, 19 (1965), 25-6.
12 Verhasselt, *Bulletin de la Société Royale Belge de Géographie*, 84 (1960), 32-5.
13 Chardonnet (1959), 80-1, 89-95. This is a useful, if dated, account of the port industries.
14 Van Buynder, *Economisch en Sociaal Tijdschrift*, 25 (1971), 21-8.

CHAPTER 7

Flanders: Oost- and West-Vlaanderen and Limburg pages 145-162

1 Vanneste, *Tijdschrift voor Economische en Sociale Geografie*, 54 (1963), 90-1.
2 de Vries, *Tijdschrift voor Economische en Sociale Geografie*, 55 (1964), 165.
3 Monkhouse, (1949), 146.
4 Ibid., 149.
5 Bekaert, *Economisch en Sociaal Tijdschrift*, 6 (1952), 14.
6 Dereyer, *Revue du Conseil Economique Wallon*, 42 (1960), 28-9.

7 'Investing in Building Land', *Weekly Bulletin of the Kredietbank*, 22nd February 1974.

8 Mérenne-Schoumaker, *La Geographie*, 96 (1973), 87.
Liekens and Goossens, *Bulletin de la Société Belge d'Etudes Géographiques*, 38 (1969), 320.

9 Ibid, 323.

10 Battesti, *Information Géographique*, 30 (1966), 218-221.

11 Ruiters, *Tijdschrift voor Economische en Sociale Geografie*, 53 (1962), 151.

12 Clout, *Geography*, 59 (1974), 147.

13 'West-Flanders: A Promising Investment Area', *Weekly Bulletin of the Kredietbank*, Brussels, 25th April 1969.

14 Vlassenbroeck, *Wetenschappelijke Tijdingen*, 30 (1971) 266.

15 'Recente Ontwikkeling van de Tewerkstelling in de Limburgse Bedrijven', *Economie in Limburg* (1974).

16 Mérenne-Schoumaker, op cit, 95.

17 Vlassenbroeck, *De Aardrijkskunde*, 72 (1967), 20.

18 Mérenne-Schoumaker, op cit, 91.

19 Liekens and Goossens, op cit, 320.

20 Mérenne-Schoumaker, op cit, 85, 97.

21 Mérenne-Schoumaker, *Bulletin de la Société Géographique de Liège*, 8 (1972), 73.

22 Vlassenbroeck and Regniers, (1968), 13.

23 Ibid, 14-17.

24 Vlassenbroeck, *Wetenschappelijke Tijdingen*, 31 (1972), 5.

25 Verburg, *Tijdschrift voor Economische en Sociale Geografie*, 55 (1964), 145.

26 Anselin, in R. Regul (Ed) (1971), 308-10.

27 Vlassenbroeck, (1972), op cit, 9.

28 De Smet, *De Aardrijkskunde* (1964), 99-102.

29 Bremer, *Geografische Tijdschrift*, 4 (1970), 51.

30 Odell, *Petroleum Times*, 6th April 1973.

CHAPTER 8

The Coalfield Provinces: Hainaut, Namur and Liège pages 163-177

1 A recent general survey of the region may be found in 'Economic Problems in Belgium's Wallonia', *European Studies*, 11 (1971), 1-4.

2 Office National de l'Emploi, *Rapport Annuel 1972*, Brussels (1973).

3   Institut National de Statistique, *Bulletin de Statistique*, No 5 (1973).
4   *Bulletin Economique du Hainaut*, no 8 (1970), 26.
5   Ministère des Affaires Economiques, *Rapport 1970*, Brussels (1971).
6   Ministère des Affaires Economiques et de l'Energie, *Rapport 1973*, Brussels (1974).
7   Debehault, *Revue Belge de Géographie*, 92 (1968), 9-60.
8   *Bulletin Economique du Hainaut*, no 4 (1969).
9   *Annales des Mines de Belgique*, various years.
10 Nols, *Revue du Conseil Economique Wallon*, no 72-3 (1965), 2-4.
11 van Hecke, (1972).
12 André, *Conseil Economique de la Province de Liège*, 22 April 1972, 62.
13 Pertinax, *Revue du Conseil Economique Wallon*, no 92-3 (1969), 41.
14 Sporck, *Information Géographique*, 34 (1970), 64-8.
15 Riley, *Geography*, 50 (1965), 261.
16 Gordon, *European Community* (September 1973), 21.
17 Thiernesse, (1967), 15.
18 Cavallo, *Revue de Géographie de Lyon*, 43 (1968), 138-9.
19 Data from Intercommunale de Développement Economique et d'Aménagement du Territoire du Hainaut Occidental (SIDEHO), Tournai (1974).
20 Celeghin, *Bulletin de la Société Belge d'Etudes Géographiques*, 33 (1964), 136.
21 La Revue Géographique Industrielle de France, *La Province de Namur*, Paris (1972), 76.
22 Romus, (1958), 260.
23 Sporck, (1957), 62.
24 Mérenne-Schoumaker, *La Géographie*, 96 (1972), 264-6.
25 Mérenne-Schoumaker, *La Géographie*, 91 (1971), 226.
26 Useful accounts of the region may be found in Paul Mingret, 'Quelques Problèmes de l'Europe à Travers l'Example de Liège et sa Règion, *Revue de Géographie de Lyon*, 37 (1962), 5-74 and in T.H. Elkins, 'Liège and the Problems of Southern Belgium', *Geography*, 41 (1956), 83-98.

Conclusion   pages 178-179

1   Tanghe, *Town and Country Planning*, 42 (1974), 277.

Bibliography

Alexandersson, G. and G. Norstom *World Shipping*, (1963).

André, Jules. 'Réflexions pour une Programmation des Infrastructures Régionales dans l'Espace et dans le Temps', *Conseil Economique de la Province de Liège, Actes de la Journée Economique et Sociale*, Liège (22nd April 1972), 57-65.

Anselin, M. 'La Fonction des Ports de Belgique et les Projets d'Investissements', in R. Regul (Ed), *The Future of European Ports*, Bruges (1971), 218-312.

Atlas de Belgique, Comité National de Géographie, Brussels (1950-1972).

Banque de Bruxelles, *Belgium, Land of Investment*, Brussels (1972), 14-21.

Baeyens, H. *La Maîtrise de la Croissance Urbaine.* Brussels (1969), 23.

Battesti, L.M. 'Une Main d'Oeuvre Temporaire en Voie de Disparition. Les Travailleurs Saisonniers Belges', *Information Géographique*, 30 (1966), 218-223.

Bauwin, E. and J. Annaert, 'La Région Industrielle Bruxelloise', *La Géographie*, 97 (1973), 113-27.

Beekers, G. *Etude Géographique de l'Industrie Textile en Région Verviétoise.* Mèmoire de Licence, Université de Liège, (1972) 134-8.

Bekaert, C.A. 'Industrialisatie in West-Vlaanderen', *Economisch en Sociaal Tijdschrift*, 6 (1952), 14-29.

Berman, M. 'The Location of the Diamond-Cutting Industry', *Annals of the Association of American Geographers*, 61 (1971), 316-28.

Bremer, J.T. 'Zeehavenproblemen in België', *Geografische Tijdschrift*, 4 (1970), 50-2.

Cavallo, Marie-Claude, 'La Vie Industrielle en Tournaisis', *Revue de Géographie de Lyon*, 43 (1968), 133-78.

Celeghin, Henri. 'Contribution à la Géographie Industrielle de la Basse-Sambre', *Bulletin de la Société Belge d'Etudes Géographiques*, 33 (1964), 125-66.

Chardonnet, Jean, *Métropoles Economiques*, Paris (1959), 80-1, 89-95.

Christians, C. 'Le Problème de l'Eau et la Liaison Escaut-Rhin', *Hommes et Terres du Nord*, (1969), 96-107.

City of Antwerp, *The Establishment of Industries in the Antwerp Port Zone*, Antwerp (1973).

Clout, H.D. 'Economic Change in Belgian Limburg', *Geography*, 59 (1974), 145-7.

Cole, J.P. and C.A.M. King, *Quantitative Geography*, Wiley (1968).

Comhaire, J.J. 'Grands Traits de la Structure de l'Industrie Sidérurgique Belge', *Tijdschrift voor Economische en Sociale Geografie*, 46 (1955), 124-30.

Coppé, Albert. *Problèmes d'Economie Charbonnière*, Bruges (1940).

Debehault, Claude. 'Les Terrils de Charbonnage du Borinage. Etude de Géographie Régionale', *Revue Belge de Géographie*, 92 (1968), 9-60.

Deboeuf, L. 'De Lokalisatie van de Stikstofnijverheid in Belgë', *De Aardrijkskunde*, 60 (1964), 7-22.

Dechesne, L. *Histoire Economique et Sociale de la Belgique*, Liège (1932).

Delwaide, L. 'L'Axe Liège-Anvers', *Revue de la Société d'Etudes et d'Expansion*, 228 (1967), 755-70.

Dereyer, A. 'La Contribution des Villes Flamandes à l'Expansion Economique', *Revue du Conseil Economique Wallon*, 42 (1960), 26-37.

De Smet, L. 'Economische Structuur en Ontwikkeling van de Stad Deinze', *Natuurwetenschappelijk Tijdschrift*, 41 (1959), 74-80.

    De Lokalisering der Nijverheid in West-Vlaanderen', *De Aardrijkskunde* (1964), 93-103.

    'Steden van Zuid-Oostvlaanderen IV, Ronse', *Bulletin de la Société Belge d'Etudes Géographiques*, 21 (1952) 126-31.

De Smet, L. Keiris, H. and W. Vlassenbroeck, *Belgiё, Luxemburg*, Roermond (1971).

De Vries, N.P.J. 'The Benelux Central Region', *Tijdschrift voor Economische en Sociale Geografie*, 55 (1964), 164-171.

Doyen, P. 'La Vallée Industrielle du Hoyoux', *Bulletin de la Société Royale Belge de Géographie*, 79 (1959), 24-33.

Duby, H. 'Court St. Etienne. Noyau Industriel en Milieu Agricole', *Bulletin de la Société Royale Belge de Géographie*, 79 (1955) III-IV, 37-54.

Dupon, E. 'L'Activité Industrielle dans la Région Anversoise', *Bulletin de la Société Royale Géographique d'Anvers*, 68 (1956), 60-142.

Elkins, T.H. 'Liège and the Problems of Southern Belgium', *Geography*, 41 (1956), 83-98.

European Coal and Steel Community High Authority, *Ninth General Report on the Activities of the Community*, Luxemburg (1961).

Evalenko, R. *Régime Economique de la Belgique*, Brussels, (1968).

Fabrimental, *Belgian Shipyards Building and Repairing Seagoing Vessels*, Brussels (1971).

Gay, Francois and Paul Wagret, *Le Benelux*, 4th edition, Paris (1970).

Gordon, Gavin, 'And Dark and Light in the Borinage', *European Community* (September 1973), 21.

Gourou, P. 'L'Agglomération Bruxelloise', *Bulletin de la Société Royale Belge de Géographie*, 82 (1958), 1-83.

Institut National de Statistique, *Bulletin de Statistique*, various issues.
    Recensement de l'Industrie et du Commerce 13-12-1961, 3 Brussels (1967).
    Statistiques Demographiques, No 1 (1973).
    Statistiques Industrielles, various issued.

International Labour Office, *Yearbook of Labour Statistics*, Geneva (1954, 1972).

Kaisin, A. 'Le Montage en Belgique des Véhicules de Transport de Personnes' *Revue Universelle des Mines*, 13 (1957), 420-9.

Kredietbank, *Antwerp as a Growth Pole*, Brussels (1971).
    Bibliothèque d'Economie d'Enpreprise, *L'Industrie Textile I*, Brussels (1966).
    The Belgian Chemical Industry, Part I, The Inorganic Chemical Products, Brussels (1969).

Lefournier, P. 'La Belgique s'est bien Vendue', *L'Expansion*, (May 1971) 116-23.

Liekens, R. and M. Goossens, 'De Vestigingsfactoren bij de Huidige Industrialisatiefase in Mideen-Limburg', *Bulletin de la Société Belge d'Etudes Géographiques*, 38 (1969), 317-45.

Linarde de Guertechin, Th. 'La Localisation des Firmes Américaines dans le Centre des Affaires de Bruxelles', *Bulletin de la Société Géographique de Liège*, 7 (1971), 109-25.

Lyon, Margot. *Belgium*, (1971).

Malburny, P. 'Considérations sur la Localisation des Industries dans la

Région de Liège', *Bulletin de la Société Belge d'Etudes Géographiques*, 20 (1951), 253-65.

Malevez, N. 'Les Industries Manufacturières de la Ville de Malines', *Bulletin de la Société Géographique de Liège*, 8 (1972), 81-93.

Mallinson, Vernon, *Belgium*, Benn (1970).

Mangelinckx, R. 'Clabecq et sa Sidérurgie', *Revue Belge de Géographie*, 87 (1963), 259-344.

Meganck, J. 'Industriële Concentratie en Deconcentratie in het Antwerpse', *Economische en Sociale Tijdschrift van Antwerpen*, 19 (1965) 31-34.

Melkin, H. 'L'Eau, Richesse Régionale et le Facteur de Développement', Conseil Economique de la Province de Liège, *Actes de la Journée Economique et Sociale*, Liège (22 April 1972), 68-84.

Mérenne, E. 'La Géographie Appliquée au Service des Chemins de Fer', *Colloque International de Géographie Appliquée*, Université de Liège (1968), 209-20.

Mérenne-Schoumaker, B. 'Aspects Industriels et Commerciaux Nouveaux du Moyen-Limbourg', *La Géographie*, 96 (1973) 83-99.

'L'Evolution Economique de la Province de Liège depuis 1960', *La Géographie*, 91 (1971) 215-34.

'Récession Charbonnière et Modifications de l'Aire de Recrutement de la Main d'Oeuvre des Charbonnages Campinois', *Bulletin de la Société Géographique de Liège*, 8 (1972), 73.

'La Région Liégeoise', *La Géographie*, 95 (1972) 257-72.

Michotte, P.L. 'L'Industrie Belge du Charbon', *Annales de Géographie* (1929), 47-66.

'L'Industrie à Domicile en Belgique', *Bulletin de la Société Belge d'Etudes Géographiques*, 8 (1938) 59-82.

Mingret, Paul. 'Les Investissements Américains en Belgique', *Revue de Géographie de Lyon*, 45 (1970), 243-78.

'Quelques Problèmes de l'Europe à Travers l'Example de Liège et de sa Région', *Revue de Géographie de Lyon*, 37 (1962), 5-74.

Ministère des Affaires Economiques, *Investissements Etrangers en Belgique, Rapport*. Various years.

Moerman, Rita. *De Belgische Verf en Vernisnijverheid*, Undergraduate Dissertation, Rijksuniversiteit Gent (1973), 55-8.

Mols, R.P. 'Où en est la Population Belge?', *Population*, 27 (1972), 985-999.

Monkhouse, F.J. *The Belgian Kempenland*, Liverpool (1949), 146.

Nadasdi, I. 'Carte de Potentiel de Population de la Belgique', *Bulletin de la Société d'Etudes Géographiques*, 40 (1971), 237-46.

Nols, Emile. 'La Reconversion des Régions Minières de Wallonie', *Revue du Conseil Economique Wallon,* no 72-3 (1965), 1-15.

Odell, P.R. 'Import Terminals and the Fundamentals of Western Europe's Future Oil Supplies', *Petroleum Times,* 6th April 1973, 29-31.

Office National de l'Emploi, *Rapport Annuel 1972,* Brussels (1973).

Office National de Sécurité Sociale, *Rapport Annuel,* various years, Bruxelles.

Olyslager, P.M. *De Localiseering der Belgische Nijverheid,* Standaard, Antwerp (1947).

Op De Beeck, R. 'L'Industrie du Port d'Anvers', *Hommes et Terres du Nord,* (1971), 5-37.

Organisation for Economic Cooperation and Development, Economic Surveys, *BLEU,* Paris (June 1972), 38.

  Manpower in Belgium, Paris (1971).

Pertinax, 'Où en est la Reconversion de l'Industrie Wallonne?', *Revue du Conseil Economique Wallon,* no 92-3 (1969), 23-58.

Pounds, N.J.G. and W.N. Parker, *Coal and Steel in Western Europe,* (1957).

La Revue Géographique Industrielle de France, *La Province de Namur,* (1972), 76.

Riley, R.C. 'Changes in the Supply of Coking Coal in Belgium since 1945', *Economic Geography,* 43 (1967), 261-70.

  'Commercial Shipbuilding in Western Europe', *European Studies,* 14 (1972), 1-4.

  Industrial Geography, (1973).

  'Recent Developments in the Belgian Borinage', *Geography,* 228 (1965), 261-73.

Riley, R.C. and G.J. Ashworth, *Benelux. An Economic Geography of Belgium, The Netherlands and Luxemburg,* (1971).

Romus, Paul, *Expansion Economique Régionale et Communauté Européenne,* Leyde (1958), 260.

Rooryck, R. 'Le Complexe Portuaire de Bruxelles', *Revue de la Société d'Etudes et d'Expansion,* 225 (1967), 191-8.

Rostow, W.W. 'The Take-off into Self-Sustained Growth', *Economic Journal,* 66 (1956), 25-48.

Ruiters, J. 'De Industrialisatie in Belgisch Limburg', *Tijdschrift voor Economische en Sociale Geographie,* 53 (1962), 149-55.

Sevrin, Robert and Pierre George, *Belgique, Pays-Bas, Luxembourg,* Paris (1967).

Sheaf, Robert, 'Multi-national Companies and the European Community', *European Community*, (January/February 1974), 16-19.

Sporck, J.A. *'L'Activité Industrielle dans la Région Liégeoise*, Liège (1957), 62.
    'La Reconversion Economique des Régions Industrielles Wallonnes', *Information Géographique* (1970) 57-70.
    'Le Rôle de l'Eau dans la Localisation de l'Industrie Verviétoise', *Bulletin de la Société Belge d'Etudes Géographiques*, 17 (1948), 154-72.

Stephenson, G.V. 'Cultural Regionalism and the Unitary State Idea in Belgium', *Geographical Review*, 62 (1972), 501-23.

Tanghe, Jan. 'Planning in Belgium', *Town and Country Planning*, 42 (1974).

Thiernesse, L. 'Problèmes de Reconversion et d'Aménagement de la Région Boraine', *Hommes et Terres du Nord* (1967), 10-25.

Tilmont, J. and M. De Roeck, *La Belgique et le Congo*, Namur (1968).

Van Buynder, E. 'Industrialisatiebeleid in de Provincie Antwerpen', *Economisch en Sociaal Tijdschrift*, 25 (1971), 21-8.

Van der Haegen, H. 'De Nieuwe Administratieve Indeling in Ingevolge de Recente Taalwetten', *Bulletin de .la Société Belge d'Etudes Géographiques*, 33 (1964) 175-8.

Vanex, F. 'La Localisation Géographique des Industries Textiles en Belgique', *Bulletin de la Société Royale de Géographie d'Anvers*, 53 (1933) 255-70.

Van Hecke, Etienne, 'Communes, Fusions, Féderations, Intercommunales', *Industrie* (1972) 2-18.

Vanneste, O. 'Problemen en Perspectieven Voortspruitend uit de Grensligging van een Belgische Streek', *Tijdschrift voor Economische en Sociale Geografie*, 54 (1963), 90-1.

Verburg, M.C. 'The Gent-Terneuzen Developmental Axis in the Perspective of the EEC', *Tijdschrift voor Economische en Sociale Geografie*, 55 (1964), 143-50.

Verhasselt, Y. 'Le Rôle de l'Escaut dans la Géographie Humaine de ses Rives, entre Termonde et Anvers', *Bulletin de la Société Royale Belge de Géographie*, 84 (1960), 7-46.

Vinck, F. 'Methods of Reconversion Policy in the Framework of the ECSC', *Tijdschrift voor Economische en Sociale Geografie*, 60 (1969), 3-11.

Vlassenbroeck, W. 'De Belgische Cementnijverheid', *Geografisch Tijdschrift*, 6 (1972), 461-8.

'De Belgische Juwelennijverheid', *De Aardrijkskunde*, 88 (1971), 29-34.

'De Belgische Lucifernijverheid', *De Aardrijkskunde*, 94 (1972) 167-72.

'De Belgische Tabakverwerkende Nijverheid. Huidige Struktuur en Lokalisatie', *De Aardrijkskunde*, 80 (1969), 5-22.

'Excursiegids Doorheen Zandig-Vlaanderen, Het Brugse, De Oostkust en de Zeepolders', *De Aardrijkskunde*, 72 (1967), 5-44.

'De Huidige Sociaal-Ekonomische Toestand in Oostvlaanderen', *Wetenschappelijke Tijdingen*, 30 (1971) 258-67.

'De Invloed van Sidmar en Texaco op het Maritiem Goederenvervoer te Gent en te Zeebrugge', *Geografisch Tijdschrift*, (1973), 300-303.

'Lokalisatie en Enkele Strukturele Kenmerken van de Belgische Geneesmiddelennijverheid', *De Aardrijkskunde*, 87 (1970), 255-63.

'De Ruimtelijke Standplaatsverklaring van de Oost-en Westvlaamse Fabrieksnijverheid', *Wetenschappelijke Tijdingen*, 31 (1972), 3-15.

'Sidmar—Le Plus Jeune des Complexes Sidérurgiques Maritimes en Europe Occidentale', *Hommes et Terres du Nord*, (1969), 87-88.

'Spreiding en Enkele Strukturele Kenmerken van een Tweetal Belgische Industrietakken', *Wetenschappelijke Tijdingen*, 29 (1970), 175-181.

De Standplaats van Fabrieksnijverheid. *Theorie en Praktijk met Toepassing op Oost-en West-Vlaanderen*, Doctoral Dissertation, Rijksuniversiteit Gent (1972), 395.

'Het Voorkomen van de Belgische Suikernijverheid', *De Aardrijkskunde*, 81 (1969), 95-110.

Vlassenbroeck W. and L. De Smet, 'De Lokaliseering der Brouwerijen en Aanverwante Bedrijven in België', *De Aardrijkskunde*, 77 (1968) 75-91.

Vlassenbroeck, W. and M. Regniers, *Het Gentse Stadsgewest, De Kanaalzone Gent-Terneuzen*, Seminaries voor Menselijke, Ekonomische en Historische Geografie, Rijksuniversiteit Gent (1968), 13.

Warntz, W. 'A New Map of the Surface of Population Potentials for the United States, 1960', *Geographical Review*, 54 (1964), 170-184.

Wever, E. 'Seaports and Physical Planning in the Netherlands. Some Comments on Policy Considerations Relating to Industrial Activities in Seaports', *Tijdschrift voor Economische en Sociale Geografie*, 65 (1974), 4-12.

Yates, M.H. *An Introduction of Quantitative Analysis in Economic Geography*, (1968), 90-2.

OTHER PUBLICATIONS (JOURNALS)

De Aardrijkskunde/La Géographie
Bulletin Economique du Hainaut
Bulletin de la Société Belge d'Etudes Géographiques
Bulletin de la Société Géographique de Liège
Economie in Limburg
Oost-Vlaanderen Groeit
Revue Belge de Géographie, until 1961 known as *Bulletin de la Société Royale Belge de Géographie*
Revue du Conseil Economique Wallon
Revue de la Société d'Etudes et d'Expansion
Tijdschrift van het Koninklijk Aardrijkskundig Genootschap van Antwerpen
Weekly Bulletin of the Kredietbank
West-Vlaanderen Werkt
Wetenschappelijke Tijdingen

Unsigned articles on specific topics in these publications may be located by consulting the Notes and References.

Acknowledgements

IN ATTEMPTING TO write about a country without being resident there, one is obliged to rely heavily on the willingness of a great many people and institutions to forward data of one sort or another. I have been fortunate enough to receive invaluable assistance from regional and provincial development associations, the administrations of the ports of Antwerp, Ghent and Zeebrugge, the Ministry of Economic Affairs, the Belgian Foreign Trade Office in Brussels, the Belgian Embassy in London and the Kredietbank in Brussels. Without their help it would have been quite impossible to have tried to present a reasonably up to date survey of industrial activity in Belgium. I have also benefited greatly from the advice and expert assistance of Professor J.A. Sporck and Dr B. Mérenne-Schoumaker at the University of Liège and Professor L. De Smet, Etienne Van Hecke and Dr W. Vlassenbroeck at the University of Ghent. Their writings have been a constant source of stimulus; in this respect I would like to acknowledge a particular debt to Dr Vlassenbroek from whose productive pen have come so many papers of especial relevance. I have learnt much from my colleagues Gregory Ashworth, David Burtenshaw and Jean-Louis Smith at Portsmouth Polytechnic, and I have watched in admiration the creation of meticulously accurate and aesthetically very pleasing maps on Gill Brady's drawing board in the Polytechnic's Cartographic Unit. I would like to record my gratitude to Portsmouth Polytechnic for financial support which enabled me to spend some time in Belgium, and to my wife Betty for her critical comments, help with phraseology, unflagging encouragement and the preparation of several thousand cups of coffee.

196

Index

Figures in italics refer to a map on the specified page.

A

Aachen 21, 65, 149
Aalst 28, 51, 63, 67, 69–70, *85*, 98, 109, 136, *148*, 155–6
Aalter 150
Aartselaar 136, *137*, 143
Abonnements scolaires 23
Abonnements sociaux 23
Aircraft production 32, 101, 124
Albatros 105, 126, *138*, 144
Albert Canal 11, 24, 33, *59*, *117*, *138*, 142, *176*
Alken *85*
Alleur 167, 175, *176*
Alsace 103
Alsemberg *96*
Aluminium, secondary 81
Amay *80*, 81
Amblève 62, 65
American investment 44, 104
Amsterdam 21, 129
Andenne 7, 9, 47, *59*, 113
Anderlecht 94, *96*, 98, *132*, 133–5
Antoing 173
Antwerp 5, 11–12, *13*, 14–17, 20–1, *22*, 23, *24*, 26, 36–7, 41, 43–4, *48*, 50–1, *52*, *53*, 54, 72, 79–80, 87, 92, 94–5, *96*, 99, *100*, 102–3, *104*, 105–6, 108, 113–6, *117*, 118–30, 136, *137*, *138*, 139–44, 150, 179
Antwerp docks 24, 26, 36, 93, 96, 103, 106–7, 120, 122, 125–6, 127, *137*, *138*, 139–42
Antwerp industrial region 136–44
Antwerp-Turnhout Canal 79
Antwerpen 10–11, 13–15, 17, *18*, 35–7, 40–1, 43–7, 51, 82, 92, 102, 108, 110, 114–6, *117*, 118–30
ARBED *see* Steel firms
Ardennes 2–5, 7, 9–10, 12, *18*, 20–3, 27, 62, 65, 70, 73, 77, 86, 110
Ardennes flamandes *18*
Arendonk 69, 127
Arlon 22, 71
Armco-Pittsburgh *see* Steel firms
Armourers 27, 70
Art et précision 129–30
Ateliers de Construction Electrique
de Charleroi (ACEC) 32, 93, 101, 134, 158, 177
Ath 28, 41, 51, 69, 102, *166*, 172–3
Athus 8, 22, 62, 71–2, *73*, 76
Auderghem *132*, 135
Auvelais 173

B

Balen 32, 79, *80*, 103, 128
Banque de Belgique 27
Base metals 127–8, 157, 160, 172–3
BASF 103, 107, 125, 126, *138*
Bastogne 5
Battice *100*, 109
Baudour 9, 82, *100*, 173
Bauwens, Lieven 68
Bayer 103, 107, 126, *138*
Beerse *80*, 103, 108, 125, 128
Bekaert, NV 76, 157, 160
Belgian Lorraine 10, 17, 22, 62
Belgochim 107
Bell 101, 122, 143, 158, 172
Belpaire 28
Benelux 152
Berchem (Brussels) *132*
Berchem (Antwerp) *137*
Beringen 8
Berlaar 129, 136, *137*
Beveren *96*, 97
Binche 29, 88, 174
Birmingham 29
Bishopric of Liège 27
Bocholt-Herentals Canal 147, 149
Boechout 72, 77, 136, *137*, 144
Bond Beter Leefmilieu—Inter-Environnement 179
Boom 9, 82, *137*, 144
Borgerhout 51, 130, *137*, 142
Borinage 9, 10, 17, 28, 31, 47, 49, 57, 58, *59*, 60, 73, 82, 101, 167–8, 170–1, 174
Botrange 3
Boudewijnkanaal *161*
Bouffioulx 82
Brabançon plateau 2
Brabant 10, 12, 13–15, 32, 34–7, 41, 43, 46, 51, 63, 86, 92, 102, 108, 110, 114–6, *117*, 118–30, 144

197

Braine l'Alleud 105, 131, 135
Brasschaat *137*
Bredene 12
Bree *96*, 97
Bremen 75
Brewing 55, 84, *85*, 86–7, 127
Brick-making 9, 82, 129, 144, 160
British Leyland 95, 97–8, 122
Bruges *13*, 14–17, *22*, *24*, 27, 29,
  46–7, *48*, *52*, 53, 62, 82, *85*, 92, *96*,
  97–8, *100*, 139, 146, 147, *148*, 150,
  154–5, 160, *161*, 162
Brussels 1, 2, 10–12, *13*, 14–17, *18*,
  19–21, *22*, 23, *24*, 32, 37, 41, 43–4,
  48, 50, *52*, *53*, 54, 66–7, 69, 82, 84,
  85, 87–8, 91, 94–5, *96*, 101–2,
  106–7, 108, 110, 112–6, *117*, 118–
  30, 131, *132*, 133–6, 172
Brussels-Antwerp axis 43, 51, 53, 91,
  95, 100, 102, 114–30, 178–9
Brussels-Charleroi Canal 59
Brussels industrial region 131–6
Brussels National Airport 20, 135
Brussels-Rupel Canal 23, 32
Brusselse Intercommunale Water-
  maatschappij 10
Buizingen *132*, 134
Burcht *137*
Bus & Car Co. 95, 97–8, 162

C

Carbochemical industry 28
Carboniferous series 8
Carpets 67, 70, 160
Cement 9, 93, 173
Centre 47, 49, 58, *59*, 60, 73, 167,
  170, 174
Ceramics 55, 82–4
Chalk 9
Channel Islands 12
Charbonnages du Borinage 58
Charleroi 7–9, *13*, 14–17, 21, *22*, 23,
  24, 28, 30–1, *48*, 49, 51, *52*, 53, 57,
  59, 70–8, 82–4, *85*, 92, 95, *100*, 101,
  111, 163, 165, *166*, 170, 172–4, 177
Charleroi industrial region 177
Châtelet *59*, 84
Chemicals 41, 101–9, 124–6, 149, 174
Chertal 74, 76, 171, 175, *176*
Chevron 44, 106–7, *138*, 177
Chooz 62
Chrysler 94, 96, *138*, 139
Cigar and cigarette manufacture 69,
  127
Citroën 33, 94, 97, 124, 134
Clabecq 71–2, *73*, 77, 78, 121, 128,
  132, 134–5
Claeys-Flandria 98, 149, 155

Clothing manufacture 29, 55, 87–8,
  89, 128, 133, 155–6, 173–5
Coal 6, 21, 26
Coalmining 7–8, 15, 16, 28, 31, 33,
  34, 50, 55, 56–8, *59*, 60–2, 145,
  156–7, *166*, 170–1, 174, *176*
Cockerill *see* Steel arms
Cockerill, John 27–8, 65, 93
Cockerill, William 65
Coefficient of specialisation 121
Coking coal 73, 74
Coking plants 32, 103
Colleye de Sarolay, Jeanne-Etienne 27
Comité de Concertation de la
  Politique Sidérurgique (CCPS) 76
Commuting 23, 47, 147, 151–2, 165,
  167
Condroz 3, 9, 10
Conseil Economique Wallon 46–7
Coo 62
Cotton 68–9
Couillet *73*, 103, 177
Court St. Etienne 71–2, 77, 121, 128
Cycles and motor cycles 30, 98, 155

D

Dampremy 74
De Chardonnet, Hilaire 109
Deerlijk 157, 160
Deinze 70
Demer, river *3*, *59*
Dender, river 2, *3*, 28–30, 67
Dendermonde 63, 67, 92, *148*, 156
Dessel 127
Deurne 32, 130, *137*, 142
Development areas 47, *48*, 91, 118
De Voerstreek *18*, 19
Diamonds 129–30
Diegem 124, 131, *132*, 135
Diest *59*, *117*
Dijle, river *see* Dyle, river
Diksmuide 51, *148*, 149–50
Dinant *166*
Doel 62, 140
Dony, J. D. 27, 79
Dour 172
Drogenbos 105, *132*
Duffel 9, 81, 110, 136, *137*, 144
Dumping 31
Dunkirk 17, 75
Durme, river 2
Dutch delta region 11, 17
Dyle, river 2, *3*

E

Ecaussinnes 9
Economische Raad voor Vlaanderen
  47

ECSC *see* European Coal and Steel Community
Edegem 17, 137
EEC *see* European Economic Community
Eeklo 51, 66, 68, *148*, 156
Ehein 79, *80*
Eiffel mountains 2
Eisden 156
Ekeren *137*
Elastic web manufacture 70
Electric power 6, 58, 62, 93, 144
Electronic products 90, 98-9, *100*, 101, 122, 175
Empain, Baron 93
Employment 33-5
Energy consumption 61-2
Enghien *18*
Engineering 28, 41, 63, 66, 91-101, 121-4, 154-5, 172-3
Engineering, heavy 5, 124
Engineering, light 92-3
England 14
Englebert 28
Entre-Sambre-et-Meuse 3, 9
Erembodegem 150
Ertvelde 103-4
Escaut, river 26
Espérance-Longdoz *see* Steel firms
Esso 105-6, 135, *138*, 139
Ethylene pipeline *104*, 107
Etterbeek *132*
Eupen 1, 19
European Coal and Steel Community (ECSC) 50, 57-8, 60-1, 170, 172
European Economic Community (EEC) 1, 62, 66, 68, 75, 76, 87, 91, 95, 107, 119, 140, 150, 152
European Economic Community Commission 49-50, 51, 119
European Investment Bank 50, 119
European Regional Development Fund 50
Europoort 105, 126, *see also* Rotterdam
Evere 32, *132*, 135
External economies 29, 32, 72, 74, 77

F

Fabrique National d'Armes de Guerre (FN) 30, 93, 162, *176*
Faille du Midi 8
Feluy 44, *104*, 105-7, *166*, 167, 170, 174, 177
Fibreglass 109
Flanders 2, 10, 12, 13, 16-*18*, 28-9, 32, 34, 36, 39, 41-2, 44-6, 51, 53, 55, 62, 64-7, 70, 90, 92-3,
95, 98, 100, 110, 113, 139, 145-62, 178-9
Flax growing 67
Flémalle 76, 175
Flemings 16-20
Flône 80
Fontaine l'Evêque *73*
Food processing 41, 126-7, 142, 156
Ford 32, 90, 94-7, 122, *138*, 139, 154
Foreign investment 43-6, 167
Forest 97, 105, *132*, 133-4
Forest resources 9-10
Frameries 99, *100*, 172
France 1, 21, 26-7, 30, 64-5, 98, 104, 111, 147, 151
Franière 173
Franks 17-18
Friction of distance 6, 51, 119
Frontaliers 17, 46, 147, 151-2
Furniture manufacture 29, 118, 121, 129, 156, 160

G

Ganshoren 17, *132*
Gaurain-Ramecroix 173
Geel *100*, *104*, *117*, 122, 125, 127
Gembloux 9, 29, 174
General Motors 32, 94, 96, 122, *138*, 139, 140
Genk *59*, 72, 76, 77-8, 95, *96*, 97, *100*, *148*, 150-1, 154
Genval 111, *112*, 129
Germany 26-7, 29, 30, 65 *see also* West Germany
Ghent 5, 11, *13*, 14-15, 17, 21, *22*, 23, *24*, 27-8, 32, 37, 44, *48*, *52*, 53, 63, 67-8, 71, 79, *85*, 93, 95, *96*, *100*, 102, *104*, 105-6, 113, 145-6, *148*, 150, 155-9, 162, 179
Ghent industrial region 157-8, *159*
Ghlin 81, 83, 84, *85*, 86, *166*, 170, 172-3
Gileppe reservoir 65
Gileppe, river 12
Glass-making 28, 30, 32, 55, 82-4, 162, 173
Glass sand 9
Glaverbel 83, 93, *161*
Glove-making 29
Gosselies 93, *100*, 101, 172, 177
Grâce Hollogne 167, *176*
Grangemouth 107
Great Britain 7, 26, 28, 46, 65, 70 *see also* England
Grimbergen 124, *132*, 134
Grivegnée 74
Grobbendonk 130

Groot-Bijgaarden *96*, 97, 124, 131, *132*, 135
Groupe l'Equerre 49
Growth industries 40–3, 90–113
Growth industry model 91, 109, 110, 113
Gueuze 87
Gun manufacture 27, 29
Gustave Boël *see* Steel firms

H

Hainaut 10, 15–16, *18*, 32, 34–7, 41, 43–6, 51, 63, 69, 70–8, 82–3, 107, 145, 163–5, *166*, 167–74
Haine, river *3*, *59*
Haine-Sambre-Meuse coalfield 7, 8, 13, 19, 26, 28, 30, 33, 37, 39, 51, 56–8, *59*, 60–2, 71–2, 73–7, 82, 100, 163–77, 178–9
Halanzy 8, 72
Halen 113
Halle *117*, *132*, 133
Halle-Vilvoorde 12, *18*, 37, 41, *53*, 54–5, 88, 102, 110, 114–6, *117*, 118–30, 133, 136, *137*, 150
Hamme 70
Haren 97, 124
Harnoncourt 111, *112*
Hasselt 40, 55, *59*, 88, 92, *100*, 147, 148, 151, 154–6, 165
Hat production 29
Hautes Fagnes 3
Hautrage 9, 82, 173
Hauts Sarts *166*, 170, *176*
Havré 107
Helchteren-Zolder pits 60
Hemiksem 124, *137*, 143
Hemp manufacture 70
Hennuyer plateau 2
Henricot, Emile 78
Hensies 171
Heppignies 108, 177
Hercynian Massif 2
Herent *100*, 101
Herentals 99, *100*, 117–8, 127
Hermalle *166*, 177
Herstal 27, 29–30, 93, 175
Herstappe *18*
Herve *100*, 171
Herve plateau 2
Hesbaye 10, 167, 176
Hesbaye plateau 2
High Ardennes 3, 5
Hoboken *80*, 103, 122, *137*, 143–4
Hoboken-Overpelt *see* Métallurgie Hoboken-Overpelt
Honda 98
Hosiery and knitwear 69

Houdeng 103, 107, 173
Houthalen 33, 60, 109
Hoyoux, river 10
Huizingen 131, *132*
Huy 28, *53*, 54, *59*, 62, 71, 74, 76, 81, 110, *166*, 173
Hydro-electric power 11, 62

I

Ieper 15, 16, 51, 88, *148*, 149, 155
Ijmuiden 75
Ijzer, river *3*
Income 37–8
Industrial estates 47, 50, 86, 97, *117*, 124, *132*, 135, 144, *148*, 150, 160, 162, *166*, 167, 170–2, 176–7
Industrial revolution 5, 7, 26–30, 82, 145
Industrial 'swarm' 29, 70, 72, 111
Industries de grande ville 133
Intercommunales 47–8, 179
International through rate 58
Iron and steel 5, 45, 55, 57, 61, 70–2, *73*, 74–9, 121, 128
Iron ore 8, 21–2, 70–5, 78
Israel 130
Italy 65, 66
Ivoz-Ramet 62, 177
Ixelles 51, *132*

J

Jaspar 28
Jemeppe *73*, 76, *104*, 105, 107, 173–5
Jette *132*
Jewellery 130, 160
Jumet 177
Jupille 87
Jute 70

K

Kallo 141
Kapellen 136, *137*
Kapelle-op-den-Bos 136, *137*, 143
Kempen coalfield 7–8, 17, 33, 37, 56–7, 58, *59*, 60–62, 74, 83
Kempen plateau 2
Kempenland 9–10, 49, 53, 79, 80–1, 89, 101
Kempense Steenkolenmijnen 60, 93
Kempische Hoogvlakte 2
Kessenich 1
Koekelberg *132*, 133
Koningshooikt 95, *96*, 97, 122, *137*, 144
Kontich *96*, *137*, 143–4

Kortrijk 9, 14–16, 21, 28, *52*, 63, 66–70, 82, 88, 130, 145–6, *148*, 154, 156–7, 160
Kortrijk industrial region 160
Kuurne *100*
Kwaadmechelen 103–4

L

La Buissière 9
Lace-making 29, 30, 62
La Hulpe 111, *112*, 113, 129
La Louvière 9, 13, 28, 71, *73*, 75, 82, 167, 172–3
Lanaken 2, 109
Lanaye 106
Land values 119, 150
Langerbrugge 72, 77, 110, *112*, 157–8
Language problem 17–20, 46, 49, 106, 135, 179
Lanklaar *100*
LD steel 74, 78
Lee, William 69
Leie, river 1, 2, *3*, 28, 63, 67, *148*, 160
Lembeek 72, 77, 104, 113, *132*
Leopold II 93
Les Fourons *18*, 19
Lesse, river 3
Lessines 9, 29
Leuven 12, 14, *18*, *22*, 49, 51, 54, 82, *85*, 87, 89, *100*, 108, *117*, 119, 121, 126–7, 135–6
Leuze 29, 69
Libin 9
Libramont *100*
Liège 7–9, 11, *13*, 14–17, *18*, 19–21, *22*, 23, *24*, 27–8, 31–2, 34–41, 43–6, *48*, 49, 51, *52*, 53, 57, 59–60, 62–3, 65–66, 70–6, 78–81, *85*, 87, 92–3, 95–8, *100*, 101, *104*, 106, 110, 113, 149, 163–5, *166*, 167–75, *176*, 177
Liège industrial region 174–5, *176*, 177
Lier 136, *137*, 144
Lilachim 104
Lille 17, 147
Limburg 11, 13, 14, 17, *18*, 34–5, 37, 40–1, 43, 45, 46–7, 51, 88, 92, 97, 101, 145–7, *148*, 149–57, 167
Limestone 9
Limon 2
Linen 30, 67–8
Lixhe 1, 177
Lixhe-Lanaye *166*, *176*
Local location quotients 133
Location quotients 41
Lokeren 67, *148*
Lommel 79, *80*, 83, *100*, 157
Loncin 167, 171, *176*

Longdoz 76
Lontzen 8
Lorenz curves 14, 42, 44
Lorraine 21, 72
Lorraine iron orefield 8, 74
Lot 124, *132*, 135
Luxembourg (Province) 10–11, 14, *18*, 34–5, 37, 41, 43, 47, 49, 51, 72, 74, 87, 92, 165
Luxemburg (Grand Duchy) 21, 72, 79, 111

M

Maas, river 1, 3, *59*
Maaseik 88, 92, 111, 147, 155, 157, 165
Maastricht 147, 149
Machelen *132*, 134
Machine tools 93
Malmédy 1, 19, 113
Malta 12
Man-made fibres 31, 67, 68–9, 108–9
Manufacture Belge des Lampes et de la Matériel Electronique (MBLE) 99, 101, 124, 135, 155, 175
Marche-en-Famenne 41
Marcinelle *73*, 76, 93
Marlois 22
Marly 103
Match production 29–30
Mater *85*
Mechelen *22*, 24, 27, 29, 46, 47, 51, *53*, 54, 69, 84, *85*, 92, *96*, 97, *100*, 114–6, *117*, 118–30, 136, *137*, 144
Mélen, J 28, 66
Mens en Ruimte 49, 136, 144
Merksem 127, *137*, 142
Metal industries 5, 37, 55, 127–8, 157, 160, 172–3
Métallurgie Hoboken-Overpelt *80*, 81, 93, 143, 157
Metalworking 41, 66, 127–8, 174
Methane 8
Meuse, river *3*, 11–12, *59*, 62, *166*, 167, *176*
Mineral resources 7–9
Ministry of Economic Affairs 46
Ministry of Public Works 20
Ministry of Regional Economy 19
Modave 10
Mol 9, 32, 62, 83–4
Molenbeek *132*, 133
Monaco 12
Monceau *73*, 76
Mons 9, *13*, 16, 21, *22*, 23, *24*, 41, 51, *52*, 53, *59*, 71, 111, 126, 164–5, *166*, 170, 172–3
Mons-Condé Canal 26

Monsanto 107, 125–6, 136, *138*, 158
Mont St. Guibert 111, *112*, 129
Mont sur Marchienne 93, 101, 177
Montignies *73*
Moresnet 8
Mortsel *137*, 142
Motorway plan 20
Mouscron *18*, 19, 29, 63, 66–7, 164, *166*, 171, 173
Moustier 83, 173
Musson 8, 72

N

Nail-making 27
Namur 7, *18*, 21, *22*, *24*, 27, 34, 41, *48*, 51, *52*, *53*, *59*, 82, 102, 110, 163–5, *166*, 167–74
Napoleon 1, 26–7
Natural gas 6, 58, 61–2
Neder-over-Heembeek 32, 105
Neotechnic industries 20, 32, 39, 40, 134
Net migration balance 51
Nete, river 2, *3*, 9, 110, 136, *137*
Netherlands 1, 5, 11–12, 20–1, 23, 26–7, 61–2, 87–8, 95, 98, 101, 107, 113, 140–1, 147, 150, 155
Niel *137*, 144
Nieupoort 2
Nijlen 129
Nimy-Blaton Canal *59*
Ninove 29, 30
Nivelles 12, 15, *18*, 37, *53*, 54, 71, 72, *100*, 111, 113, *117*, 118–9, 121, 126, 128–9, 131, 136
Non-ferrous metals 32, 79, *80*, 81, 103, 149
Non-metallic minerals 55, 129, 172–3
Nord (France) 21
North Atlantic Treaty Organisation (NATO) 124
North European Plain 2
North Sea 1, 5, 126
Nottingham 69
Nuclear power 62

O

Obourg 109, 173
Oelegem 24, 104, 140
Oevel *96*, 97, 122
Office employment in manufacturing 115–6, 135
Oil 6, 58, 61
Oil refining 44, *104*, 105–6
Olen *80*, 81, 128
Oost-Vlaanderen 13–14, 16, *18*, 22, 26, 34–7, 41, 43–7, 49, 51, 63–70 71, 92, 109–10, 145–7, *148*, 149–59

Oostkamp *100*, 162
Oostmalle *100*
Opglabbeek 156
Organisation for Economic Cooperation and Development (OECD) 50
Ostend 2, 5, 14, 21, 22, 52–3, 83, 102–3, *104*, 107, *148*, 149–50
Ottignies 17, 131, 135
Oudegem 110
Oudenaarde 28–9, 51, 63, 66–8, *148*
Ougrée *73*, 76, 175–7
Our, river 1
Ourthe, river *3*, 11–12, 65, 175, *176*
Overboelare 29
Overpelt 79, *80*, 103, *148*, 157
Oxygen pipeline *73*, 75, 126

P

Paint and varnish production 125
Paliseul 72, 77
Paper 10, 41, 109–111, *112*, 113, 128–9
Papeteries de Genval 111
Paris 21, 50
Paris Basin 2
Part-time farming 3
Pas-de-Calais 31
Peruwelz 109
Petit granit 9
Petrochemicals 36, 44, 90, 106–8
Petrochim 107, 126, *138*
Pharmaceuticals 91, 108
Philippeville 9, 82, *166*
Philips 93, 99, 101, 122, 124, 150, 155
Playing card manufacture 111
Polders 2
Population 12–17
Population migration 16–17, 147
Population potential 51
Portugal 65
Pottery 9, 28
Prayon *80*
Prince Bishops of Liège 65
Printing 128–9
Produits Chimiques de Limbourg 103
Publishing 41, 90
Push barges 24, 140

Q

Quaregnon 168
Quarrying 9
Quenast 9
Quevaucamps 69, *100*

R

Raeren 81
Railway travel, cheap 16, 23, 165

Rank correlation, Spearman 85–6
Rassemblement Wallon 17
Reconversion aid 50
Régional employment premiums 49
Regional policy 46–7, *48*, 49–51, 116–8, 179
Rekken 1
Relief and drainage 2–4
Remi-Claeys 98
Renault 33, 94, 97, 124, 173
Reservoirs 12
Ribbon and tape manufacture 70
Rieme 158, *159*
Rodenhuize 158
Roeselare 63, 67, 92, *100*, *148*, 149, 154, 155–6
Romans 17–18
Ronquièrres 134
Ronse 28, 66, 68, *148*
Rostow, W 26
Rotterdam 20, 50, 107, 140 *see also* Europoort
Rotterdam-Antwerp pipeline (RAPL) 106, 142
Roubaix 17
Ruhr 21, 31, 56, 72, 107
Ruisbroek *132*, 134, 144
Rumst 136, *137*, 144
Rupel, river 9, 23, 82, 134, 136, 143–4
Rupelmonde 23

S

SA Belge de Constructions Aéronautiques (SABCA) 101, 124, 177
SABENA (SA Belge d'Exploitation de la Navigation Aérienne) 20
Sambre, river *3*, 11, *59*, 166
Sambre-Meuse valley 2, 5, 21, 23, 27, 73 *see also* Haine-Sambre-Meuse coalfield
Saxony 65
Schaerbeek *132*, 133
Schelde-Maas Canal 79
Scheldt, river 2, *3*, 5, 11–12, 14, 23, 32, 36, 63, 67, 105, 107, 113, 120, 122, 124–5, 134, 136, *137*, *138*, 139, 141, 143, *148*, *166*
Scheldt-Rhine Canal 11, 17, *138*, 140
Schelle *137*, 144
Schoten 72, 77, *137*, 142
Semois, river *3*, 5, 11
Seneffe 95, *96*, *100*, 101, 177
Senne, river 131–4 *see also* Zenne, river
Seraing 28, *73*, 76, 93, 175, 177
Service de la Politique Générale d'Aménagement du Territoire 49

Sewing thread 69
Shaft-freezing process 8
SHAPE (Supreme Headquarters Allied Powers in Europe) 119
Sheffield cutlers 70
Shell 158, *159*
Shipbuilding 93, 122, 124, 143
SIDMAR (Sidérurgie Maritime) *see* Steel firms
Société Générale 76, 84
Société Industrielle Belge des Pétroles (SIBP) 105, *138*, 139, 140
Sociétés d'équipement économique régionale 48
Soignies 9, 53, 71, 111, 165, *166*, 170, 172
Solvay 101, 105, *138*
Solvay, Ernest 28, 103
South Africa 94
Spain 65
Sprimont 9
St. Etienne 29
St. Ghislain 173
St. Gilles *132*, 133, 135
St. Gillis-bij-Dendermonde 110
St. Josse *132*
St. Niklaas 46, 63, 66–7, 69, 70, *100*, *148*, 150, 152, 155–6
St. Pieters-Leeuw *132*
St. Truiden *148*
St. Vith 1, 19
Steel firms
  Allegheny Ludlum 76, 78
  Armco-Pittsburgh 74, 75, *176*
  Cockerill 72, 74, 75, 76, 79, 93, 122, *138*, 143, 171, 175, *176*
  Espérance-Longdoz 74–6
  Forges de Clabecq *73*, 77–8, 135
  Forges de Thy-Marcinelle et Monceau 75, 177
  Gustave Boël 75, 172
  Hainaut-Sambre 75, 76, 177
  Sadacem 77, *159*
  SIDMAR (Sidérurgie Maritime) 36, 72, 78, 93, 152, 157–8, *159*
Suburbanisation 16–17, 54, 119, 133–6
Sugar refining 127
Sugical instrument production 29, 174
Swarming *see* Industrial swarm

T

Tailles, plateau des 3
'Take-off' 26
Tapestry weaving 29
Tariff protection 31, 94, 127
Temse 143, 155
Terhagen *137*

Termonde 66–7
Terneuzen 23, *104*, *148*
Terneuzen-Ghent Canal 24, 32, 78, 96, 103, 105, 107, 112, 157, *159*
Tertre 103, 105, 107, 172
Tessenderlo *100*, 103, *104*, 107, *148*, 150
Texaco 105, 158, *159*
Textiles 27–8, 30–1, 55, 62–70, 128, 133, 157–8, 173–4
Thuin 39, 51, *59*, 71, 166, 170, 173
Tielt 16, 51, 68, 88, *148*, 156
Tienen *100*, *117*, 126
Tihange 62
Tilleur 76
Tisselt 136, *137*, 143–4
Tobacco 127
Toit du Samson 7, 8
Tongeren *59*, 88, 92, 111, *148*, 155
Tourcoing 17
Tournai 9, 10, 21, 29, 63, 66–7, 69, 81, 111, 165, *166*, 173
Trade unions 66
Trans-Europe Express 22
Transport 20–5
Tubize 31, 109, 131, *132*, 134
Turnhout 8, 9, 15, 69, 89, 92, *100*, 111, 114–6, *117*, 118–30

U

Uccle *132*, 133–5
UCO 69, 158
Unemployment 36–7
Union Carbide 107, 125, 126, *138*, 140
Union Chimique Belge (UCB) 103, 105, 107, 109, 158, *159*, *161*
USA 30, 58, 68, 74, 94, 95, 98

V

Val St. Lambert 83–4, 93, 175, *176*
Valenciennes 17
Van Hool 95, 97–8, 122, 144
Vatican 12
Vaulx 173
Vehicle production 32–3, 90, 94–5, *96*, 97–8, 122
Verviers 16, 27, 28, 31, 47, *59*, 63, 64–7, 100, 110, 165, *166*, 173
Vesdre, river *3*, 12, *59*, 65, 175, *176*
Veurne 51, *148*, 149, 150, 151
Vichte 160
Vieille Montagne 32, 79, *80*, 81, *176*
Vierre, river 12
Vilvoorde 78, 103–5, 125, 131, *132*, 133, 134

Virginal 113
Virton 111
Visé *176*, 177
Volksunie 17
Volkswagen 97, 124, 134
Volvo 95–7, 158, *159*

W

Waarloos *85*, 87, *137*
Waasland 67
Wage rates 45–6, 66, 88, 101, 108, 109, 118, 127, 129, 150–1, 165
Walchaerts 28
Wallonie 16–18, 21, 32, 36, 41–2, 44–6, 51, 53, 55, 56–8, 60, 74, 84, 92–3, 95, 98, 103, 106, 109, 110, 139, 163–77, 178–9
Walloons 16–20, 45–6
Wandre 175–6
Warche, river 12, 62, 65
Waregem 160
Waremme *53*, 54, *166*
Wasmes *100*
Water resources 10–12
Waterloo 95
Watermael-Boitsfort *132*, 135
Welkenraedt 19
Wervik 152, 160
West Germany 2, 21–2, 74, 101, 104, 107, 150, 154 *see also* Germany
West-Vlaanderen 1, 2, 14, 16–17, *18*, 22, 26, 34–5, 40–1, 45–6, 47, 49, 51, 53, 63–70, 71, 88, 92, 101, 109, 145–7, *148*, 149–57, 160–2
Westhoek 49, 89
Westinghouse 93, 99, *176*, 177
Westphalia 14, 65
Wetteren 68
Wieze *85*, 87
Wijnegem *137*
Willebroek 103, 110, *112*, 129, 136, 144
Willebroek Canal 107, 131, 134–5, 136, 143–4
William I of the Netherlands 26–7, 93
Wilrijk 113, 136, *137*, 142–3
Winterslag 33
Woollens and worsteds 30–1, 64–7
Woluwe St. Lambert *132*
Woluwe St. Pierre 17, *132*, 135

Z

Zandvliet 24, 139, 140
Zandvoorde 32, 103, 109
Zaventem 20, 124, 131, *132*, 135

Zedelgem 98, 149, 155
Zeebrugge 17, 32, 83–4, *104*, 105, 107, *148*, 149–50, 158, 160, *161*, 162, 179
Zele *100*
Zellik *132*, 135
Zelzate 9, 24, 32, 36, 72, *73*, 78, 103, 105, *148*, 158
Zenne, river 2, *3*, 110 *see also* Senne, river
Zinc ore 8, 79
Zinc refining 8, 32, 79, 81

Zolder 155
Zolder-Lummen 150
Zottegem 69
Zuid-Limburg (Netherlands) 57, 106
Zuid-Willems Canal 147
Zulte 66, *85*, 160
Zwartberg 17, 60
Zwevegem 157, 160
Zwevezele 98
Zwijnaarde 158
Zwijndrecht 120, 140